TWO ESOTERIC SUTRAS

BDK English Tripiṭaka 29-II, 30-II

TWO ESOTERIC SUTRAS

The Adamantine Pinnacle Sutra

The Susiddhikara Sutra

Translated from the Chinese
(Taishō Volume 18, Numbers 865, 893)

by

Rolf W. Giebel

Numata Center
for Buddhist Translation and Research
2001

First Printing, 2001
ISBN: 978-1-886439-15-3
Library of Congress Catalog Card Number: 2001088183

Published by
Numata Center for Buddhist Translation and Research
2620 Warring Street
Berkeley, California 94704

Printed in the United States of America

A Message on the Publication of the English Tripiṭaka

The Buddhist canon is said to contain eighty-four thousand different teachings. I believe that this is because the Buddha's basic approach was to prescribe a different treatment for every spiritual ailment, much as a doctor prescribes a different medicine for every medical ailment. Thus his teachings were always appropriate for the particular suffering individual and for the time at which the teaching was given, and over the ages not one of his prescriptions has failed to relieve the suffering to which it was addressed.

Ever since the Buddha's Great Demise over twenty-five hundred years ago, his message of wisdom and compassion has spread throughout the world. Yet no one has ever attempted to translate the entire Buddhist canon into English throughout the history of Japan. It is my greatest wish to see this done and to make the translations available to the many English-speaking people who have never had the opportunity to learn about the Buddha's teachings.

Of course, it would be impossible to translate all of the Buddha's eighty-four thousand teachings in a few years. I have, therefore, had one hundred thirty-nine of the scriptural texts in the prodigious Taishō edition of the Chinese Buddhist canon selected for inclusion in the First Series of this translation project.

It is in the nature of this undertaking that the results are bound to be criticized. Nonetheless, I am convinced that unless someone takes it upon himself or herself to initiate this project, it will never be done. At the same time, I hope that an improved, revised edition will appear in the future.

It is most gratifying that, thanks to the efforts of more than a hundred Buddhist scholars from the East and the West, this monumental project has finally gotten off the ground. May the rays of the Wisdom of the Compassionate One reach each and every person in the world.

NUMATA Yehan
Founder of the English
Tripiṭaka Project

August 7, 1991

Editorial Foreword

In January 1982, Dr. NUMATA Yehan, the founder of the Bukkyō Dendō Kyōkai (Society for the Promotion of Buddhism), decided to begin the monumental task of translating the complete Taishō edition of the Chinese Tripiṭaka (Buddhist canon) into the English language. Under his leadership, a special preparatory committee was organized in April 1982. By July of the same year, the Translation Committee of the English Tripiṭaka was officially convened.

The initial Committee consisted of the following members: (late) HANAYAMA Shōyū (Chairperson), BANDŌ Shōjun, ISHIGAMI Zennō, KAMATA Shigeo, KANAOKA Shūyū, MAYEDA Sengaku, NARA Yasuaki, SAYEKI Shinkō, (late) SHIOIRI Ryōtatsu, TAMARU Noriyoshi, (late) TAMURA Kwansei, URYŪZU Ryūshin, and YUYAMA Akira. Assistant members of the Committee were as follows: KANAZAWA Atsushi, WATANABE Shōgo, Rolf Giebel of New Zealand, and Rudy Smet of Belgium.

After holding planning meetings on a monthly basis, the Committee selected one hundred thirty-nine texts for the First Series of translations, an estimated one hundred printed volumes in all. The texts selected are not necessarily limited to those originally written in India but also include works written or composed in China and Japan. While the publication of the First Series proceeds, the texts for the Second Series will be selected from among the remaining works; this process will continue until all the texts, in Japanese as well as in Chinese, have been published.

Frankly speaking, it will take perhaps one hundred years or more to accomplish the English translation of the complete Chinese and Japanese texts, for they consist of thousands of works. Nevertheless, as Dr. NUMATA wished, it is the sincere hope of the Committee that this project will continue unto completion, even after all its present members have passed away.

It must be mentioned here that the final object of this project is not academic fulfillment but the transmission of the teaching of the

Buddha to the whole world in order to create harmony and peace among humankind. To that end, the translators have been asked to minimize the use of explanatory notes of the kind that are indispensable in academic texts, so that the attention of general readers will not be unduly distracted from the primary text. Also, a glossary of selected terms is appended to aid in understanding the text.

To my great regret, however, Dr. NUMATA passed away on May 5, 1994, at the age of ninety-seven, entrusting his son, Mr. NUMATA Toshihide, with the continuation and completion of the Translation Project. The Committee also lost its able and devoted Chairperson, Professor HANAYAMA Shōyū, on June 16, 1995, at the age of sixty-three. After these severe blows, the Committee elected me, Vice President of Musashino Women's College, to be the Chair in October 1995. The Committee has renewed its determination to carry out the noble intention of Dr. NUMATA, under the leadership of Mr. NUMATA Toshihide.

The present members of the Committee are MAYEDA Sengaku (Chairperson), BANDŌ Shōjun, ISHIGAMI Zennō, ICHISHIMA Shōshin, KAMATA Shigeo, KANAOKA Shūyū, NARA Yasuaki, TAMARU Noriyoshi, URYŪZU Ryūshin, YUYAMA Akira, Kenneth K. Tanaka, WATANABE Shōgo; and assistant member YONEZAWA Yoshiyasu.

The Numata Center for Buddhist Translation and Research was established in November 1984, in Berkeley, California, U.S.A., to assist in the publication of the BDK English Tripiṭaka First Series. In December 1991, the Publication Committee was organized at the Numata Center, with Professor Philip Yampolsky as the Chairperson. To our sorrow, Professor Yampolsky passed away in July 1996. In February 1997, Dr. Kenneth K. Inada became Chair and served in that capacity until August 1999. The current Chair, Dr. Francis H. Cook, has been continuing the work since October 1999. All of the remaining texts will be published under the supervision of this Committee, in close cooperation with the Editorial Committee in Tokyo.

MAYEDA Sengaku
Chairperson
Editorial Committee of
the BDK English Tripiṭaka

Publisher's Foreword

The Publication Committee shares with the Editorial Committee the responsibility of realizing the vision of Dr. Yehan Numata, founder of Bukkyō Dendō Kyōkai, the Society for the Promotion of Buddhism. This vision is no less than to make the Buddha's teaching better known throughout the world, through the translation and publication in English of the entire collection of Buddhist texts compiled in the *Taishō Shinshū Daizōkyō,* published in Tokyo in the early part of the twentieth century. This huge task is expected to be carried out by several generations of translators and may take as long as a hundred years to complete. Ultimately, the entire canon will be available to anyone who can read English and who wishes to learn more about the teaching of the Buddha.

The present generation of staff members of the Publication Committee are Diane Ames, Marianne Dresser, Eisho Nasu, Koh Nishiike, and Reverend Kiyoshi Yamashita, president of the Numata Center for Buddhist Translation and Research, Berkeley, California. The Publication Committee is headquartered at the Numata Center and, working in close cooperation with the Editorial Committee, is responsible for the usual tasks associated with preparing translations for publication.

In October 1999, I became the third chairperson of the Publication Committee, on the retirement of its very capable former chair, Dr. Kenneth K. Inada. The Committee is devoted to the advancement of the Buddha's teaching through the publication of excellent translations of the thousands of texts that make up the Buddhist canon.

Francis H. Cook
Chairperson
Publication Committee

Contents

THE ADAMANTINE PINNACLE SUTRA

Translated from the Chinese of Amoghavajra
(Taishō Volume 18, Number 865)

by

Rolf W. Giebel

Contents

Translator's Introduction

This volume contains two of the three most important scriptures in the Esoteric or Tantric Buddhism of East Asia (the third being the *Vairocanābhisaṃbodhi-sūtra,* which is to appear as a separate volume in this series). Chronologically speaking, the *Susiddhikara Sutra* probably antedates what has here for convenience' sake been called the *Adamantine Pinnacle Sutra,* but because of the latter's great importance it has been placed first. The rest of this introduction deals specifically with the *Adamantine Pinnacle Sutra,* while the *Susiddhikara Sutra* is dealt with in a separate introduction immediately preceding the translation itself (page 113).

The Text

The text with the unwieldy title translated here as *The Adamantine Pinnacle: The Compendium of the Truth of All the Tathāgatas and the Realization of the Great Vehicle, Being the Scripture of the Great King of Teachings* represents the Chinese translation by Amoghavajra (705–774) of the Buddhist Tantric scripture known in Sanskrit as the *Sarvatathāgatatattvasaṃgraha* (*Compendium of the Truth of All the Tathāgatas*). This *Sarvatathāgatatattvasaṃgraha* belongs to that division of Buddhist Tantric scriptures designated in India and Tibet as the "Yoga Tantras," corresponding to the third category of what was to become the standard fourfold classification of Buddhist tantras, and the *Sarvatathāgatatattvasaṃgraha* represents the basic text of this category. In Sino-Japanese traditions, on the other hand, this same work is regarded as one of the two (or three) basic texts of Esoteric

Buddhism, standing on a par with the *Vairocanābhisaṃbodhi-sūtra,* and it is more commonly known by its abbreviated title of *Chin-kang-ting ching* (Japanese: *Kongōchō-gyō[/-kyō] = Vajraśekhara-sūtra: Adamantine Pinnacle Sutra*). Thus, in spite of these differences in classification, deriving to a large extent from historical circumstances, it should be evident that considerable importance has been and still is attached to this work in both the Indo-Tibetan and Sino-Japanese traditions of Buddhist Esotericism, and it may be stated without undue exaggeration that it is one of the most important works in the entire corpus of Buddhist Tantric literature.

In the case of such an important text as this it is indeed fortunate that we have available to us a variety of source materials from which to work: in addition to Amoghavajra's Chinese translation there are also extant the original Sanskrit text, available in several editions (see Bibliography, page 107); a Tibetan translation by Śraddhākaravarma and Rin-chen bzang-po dating from the early eleventh century (Peking No. 112); and two further Chinese translations, one in four fascicles and translated ca. 723 by Amoghavajra's teacher Vajrabodhi (Taishō No. 866; originally in six fascicles), and the other in thirty fascicles completed in 1015 by Dānapāla (Taishō No. 882), as well as a wealth of ancillary texts and exegetical works.

The Sanskrit original, of which the Tibetan translation and the Chinese translation by Dānapāla are reasonably faithful renditions, consists of four major sections followed by what is termed in the commentarial literature as the *Uttara-tantra* (*Continuation Tantra*) and *Uttarottara-tantra* (*Continuation of the Continuation Tantra*). Judging from the fact that there exist Tibetan translations of Sanskrit commentaries on the *Sarvatathāgatatattvasaṃgraha* by Śākyamitra (Peking No. 3326) and Ānandagarbha (Peking No. 3333), as well as an introduction to the Yoga Tantras by Buddhaguhya containing quotations from the same (Peking No. 3324), it is to be surmised that since these three scholar-monks were active in the eighth century, the final codification of the Sanskrit *Sarvatathāgatatattvasaṃgraha* in a form close to that extant today had also been completed around the end of the eighth century, probably in southern India.

Amoghavajra's translation was completed ca. 754 on the basis of a text that he himself had brought back to China from Ceylon (present-day Sri Lanka) or southern India, and which he elsewhere declares to represent only the first assembly of a vast work consisting of eighteen assemblies, and although his translation corresponds to only the first chapter of the first section of the Sanskrit version, it tallies very closely with the corresponding portion of the Sanskrit text, the Tibetan translation, and Dānapāla's Chinese translation. It is clear from Amoghavajra's own testimony that his Sanskrit text consisted of the four major sections mentioned above, and so it would seem that although he had in his possession a Sanskrit original similar to that extant today (with the possible exception of the final *Uttara-tantra* and *Uttarottara-tantra*), he was able to complete a translation of only the first chapter of the first section. The translation by Vajrabodhi, on the other hand, although purporting to present the essentials of a larger text consisting of one hundred thousand verses, would in fact appear to be a translation (perhaps abridged) of a text corresponding to the first section of the *Sarvatathāgatatattvasaṃgraha* and representing a stage of development slightly different from that of the text used by Amoghavajra.

It has been necessary to dwell at some length on the textual aspects of the *Sarvatathāgatatattvasaṃgraha* in order to clarify the position occupied by Amoghavajra's translation within this body of Buddhist Tantric literature. In passing, it might be noted that Amoghavajra, one of the most prolific of all translators involved in the transmission of Buddhism to China and arguably the most important figure in the history of Chinese Esoteric Buddhism, translated and composed many other works related to the traditions of the *Sarvatathāgatatattvasaṃgraha*.

There exist Japanese word-for-word commentaries on Amoghavajra's translation of the *Sarvatathāgatatattvasaṃgraha* by Ennin (794–864) of the Tendai sect (*Kongōchō-daikyōō-kyō sho,* seven fascicles; Taishō No. 2223) and Donjaku (1674–1742) of the Shingon sect (*Kongōchō-daikyōō-kyō shiki,* nineteen fascicles; Taishō No. 2225), but the former covers only the first two fascicles of Amoghavajra's translation, passing over the third fascicle on the grounds that its contents are not to be divulged to the uninitiated. A representative, although not very reliable, Japanese rendition in the pseudoclassical *kundoku* style may be found in the *Kokuyaku Issaikyō* series ("Mikkyō-bu" 2), and there is also a modern Japanese commentary by Nasu Seiryū (1976).

Contents

It has already been pointed out that Amoghavajra's translation of the *Sarvatathāgatatattvasaṃgraha* represents a translation of only the first chapter ("Vajradhātumahāmaṇḍalavidhivistara": Extended Rules for the Great Maṇḍala "Adamantine Realm") of the first section (*Sarvatathāgatamahāyānābhisamaya*: Realization of the Great Vehicle of All the Tathāgatas; more commonly known as **Vajradhātu-khaṇḍa:* "Adamantine Realm" Section) of this voluminous work. However, it is this first chapter that may be considered pivotal to the work as a whole, and so it is by no means unnatural that Amoghavajra should have terminated his translation where he did. Let us now consider briefly the contents of this portion of the *Sarvatathāgatatattvasaṃgraha* as translated by Amoghavajra.

But first a word about the title. I have for the sake of convenience translated the title of Amoghavajra's translation (*Chin-kang-ting i-ch'ieh ju-lai chen-shih she ta-ch'eng hsien-cheng ta-chiao-wang ching*) as if it were a single, integrated title. It is, however, equally possible that it is a composite title analyzable into a number of units. It will be recalled that Amoghavajra states elsewhere that the text on which he based his translation corresponds to only the first assembly of a vast work consisting of eighteen assemblies (and one hundred thousand verses). These eighteen assemblies (some of which have been identified with other extant works) he refers to collectively as the *Chin-kang-ting ching* (**Vajraśekhara-sūtra: Adamantine Pinnacle Scripture; Vajraśekhara*[*-mahāguhya-yogatantra*] also happens to be the name of an explanatory tantra of the *Sarvatathāgatatattvasaṃgraha* [Peking No. 113]). The first assembly, on the other hand, he calls *I-ch'ieh ju-lai chen-shih she* (*chiao-wang*) (Compendium of the Truth of All the Tathāgatas [King of Teachings]), which clearly corresponds to the Sanskrit title *Sarva-tathāgatatattvasaṃgraha* and is also present in the Chinese title of our text. This being the case, *ta-ch'eng hsien-cheng* (*mahāyānā-bhisamaya*) may represent an abridgement of the title of the first section of the Sanskrit text (*Sarvatathāgatamahāyānābhisamaya*), with *ta-chiao-wang* ("great king of teachings") corresponding to *mahākalparāja* found appended to the titles of each of the four major sections. To sum up, the title of our text may be broken up into three principal units: (1) "Adamantine Pinnacle" (= generic title), (2) "Compendium of the Truth of All the Tathāgatas" (= specific title), and (3) "Realization of the Great Vehicle" (= abridged section title). It will be further noted that the same chapter title (tallying with the title of the first chapter of the Sanskrit text) is to be found at the head of each of the three fascicles of Amoghavajra's translation. This could possibly suggest that Amoghavajra may indeed have perhaps intended to translate further chapters of this work.

Let us now move on to the actual contents of the text. The Introduction may be divided into two parts: a general introduction in the conventional format of Buddhist scriptures that sets the scene, as it were; and a supplementary introduction that describes the nature of Mahāvairocana, equatable with the Dharma-body (*dharma-kāya*), first primarily from the perspective of his aspect as the essence of the Sixteen Bodhisattvas in the Dharma, Great, and Samaya Maṇḍalas, and then in his capacity as the essence of the Dharma-realm (*dharma-dhātu*).

The Introduction is followed by the main body of the text itself, beginning with a description of three *samādhis* characteristic of the Yoga Tantras. The first of these presents an account of the five-stage process (*pañcākārābhisaṃbodhikrama*) whereby the Bodhisattva Sarvārthasiddhi attains enlightenment. The name Sarvārthasiddhi is obviously a play on Siddhārtha, Śākyamuni's name prior to his enlightenment, and so the process of enlightenment described here may be regarded as a recasting in Tantric terms of Śākyamuni's own enlightenment. The second *samādhi,* in which the stage has now shifted from our world of Jambūdvīpa to the summit of Mount Sumeru, accounts for a full one-half of Amoghavajra's translation and it describes the process whereby the thirty-seven deities (except the Five Tathāgatas) constituting the nucleus of the different *maṇḍala*s appearing in the *Sarvatathāgatatattvasaṃgraha* are generated. The *Sarvatathāgatatattvasaṃgraha* and Yoga Tantras in general have traditionally been defined as attaching prime importance to "inner *yoga*" or meditation rather than to "outer action" or ritual, and the process of generation described here may be considered indicative of this characteristic. The third *samādhi,* described only in brief, deals with the empowerment of the assembly of deities and, according to Ānandagarbha's commentary, the above three *samādhi*s explain "the means for attaining [the state of] Vairocana and Mahāvairocana."

Next follows an exposition of the rites of initiation, beginning with an invocation of Vairocana in which he is extolled with the so-called "one hundred and eight names" and entreated to expound the Great Maṇḍala (*mahā-maṇḍala*) and the rites associated therewith. The Great Maṇḍala (here a taxonomical designation representing one of the six types of *maṇḍala*s found in the *Sarvatathāgatatattvasaṃgraha*), called "Adamantine Realm" (*Vajradhātu*), is then described, although in somewhat abbreviated terms. Next follows a description of the rites to be performed by the teacher in the *maṇḍala* and the manner in which he is to initiate the disciple.

Having been initiated, the disciple is taught how to obtain various types of "success" (*siddhi*), after which he is initiated into the four varieties of "seal-knowledge" (*mudrā-jñāna*) essential for performing the rituals associated with the Great Maṇḍala "Adamantine Realm," and instructed in the benefits accruing from the individual seals. The four types of seals described here are: (1) "great seals" (*mahā-mudrā*), corresponding to the images of the deities as they are visualized in their physical form (and represented in the Great Maṇḍala); (2) "*samaya* seals" (*samaya-mudrā*), that is, seals in the sense of hand gestures and considered to represent both a "coming together" (*samaya*) of the deity and practitioner and the respective "pledges" (*samaya*) of the individual deities; (3) "*dharma* seals" (*dharma-mudrā*), expressed in the form of incantatory formulae (*mantra*) or seed-syllables (*bīja*) and representing the verbal counterparts of the deities; and (4) "*karma* seals" (*karma-mudrā*), which symbolize the activities characteristic of each deity. The descriptions of these seals are very succinct, and they were obviously intended to be supplemented by direct verbal instruction.

The final section consists of some miscellaneous rules. The conclusion to our text may seem rather abrupt, but this is because, as has already been pointed out, the Sanskrit text upon which Amoghavajra is thought to have based his translation does not in fact end at this point but continues on to the second chapter ("Vajraguhyavajramaṇḍalavidhivistara": Extended Rules for the Adamantine Maṇḍala "Adamantine Secret").

Such is the basic content of our text. In view of the nature of this work, however, reference to the commentarial literature, especially in regard to passages dealing with ritual matters, is indispensable. But the aim of the present translation is not to provide a detailed commentary on the text, and any attempt to do so would go well beyond the scope of this translation series. Therefore, the notes have been kept to a bare minimum, but full use has been made of bracketed interpolations to assist the reader's understanding. It may thus be helpful to bring this summary to a close with a brief word on the *maṇḍala*.

A total of twenty-eight *maṇḍalas* are described in the *Sarvatathāgatatattvasaṃgraha*, but underlying them all is the Great Maṇḍala "Adamantine Realm" (*Vajradhātu-mahā-maṇḍala*), consisting of thirty-seven deities and described in the first chapter translated here. The description of the *maṇḍala* as given in the text itself is very cursory, and there exist different schemes of representation, a standard example of which is illustrated below.

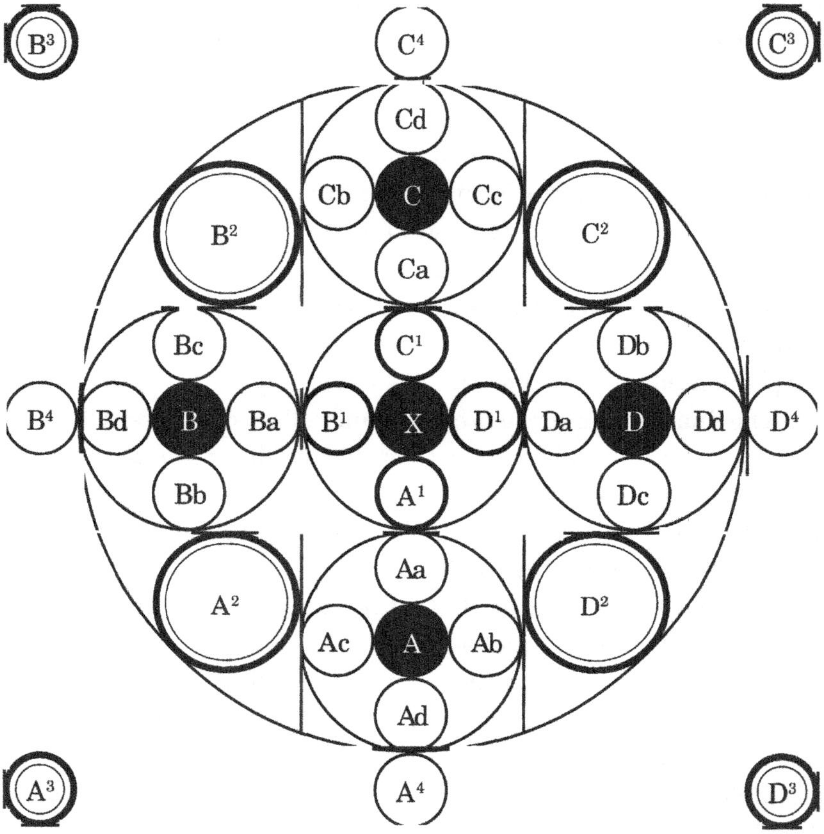

List of the Thirty-Seven Chief Deities Appearing in the *Vajradhātu-mahā-maṇḍala*

The majority of these deities are referred to by more than one name in the *Sarvatathāgatatattvasaṃgraha;* the names given here are the standard names, based on their respective mantras.

The letter accompanying each name is used throughout the translation to mark passages referring to the corresponding deity.

X Vairocana

A Akṣobhya		
Aa Vajrasattva		
Ab Vajrarāja	Attendant	
Ac Vajrarāga	Bodhisattvas	
Ad Vajrasādhu		
B Ratnasaṃbhava		
Ba Vajraratna		
Bb Vajrateja	Attendant	
Bc Vajraketu	Bodhisattvas	
Bd Vajrahāsa		Sixteen (Great) Bodhisattvas
C Lokeśvararāja/Amitāyus		
Ca Vajradharma		
Cb Vajratīkṣṇa	Attendant	
Cc Vajrahetu	Bodhisattvas	
Cd Vajrabhāṣa		
D Amoghasiddhi		
Da Vajrakarma		
Db Vajrarakṣa	Attendant	
Dc Vajrayakṣa	Bodhisattvas	
Dd Vajrasandhi		

A^1 Sattvavajrī	
B^1 Ratnavajrī	Four Pāramitās
C^1 Dharmavajrī	
D^1 Karmavajrī	

A^2 Vajralāsyā		
B^2 Vajramālā	Four Inner Goddesses	
C^2 Vajragītā	of Offering	
D^2 Vajranṛtyā		
		Eight Goddesses of Offering
A^3 Vajradhūpā		
B^3 Vajrapuṣpā	Four Outer Goddesses	
C^3 Vajrālokā	of Offering	
D^3 Vajragandhā		
A^4 Vajrāṅkuśa		
B^4 Vajrapāśa	Four Gatekeepers	
C^4 Vajrasphoṭa		
D^4 Vajrāveśa		

A Note on the Translation

In the English translation presented here it has been my aim to provide a rendition as faithful as possible to the Taishō Edition (No. 865) of Amoghavajra's Chinese translation. This means that when Amoghavajra translates, I generally also translate, and when he transliterates, I generally also transliterate. One major exception to this is proper names, for which I give the Sanskrit, followed on first appearance by a translation conforming with Amoghavajra's Chinese rendering (which may in some instances appear to deviate somewhat from the Sanskrit). Other exceptions include the terms "mantra" and "Tathāgata," which Amoghavajra translates, and *"bhagavān"* and *"bodhi,"* which he transliterates but I translate as "Lord" and "enlightenment" respectively, and also the treatment of the Chinese equivalents of *"dharma"* and *"vajra,"* which at the risk of some inconsistency are only sometimes translated and otherwise reconverted to Sanskrit. All headings (except for the chapter title appearing at the start of each fascicle) have been added and generally follow those given in the edition of the Sanskrit text by Horiuchi Kanjin (1983).

As was noted earlier, Amoghavajra's translation tallies well with the Sanskrit text, but sometimes, it would seem, too well, for there are instances where Amoghavajra's rendering gives the impression of being little more than a mechanical substitution of Chinese for Sanskrit with scant regard for the syntactic differences between the two languages. In such cases a translation faithful to the conventions of the Chinese language would result in a version quite unfaithful to what may be assumed to have been the intended meaning of the Sanskrit original. Opting for comprehensibility of the text rather than fidelity to the Chinese, I have in such cases taken the liberty of construing Amoghavajra's Chinese so as to reflect the meaning of the Sanskrit. In this respect the English translation represents in some passages a compromise, but this was thought to be preferable to the confusion and misunderstanding that might otherwise ensue. When, however, discrepancies between the Sanskrit text and Amoghavajra's translation appear to be due to a difference of interpretation on the part of Amoghavajra or other factors, I have of course followed Amoghavajra.

The Adamantine Pinnacle: The Compendium of the Truth of All the Tathāgatas and the Realization of the Great Vehicle, Being the Scripture of the Great King of Teachings 207a2

Respectfully translated on Imperial Mandate by Pu-k'ung (Amogha[vajra]), a Tripiṭaka [Master] and *śramaṇa* of Ta-hsing-shan Monastery; a Commander with Honorary Rank Equal to That of the Three Dignitaries, a [Lord] Specially Advanced, and Probationary Chief Minister of the Court of State Ceremonial, he was Duke of the region of Su with a fief of three thousand households, upon whom was [also] bestowed the purple [robe]; he was posthumously appointed a Minister of Works, posthumously called Ta-chien-cheng, and entitled Ta-kuang-chih ("Great and Extensive Wisdom").[1]

Fascicle One

Extended Rules for the Great Maṇḍala "Adamantine Realm" (I)

General Introduction

Thus have I heard. At one time the Lord, who had accomplished the most excellent knowledge of the *samaya* of adamantine empowerment of All the Tathāgatas,[2] who had obtained consecration as the Dharma-king of the three realms [of desire, form, and nonform] with the gemmed diadem of All the Tathāgatas, who had realized the mastery of the *yoga* of the knowledge of the omniscient one of All the Tathāgatas, and who was skilled in performing manifold deeds [based upon] the equality of all seals (*mudrā*) of All the Tathāgatas by which all wishes and activities in all realms of sentient beings, inexhaustible and without exception, are all accomplished—[this same Lord, namely,] Vairocana of great compassion, the Tathāgata who eternally abides throughout the three ages [of past, present, and future] and is the *vajra* of all body, speech, and mind, was residing in the Great Maṇi (Jewel) Hall within the palace of the king of the Akaniṣṭha Heaven, a place frequented by All the Tathāgatas. [This palace] was variously adorned, with bells large and small and silken banners swaying in the gentle breeze, and it was bedecked with chaplets of pearls, strings of precious stones, half and full moons, and the like. [Vairocana] was together with an assembly of ninety *koṭi* (nine hundred million) bodhisattvas, headed by the following bodhisattvas: namely, the Bodhisattva and Mahāsattva Vajrapāṇi (Vajra-in-Hand), the Bodhisattva and Mahāsattva Noble Avalokiteśvara (Self-Master of Vision), the Bodhisattva and Mahāsattva Youthful Mañjuśrī, the Bodhisattva and Mahāsattva Ākāśagarbha (Matrix of Empty Space), the Bodhisattva and Mahāsattva Vajramuṣṭi (Adamantine Fist), the

Bodhisattva and Mahāsattva Sahacittotpādadharmacakrapravartin (He Who Immediately upon Generating the Intent Turns the Dharma-Wheel), the Bodhisattva and Mahāsattva Gaganagañja (Treasury of Empty Space), and the Bodhisattva and Mahāsattva Sarvamārabalapramardin (He Who Destroys the Power of all Mā[ras]). He was [also] with Tathāgatas equal in number to the sands of the Ganges River, who appeared and filled [the land of] Jambūdvīpa just like sesame [seeds packed closely together in a sesame pod]; it was the same in the Akaniṣṭha Heaven. From each of the bodies of these Tathāgatas of immeasurable numbers there appeared immeasurable *asaṃkhyeya* (incalculable) Buddha-*kṣetra*s (-lands), and in those Buddha-*kṣetra*s too the guiding principles of this teaching were being expounded.

Supplementary Introduction: Own-Nature of Mahāvairocana

Now, the Lord, the Tathāgata Mahāvairocana, who abides forever throughout all empty space and is the *vajra* of the body, speech, and mind of All the Tathāgatas, is [through] mutual interpenetration with All the Tathāgatas the knowledge-*sattva* (-being) who
207b enlightens all Adamantine Realms [A1]; he is the knowledge-matrix born of adamantine empowerments [equal in number to] the dust-motes in the entire realm of empty space, and owing to the infinitude of All the Tathāgatas he is the gem of the great adamantine knowledge consecration [B1]; [by means of] the knowledge of thusness pervading all empty space he has actually realized *saṃbodhi* (enlightenment), and because All the Tathāgatas are themselves by nature pure, all *dharma*s are [for him] pure by nature [C1]; [by means of] the knowledge that manifests all forms throughout all empty space, he is supreme in the act of subduing all realms of sentient beings without exception, and through his infallible execution of the commands of All the Tathāgatas [he is endowed with] all [un]equaled and unsurpassed skillful knowledge

[D[1]];[3] he is the *sattva* firm in great enlightenment of All the Tathāgatas [Aa]; he is the *samaya* of hook-summoning of All the Tathāgatas [Ab]; he is self-master of the knowledge of enrapturement of All the Tathāgatas [Ac]; he is the applause of All the Tathāgatas [Ad]; he is the gem of consecration of All the Tathāgatas [Ba]; he is the halo of light of the solar disc of All the Tathāgatas [Bb]; he is the banner of the *maṇi*-gem "thought-king" (*cintā-rāja*) of All the Tathāgatas [Bc]; he is the great laugh of All the Tathāgatas [Bd]; he is the great pure Dharma of All the Tathāgatas [Ca]; he is the *prajñā*(wisdom)-knowledge of All the Tathāgatas [Cb]; he is the wheel of All the Tathāgatas [Cc]; he is the secret speech of All the Tathāgatas [Cd]; he is the infallible and manifold deeds of All the Tathāgatas [Da]; he is the very firm armor of great energy of All the Tathāgatas [Db]; he is the adamantine *yakṣa* (type of semi-divine being) of universal protection of All the Tathāgatas [Dc]; and he is the knowledge of the seal of the *vajra* of body, speech, and mind of All the Tathāgatas [Dd].[4]

He is the universally worthy one [Aa], the most infallible one [Ab], *māra* [Ac], the lord of extreme joy [Ad],
The matrix of space [Ba], the wondrous great light [Bb], the gemmed banner [Bc], the great smile [Bd],
The great self-master of vision [Ca], *mañju* (pleasant) [Cb], every altar [Cc],
The speechless one [Cd], the manifold doer [Da], energy [Db], anger [Dc], and firm hold [Dd].[5]
He is *vajra* [Aa], hook [Ab], arrow [Ac], joy [Ad], gem [Ba], sun [Bb], banner [Bc], laugh [Bd],
Lotus [Ca], sword [Cb], wondrous wheel [Cc], speech [Cd], *karman* (action) [Da], armor [Db], fear [Dc], and hold [Dd].[6]
He is without beginning, without end, the quiet one, the violent one, the wrathful one, and of great calm patience.
He is a *yakṣa*, a *rākṣasa* (type of demon), the valiant one, the majestic one, the fierce one, and of great opulence.

He is [lord of] the goddess Umā, lord of the world, Viṣṇu, the victorious one, and the great silent one.
He is protector of the world, empty space, the earth, the three worlds, and the three realms.
He is the great elements, of good benefit to people, all, Śarva, and the paternal grandfather (i.e., Brahmā).
He is transmigration, nirvana, the eternal one, proper conduct, and great among the great.
He is the enlightened one, the pure one, the Great Vehicle (Mahāyāna), the three existences, and the perpetual one.
He is the vanquisher of the three worlds, one who enjoys happiness, ruler, and the subduer of all.
He is the steadfast lord, the foremost of the wondrous stages, knowledge, and the guiding principle of the further shore.
207c He is liberation, the sentient being of enlightenment (*bodhisattva*), practice, and All-Tathāgata.
He is the benefit of the enlightened one, the heart of the Buddha, all enlightenment, and the unsurpassed one.
He is the universally illuminating one (*vairocana*), the supreme one, the lord, the spontaneous[ly born] one, the all-retaining one, and mindfulness.
He is the great *sattva,* the great seal, mental equipoise (*samādhi*), and [doer of] the activity of the Buddhas.
He has all the Buddhas for a body, he is a *sattva,* and awakens [others] to the eternal weal.
He is the great foundation, the great black one, great passionate desire, and great bliss.
He is the great expedient means, the great supreme one, the all-supreme one, and self-master of the palace.[7]

[This same] Lord, the great mind of enlightenment (*bodhicitta*) and Great Bodhisattva Samantabhadra (Universally Worthy), was residing in the hearts of All the Tathāgatas.

I. *Samādhi* of the First Yoga (*Ādiyoga-nāma-samādhi*)

At that time All the Tathāgatas filled this Buddha-world just like sesame [seeds packed closely together in a sesame pod]. Then All the Tathāgatas gathered as if in a cloud and betook themselves to where the Bodhisattva and Mahāsattva Sarvārthasiddhi (Accomplishment of All Objectives) was seated at the place of enlightenment (*bodhimaṇḍa*). Manifesting the body of enjoyment (*saṃbhoga-kāya*), they spoke all together as follows: "Good sir, how will you, who endure ascetic practices without knowing the truth of All the Tathāgatas, realize unsurpassed perfect enlightenment?"

Thereupon the Bodhisattva and Mahāsattva Sarvārthasiddhi, having been aroused by All the Tathāgatas, arose from the *āsphānaka-samādhi*,[8] made obeisance to All the Tathāgatas, and said, "World-honored Tathāgatas, please instruct me! How should I practice? What is the truth?"

When he had finished speaking thus, All the Tathāgatas addressed the bodhisattva in unison, saying, "Good sir, abiding in the *samādhi* of observing one's mind, you should chant as [many times as] you please with the [following] mantra, which is effective of its own nature: *Oṃ cittaprativedhaṃ karomi* (*Oṃ*, I penetrate the mind)."

Then the bodhisattva said to All the Tathāgatas, "World-honored Tathāgatas, I have understood it completely. I see my heart to be like a lunar disc in shape."

All the Tathāgatas addressed him all together, saying, "Good sir, the mind is by nature radiant. It is just as, when you make extensive efforts, the result obtained is in proportion to the action, or when you dye a white garment, it changes color according to the dye."

Then, in order to increase his knowledge of the mind radiant by nature, All the Tathāgatas again commanded the bodhisattva, saying, "*Oṃ bodhicittam utpādayāmi* (*Oṃ*, I generate the mind

208a of enlightenment)," and caused him to generate the mind of enlightenment with this mantra, which is effective by nature.

Thereupon the bodhisattva, having generated the mind of enlightenment in accordance with the instructions of All the Tathāgatas, again spoke as follows: "That which was like a lunar disc in shape I again see to be [really] like a lunar disc in shape."[9]

All the Tathāgatas addressed him, saying, "You have already generated the mind of Samantabhadra of All the Tathāgatas. [In order to] obtain firmness equal to that of a *vajra,* duly abiding in this generation of the mind of Samantabhadra of All the Tathāgatas, contemplate the form of a *vajra* on the lunar disc in your heart with this mantra: *Oṃ tiṣṭha vajra* (*Oṃ,* stand, O *vajra!*)."

The bodhisattva said, "World-honored Tathāgatas, I see a *vajra* on the lunar disc."

All the Tathāgatas addressed him all together, saying, "Make firm the *vajra* in the mind of Samantabhadra of All the Tathāgatas with this mantra: *Oṃ vajrātmako 'ham* (*Oṃ,* I am of the nature of a *vajra*)."

[Thereupon] the Adamantine Realms of the body, speech, and mind of All the Tathāgatas such as pervade the entire realm of empty space all entered the *sattva-vajra* [represented by the *vajra* on the lunar disc] through the empowerment of All the Tathāgatas. Then All the Tathāgatas consecrated the Bodhisattva and Mahāsattva Sarvārthasiddhi with an adamantine name, calling him "Vajradhātu (Adamantine Realm), Vajradhātu." Then the Bodhisattva and Mahāsattva Vajradhātu said to All those Tathāgatas, "World-honored Tathāgatas, I see All the Tathāgatas as myself."

All the Tathāgatas addressed him again, saying, "Therefore, Mahāsattva, the whole *sattva-vajra,* perfected with all [excellent] forms, you visualize as yourself in the form of a Buddha with this mantra, which is effective of its own nature, reciting it at will: *Oṃ yathā sarvatathāgatās tathāham* (*Oṃ,* as are All the Tathāgatas, so am I)."

Having said this, the Bodhisattva and Mahāsattva Vajradhātu actually realized himself to be a Tathāgata, and after having made full obeisance to All the Tathāgatas, he said, "World-honored Tathāgatas, I beg you to empower me and make this actual realization of enlightenment firm." When he had finished saying this, All the Tathāgatas entered into the *sattva-vajra* of the Tathāgata Vajradhātu. Then, at that very moment, the World-honored One, the Tathāgata Vajradhātu, actually realized with perfect enlightenment the knowledge of equality of All the Tathāgatas, entered the *samaya* of the knowledge of equality of All the Tathāgatas, was pure by nature, having realized the knowledge of the equality of *dharmas* of All the Tathāgatas, became the matrix of the knowledge of the natural radiance of equality of All the Tathāgatas, and [became] a Tathāgata, one worthy of worship (*arhat*), and a perfectly all-knowing one (*samyaksaṃbuddha*).

Then All the Tathāgatas came forth again from the *sattva-vajra* of All the Tathāgatas and consecrated [him] with the great *maṇi*-gem of Ākāśagarbha, generated [in him] the Dharma-knowl- 208b
edge of Avalokiteśvara, and established [him in] the *viśvakarma*[*tā*] (universal activity) of All the Tathāgatas. From here (i.e., the *bodhimaṇḍa*) they proceeded to a pavilion with a pinnacle [made] of *vajras* and *maṇi*-gems on the summit of [Mount] Sumeru. Upon arriving there, the Tathāgata Vajradhātu was established by the empowerment of All the Tathāgatas on the lion-throne of All the Tathāgatas, facing all directions. Then All the Tathāgatas, [represented by] the Tathāgata Akṣobhya (Immovable One), the Tathāgata Ratnasaṃbhava (Gem-Born One), the Tathāgata Lokeśvararāja (King of the Self-Mastery of Vision), and the Tathāgata Amoghasiddhi (Infallible Accomplishment), empowered themselves as All the Tathāgatas, and since the Lord, the Tathāgata Śākyamuni, had fully mastered the equality of everything, observing the equality of all directions they seated themselves in the four quarters.

II. *Samādhi* of the Supreme King of the *Maṇḍala* (*Maṇḍalarājāgrī-nāma-samādhi*)

Then, not long after the World-honored One, the Tathāgata Vairocana, had actually realized with perfect enlightenment the mind of Samantabhadra of All the Tathāgatas, had obtained the consecration of the great *maṇi*-gem born of empty space of All the Tathāgatas, had obtained the further shore of the Dharma-knowledge of Avalokiteśvara of All the Tathāgatas, had become infallible and unobstructed in teaching [on account of] the *viśvakarma*[*tā*] of All the Tathāgatas, had consummated his deeds, and had consummated the mind's desires, he empowered himself as being of the nature of All the Tathāgatas.[10]

[Aa] Then he entered the *samādhi* [called] "Vajra of the Sattva-Empowerment Born of the Samaya of the Great Bodhisattva Samantabhadra of All the Tathāgatas," whereupon there came forth from his heart the heart[-mantra] of All the Tathāgatas called "Realization of the Great Vehicle of All the Tathāgatas":

Vajrasattva. (Adamantine Being!)

As soon as it had come forth from the hearts of All the Tathāgatas, he, the Lord Samantabhadra, became a multitude of lunar discs which universally purified the great mind of enlightenment of all sentient beings and took up their places all around the Buddhas. From that multitude of lunar discs knowledge-*vajras* of All the Tathāgatas came forth and entered the heart of the Lord, the Tathāgata Vairocana. Owing to the firmness of their universal worth[iness], to the Vajrasattva-*samādhi*, and to the empowerment of All the Tathāgatas, they united and became one. In size such as to completely pervade empty space, this took the form of a *vajra* with five prongs, radiant, and born of the body, speech, and mind of All the Tathāgatas. Coming forth from the heart of All the Tathāgatas (i.e., Vairocana), it settled on the Buddha's palm.

Then, from this *vajra* there appeared [light rays in] the form

of *vajras* and of various colors and aspects, which pervaded and illuminated all world-systems. From the tips of these *vajra*[-like] light rays there appeared the figures of Tathāgatas equal [in number] to the dust-motes of all world-systems: they pervaded the Dharma-realm, went to the extremities of all empty space, pervaded the oceanlike clouds of all world-systems, and completely realizing the knowledge of equality and the supernatural faculties (*abhijñā*) of All the Tathāgatas, they generated the great mind of enlightenment of All the Tathāgatas, accomplished the various practices of Samantabhadra, served All the Tathāgatas, 208c
proceeded to the great place of enlightenment, destroyed the hosts of Mā[ra], realized the great enlightenment of equality of All the Tathāgatas, and turned the wheel of the true Dharma, as well as saving and bringing all benefit and well-being to all realms of sentient beings without exception and accomplishing the knowledge, supreme supernatural faculties, *siddhi* (accomplishment), and so forth of All the Tathāgatas, [thereby] displaying the play of the supernatural powers (*ṛddhi*) of All the Tathāgatas. [Then] owing to their universal worth[iness] and the wondrous firmness of the Vajrasattva-*samādhi*, they combined and became one, producing the figure of the Great Bodhisattva Samantabhadra, who settled in the heart of the World-honored One, the Buddha Vairocana, and uttered the [following] *udāna* (inspired verse):

> "How wonderful! I am Samantabhadra, the firm *sattva* of
> the spontaneous[ly born] ones;
> Owing to my firmness I have no body, [yet] I have obtained
> the *sattva*-body."

Then the figure of the Great Bodhisattva Samantabhadra descended from the heart of the World-honored One and took up his place on a lunar disc in front of All the Tathāgatas, where he again requested instructions.

Then the Lord entered the adamantine *samādhi* called "Samaya of Knowledge of All the Tathāgatas," and for the salvation of the realms of sentient beings inexhaustible and without exception, their lordship over all, and their well-being and happiness, as well as for the obtaining of the fruit of the supreme *siddhi* of the knowledge of equality, the supernatural faculties, and the realization of the unsurpassed Great Vehicle of All the Tathāgatas, he conferred upon the Great Bodhisattva Samantabhadra the *samaya* for experiencing the morality, meditation, wisdom, liberation, and knowledge-and-vision of liberation of All the Tathāgatas,[11] the turning of the wheel of the true Dharma, the benefiting of sentient beings, great expedient means, strength, energy, and great knowledge [in the form of] the *vajra* of success of All the Tathāgatas; when he had invested him with the gemmed diadem [representing] the body of all Buddhas and a colored silken scarf, consecrating him as the Wheel-Turning King of All the Tathāgatas, he placed [the *vajra*] in both his hands, whereupon All the Tathāgatas consecrated him with an adamantine name, calling him "Vajrapāṇi (Vajra-in-Hand) Vajrapāṇi." Then the Bodhisattva and Mahāsattva Vajrapāṇi, with his left [hand making the gesture "adamantine fist," indicating] pride, and brandishing the *vajra* in his right [hand], placed the *vajra* on his heart, holding it as if to thrust it upward, and uttered this *udāna:*

> "This is the *vajra* of success of all Buddhas, unsurpassed;
> Given in the palm of my hand, *vajra* is added to *vajra*."

[Ab] Then the World-honored One again entered an adamantine *samādhi*, called the "Sattva-Empowerment Born of the Samaya of the Great Bodhisattva Amogharāja (Infallible King)," whereupon there came forth from his heart the heart[-mantra] of All the Tathāgatas called the "Samaya of Hook-Summoning of All the Tathāgatas":

> *Vajrarāja.* (Adamantine King!)

As soon as it had come forth from the hearts of All the Tathāgatas,
209a he, the Lord Vajrapāṇi, became the great hooks of All the Tathāgatas. When they had appeared, they entered the heart of the World-honored One Vairocana, where they combined and became one,

producing the form of a great adamantine hook, which settled on the Buddha's palm.

From [this] form of a great adamantine hook there appeared the figures of Tathāgatas equal [in number] to the dust-motes of all world-systems, and they performed the play of the supernatural powers of all Buddhas, such as the summoning of All the Tathāgatas. [Then] owing to their fine [nature as] infallible king and the extreme firmness of the Vajrasattva-*samādhi,* they combined and became one, producing the figure of the Great Bodhisattva Amogharāja, who settled in the heart of the Buddha Vairocana and uttered this *udāna:*

> "How wonderful! [I am] Amogharāja, the hook, and born of the *vajra*,
> Whereby the all-pervading Buddhas summon by hook for the sake of success."

Then the figure of the Great Bodhisattva Amogharāja descended from the Buddha's heart and took up his place on a lunar disc to the right of All the Tathāgatas, where he again requested instructions.

Then the Lord entered the adamantine *samādhi* called "Samaya of Hook-Summoning of All the Tathāgatas," and for the complete hook-summoning and complete well-being and happiness of all realms of sentient beings without exception, as well as for the supreme *siddhi* of the empowerment of the assembly of All the Tathāgatas, he conferred upon the Great Bodhisattva Amogharāja the *samaya* of hook-summoning of All the Tathāgatas [in the form of] the adamantine hook, [placing it] in both his hands, whereupon All the Tathāgatas consecrated him with an adamantine name, calling him "Vajrākarṣa (Adamantine Hook-Summons), Vajrākarṣa." Then the Bodhisattva and Mahāsattva Vajrākarṣa summoned All the Tathāgatas with the adamantine hook and uttered this *udāna:*

> "This is the unsurpassed adamantine knowledge of all Buddhas;

> Performing the beneficial activity of the Buddhas, it is the foremost hook-summoner."

[Ac] Then the Lord again entered an adamantine *samādhi*, called "Sattva-Empowerment Born of the Samaya of the Great Bodhisattva Māra," whereupon there came forth from his heart the heart[-mantra] of All the Tathāgatas called "Samaya of Enrapturement of All the Tathāgatas":

> *Vajrarāga*. (Adamantine Passion!)

As soon as it had come forth from the hearts of All the Tathāgatas, he, the Lord Vajradhara (Vajra-Holder), became the flower[-tipped] weapons of All the Tathāgatas. When they had appeared, they entered the heart of the World-honored One, the Buddha Vairocana, where they combined and became one, producing the form of a great adamantine arrow, which settled on the Buddha's palm.

From this form of an adamantine arrow there appeared the figures of Tathāgatas equal [in number] to the dust-motes of all world-systems, and they performed the play of the supernatural powers of all Buddhas, such as the enrapturement of All the
209b Tathāgatas. [Then] owing to their extreme [nature of] killing and the extreme firmness of the Vajrasattva-*samādhi*, they combined and became one, producing the figure of the Great Bodhisattva Māra, who settled in the heart of the World-honored One, the Buddha Vairocana, and uttered this *udāna:*

> "How wonderful! [I am] pure by nature, the desire for enrapturement of the spontaneous[ly born] ones;
> For the purity of those free from desire, I subdue by means of passion."

Then the figure of the Great Bodhisattva Māra descended from the heart of the World-honored One and took up his place on a lunar disc to the left of All the Tathāgatas, where he again requested instructions.

Then the World-honored One entered the adamantine *samādhi* called "Empowerment of Enrapturement of All the Tathāgatas," and for the enrapturement and complete well-being and happiness of all realms of sentient beings without exception, as well as for the obtaining of the fruit of the supreme *siddhi* of the Māra[-like] activity of All the Tathāgatas, he conferred upon the Great Bodhisattva Māra the *samaya* of killing of All the Tathāgatas [in the form of] the adamantine arrow, [placing it] in both his hands, whereupon All the Tathāgatas consecrated him with an adamantine name, calling him "Vajradhanu (Adamantine Bow), Vajradhanu." Then the Bodhisattva and Mahāsattva Vajradhanu killed All the Tathāgatas with the adamantine arrow and uttered this *udāna:*

> "This is the knowledge of passion of all Buddhas, without blemish;
> By means of passion it impairs renunciation and is able to bestow all well-being."

[Ad] Then the Lord again entered an adamantine *samādhi*, called "Sattva-Empowerment Born of the Samaya of the Great Bodhisattva Prāmodyarāja (King of Extreme Joy)," whereupon there came forth from his heart the heart[-mantra] of All the Tathāgatas called "Samaya of Extreme Joy of All the Tathāgatas":

Vajrasādhu. (Adamantine Applause!)

As soon as it had come forth from the hearts of All the Tathāgatas, he, the Lord Vajradhara, assumed the shapes of applause of All the Tathāgatas. They entered the heart of the World-honored One, the Buddha Vairocana, where they combined and became one, producing the form of great joy, which settled on the Buddha's palm.

From this form of [adamantine] joy, there appeared the figures of Tathāgatas equal [in number] to the dust-motes of all world-systems, and they performed the play of the supernatural powers of all Buddhas, such as the applauding of All the Tathāgatas. [Then] owing to their extreme joy and the extreme firmness of the Vajrasattva-*samādhi*, they combined and became one, producing the figure of the Great Bodhisattva Prāmodyarāja, who settled in the heart of the World-honored One, the Buddha Vairocana, and uttered this *udāna:*

> "How wonderful! I am the applause of those of all-superior knowledge;
> [For] those free from discrimination, I am able to produce ultimate joy."

209c Then the figure of the Great Bodhisattva Prāmodyarāja descended from the heart of the World-honored One and took up his place on a lunar disc behind All the Tathāgatas, where he again requested instructions.

Then the World-honored One entered the adamantine *samādhi* called "Empowerment of Contentment of All the Tathāgatas," and so that all realms of sentient beings without exception might experience complete contentment and complete well-being and happiness, as well as for the obtaining of the fruit of the supreme *siddhi* of the taste of unsurpassed joy of All the Tathāgatas, he conferred upon the Great Bodhisattva and Mahāsattva Prāmodyarāja the *samaya* of the knowledge-*vajra* of extreme joy of All the Tathāgatas [in the form of] adamantine joy, [placing it] in both his hands, whereupon All the Tathāgatas consecrated him with an adamantine name, calling him "Vajraharṣa (Adamantine Joy), Vajraharṣa." Then the Bodhisattva and Mahāsattva Vajraharṣa delighted All the Tathāgatas by applauding with the adamantine joy and uttered this *udāna:*

> "This is the form of that of all Buddhas which effects applause;
> It is the *vajra* that produces all joy, it is sublime and promotes [extreme] joy."

Great Mind of Enlightenment [Aa], Samaya of Hook-Summoning of All the Tathāgatas [Ab], Knowledge of Enrapturement of All the Tathāgatas [Ac], and Great Joy [Ad]: these are the Great Samaya Sattvas of All the Tathāgatas.

[Ba] Then the Lord again entered an adamantine *samādhi*, called "Gem-Empowerment Born of the Samaya of the Great Bodhisattva

Ākāśagarbha (Matrix of Empty Space)," whereupon there came forth from his heart the heart[-mantra] of All the Tathāgatas called "Samaya of Consecration of All the Tathāgatas":

Vajraratna. (Adamantine Jewel!)

As soon as it had come forth from the hearts of All the Tathāgatas, it [then], owing to full mastery of knowledge of the equality of all empty space and the firmness of the Vajrasattva-*samādhi*, condensed and became one. Then he, the Lord Vajradhara, became light rays [filling] all empty space, and when they had appeared, all the realms of sentient beings were illuminated by these light rays [filling] all empty space and became a realm [composed] entirely of empty space. On account of the empowerment of All the Tathāgatas, this entire realm of empty space entered the heart of the World-honored One, the Buddha Vairocana. Owing to good cultivation of the Vajrasattva-*samādhi*, the form of a great adamantine gem was produced, composed of the matrix of the entire realm of empty space and in size such as to pervade all world-systems, which settled on the Buddha's palm.

From this form of an adamantine gem there appeared the figures of Tathāgatas equal [in number] to the dust-motes of all world-systems. When they had appeared, they performed the play of the supernatural powers of All the Tathāgatas, such as performing the consecration of All the Tathāgatas, in all world-systems. 210a
[Then] owing to the wondrous generation of the matrix of the [entire] realm of empty space and to the extreme firmness of the Vajrasattva-*samādhi*, they combined and became one, generating the figure of the Great Bodhisattva Ākāśagarbha, who settled in the heart of the World-honored One, the Buddha Vairocana, and uttered this *udāna*:

"How wonderful! [I am] the wondrous consecration, the
  unsurpassed adamantine gem,
On account of which the Buddhas, [although] without
  attachment, are called 'Lords of the Three Realms.'"

Then the figure of the Great Bodhisattva Ākāśagarbha descended from the heart of the World-honored One and took up his place on a lunar disc in front of All the Tathāgatas, where he again requested instructions.

Then the World-honored One entered the adamantine *samādhi* called "Great Maṇi-Gem of All the Tathāgatas," and so that all realms of sentient beings without exception might acquire all objectives and experience complete well-being and happiness, as well as for the obtaining of the supreme *siddhi* of the abundance of benefits of All the Tathāgatas, he conferred upon the Great Bodhisattva and Mahāsattva Ākāśagarbha the *samaya* of the fulfillment of the mind's desires of All the Tathāgatas [in the form of] the adamantine *maṇi;* when he had bestowed upon him the consecration of the shoot of the adamantine gem, [consecrating him] as the Wheel-Turning King of the Adamantine Gem, he placed [the adamantine *maṇi*] in both his hands, whereupon All the Tathāgatas consecrated him with an adamantine name, calling him "Vajragarbha (Adamantine Matrix), Vajragarbha." Then the Bodhisattva and Mahāsattva Vajragarbha placed the adamantine *maṇi* on his place of consecration (i.e., forehead) and uttered this *udāna:*

> "This is that of all the Buddhas which consecrates the realms of sentient beings;
> Given in the palm of my hand, gem is placed within gem."

[Bb] Then the Lord again entered an adamantine *samādhi,* called "Gem-Empowerment Born of the Samaya of the Great Bodhisattva Mahāteja (Great Splendor)," whereupon there came forth from his heart the heart[-mantra] of All the Tathāgatas called "Samaya of Light of All the Tathāgatas":

Vajrateja. (Adamantine Splendor!)

As soon as it had come forth from the hearts of All the Tathāgatas, he, the Lord Vajrapāṇi, became a multitude of great solar discs. When they had appeared, they entered the heart of the World-honored One, the Buddha Vairocana, where they combined and became one, producing the form of a great adamantine sun, which settled on the Buddha's palm.

From this adamantine solar disc there appeared the figures of Tathāgatas equal [in number] to the dust-motes of all world-systems, and they performed the play of the supernatural powers of all Buddhas, such as emitting the light rays of All the Tathāgatas. [Then] owing to their extremely great splendor and the extreme firmness of the Vajrasattva-*samādhi,* they combined and became one, producing the figure of the Bodhisattva and Mahāsattva Mahāteja, who settled in the heart of the World-honored One, the Buddha Vairocana, and uttered this *udāna:*

> "How wonderful! [I am] the incomparable light that illuminates the realms of sentient beings, 210b
> And purifies [even] the pure ones, [namely,] the Buddhas, saviors of the world."

Then the figure of the Bodhisattva Vimalamahāteja (Untainted Great Splendor) descended from the heart of the World-honored One and took up his place on a lunar disc to the right of All the Tathāgatas, where he again requested instructions.

Then the World-honored One entered the adamantine *samādhi* called "Empowerment of the Halo of Light of All the Tathāgatas," and for the incomparable light and the complete well-being and happiness of all realms of sentient beings without exception, as well as for the obtaining of the supreme *siddhi* of the own light of All the Tathāgatas, he conferred upon the Bodhisattva and Mahāsattva Mahāteja the *samaya* of light of All the Tathāgatas [in the form of] the adamantine sun, [placing it] in both his hands, whereupon All the Tathāgatas consecrated him with an adamantine name, calling him "Vajraprabha (Adamantine Light), Vajraprabha." Then the Bodhisattva and Mahāsattva Vajraprabha illuminated All the Tathāgatas with this adamantine sun and uttered this *udāna:*

> "This is that of all Buddhas which is able to destroy the darkness of ignorance;

> Supposing there were suns like dust-motes [in number], its
> light would [still] surpass theirs."

[Bc] Then the Lord again entered an adamantine *samādhi*, called "Gem-Empowerment Born of the Samaya of the Great Bodhisattva Ratnaketu (Gemmed Banner)," whereupon there came forth from his heart the heart[-mantra] of All the Tathāgatas called "Samaya of Wish Fulfillment of All the Tathāgatas":

> *Vajraketu.* (Adamantine Banner!)

As soon as it had come forth from the hearts of All the Tathāgatas, he, the Lord Vajradhara, became multicolored banners of ornate form. When they had appeared, they entered the heart of the World-honored One, the Buddha Vairocana, where they combined and became one, producing the form of an adamantine banner, which settled on the Buddha's palm.

From this form of an adamantine banner there appeared the figures of Tathāgatas equal [in number] to the dust-motes of all world-systems, and they performed the play of the supernatural powers of all Buddhas, such as raising the gemmed banners of All the Tathāgatas. [Then] owing to their [nature as] great gemmed banners and the extreme firmness of the Vajrasattva-*samādhi*, they combined and became one, producing the figure of the Great Bodhisattva Ratnaketu, who settled in the heart of the World-honored One, the Buddha Vairocana, and uttered this *udāna:*

> "How wonderful! [I am] the incomparable banner of the
> accomplishment of all benefit,
> Which causes those who have fulfilled all wishes to fulfill all
> the desires [of others]."

Then the figure of the Great Bodhisattva Ratnaketu descended from the heart of the World-honored One and took up his place on a lunar disc to the left of All the Tathāgatas, where he again requested instructions.

Then the World-honored One entered the adamantine *samādhi*
210c called "Empowerment of Raising of All the Tathāgatas," and in

order to cause all realms of sentient beings without exception [to experience] the fulfillment of all wishes and complete well-being and happiness, as well as for the obtaining of the fruit of the supreme *siddhi* of great benefit of All the Tathāgatas, he conferred upon the Bodhisattva and Mahāsattva Ratnaketu the *samaya* for raising the banner of the *maṇi* "thought-king" of All the Tathāgatas [in the form of] the adamantine banner, [placing it] in both his hands, whereupon All the Tathāgatas consecrated him with an adamantine name, calling him "Vajrayaṣṭi (Adamantine Banner), Vajrayaṣṭi." Then the Bodhisattva and Mahāsattva Vajrayaṣṭi established All the Tathāgatas in the *dāna-pāramitā* (perfection of giving) with the adamantine banner and uttered this *udāna:*

> "This is that of all Buddhas which is able to fulfill all the mind's desires;
> It is called 'banner of the wish-fulfilling gem' and represents the guiding principle of the perfection of *dāna* (giving)."

[Bd] Then the Lord again entered an adamantine *samādhi*, called "Gem-Empowerment Born of the Samaya of the Great Bodhisattva Nityaprītipramuditendriya (Faculty of Permanent Joy and Gladness)," whereupon there came forth from his heart the heart[-mantra] of All the Tathāgatas called "Samaya of Joy of All the Tathāgatas":

Vajrahāsa. (Adamantine Laughter!)

As soon as it had come forth from the hearts of All the Tathāgatas, he, the Lord Vajradhara, became the smiles of All the Tathāgatas. When they had appeared, they entered the heart of the World-honored One, the Buddha Vairocana, where they combined and became one, producing the form of an adamantine smile, which settled on the Buddha's palm.

From this form of an adamantine smile there appeared the figures of Tathāgatas equal [in number] to the dust-motes of all world-systems, and they performed the play of the supernatural powers of all Buddhas, such as performing the marvels of All the

Tathāgatas. [Then] owing to their faculty of permanent joy and gladness and to the extreme firmness of the Vajrasattva-*samādhi*, they combined and became one, producing the figure of the Great Bodhisattva Nityaprītipramuditendriya, who settled in the heart of the World-honored One, the Buddha Vairocana, and uttered this *udāna:*

"How wonderful! I am the great laugh, the great marvel of all the supreme ones,
[Whereby] those who always abide in wondrous mental equipoise establish the Buddha's benefit."

Then the figure of the Great Bodhisattva Nityaprītipramuditendriya descended from the heart of the World-honored One and took up his place on a lunar disc behind All the Tathāgatas, where he again requested instructions.

Then the World-honored One entered the adamantine *samādhi* called "Empowerment of the Marvels of All the Tathāgatas," and for the unsurpassed well-being and happiness of all sense organs in all realms of sentient beings without exception, as well as for the obtaining of the fruit of the knowledge of the purity of sense organs
211a and the supernatural faculties of All the Tathāgatas, he conferred upon the Great Bodhisattva and Mahāsattva Nityaprītipramuditendriya the *samaya* of the manifestation [of marvels] of All the Tathāgatas [in the form of] the adamantine smile, [placing it] in both his hands, whereupon All the Tathāgatas consecrated him with an adamantine name, calling him "Vajraprīti (Adamantine Joy), Vajraprīti." Then the Bodhisattva and Mahāsattva Vajraprīti delighted All the Tathāgatas with the adamantine smile and uttered this *udāna:*

"This is that of all Buddhas which demonstrates the manifestation of marvels;
It is able to cause great joy and is unknowable to other teachers."

Great Consecration [Ba], Halo of Light of One Fathom [Bb], Great

Benefit of Sentient Beings [Bc], and Great Laughter [Bd]: these are the Great Consecration Sattvas of All the Tathāgatas.

[Ca] Then the Lord again entered an adamantine *samādhi*, called "Dharma-Empowerment Born of the Samaya of the Great Bodhisattva Avalokiteśvara (Self-Master of Vision)," whereupon there came forth from his heart the heart[-mantra] of All the Tathāgatas called "Samaya of Dharma of All the Tathāgatas":

Vajradharma. (Adamantine Dharma!)

As soon as it had come forth from the hearts of All the Tathāgatas, he, the Lord Vajradhara, owing to full mastery, in the Vajrasattva-*samādhi,* of knowledge of the equality of all *dharmas* pure by nature, became light rays of the true Dharma. When they had appeared, all world-systems were illuminated by these light rays of the true Dharma and were transformed into the Dharma-realm. This Dharma-realm in its entirety entered the heart of the World-honored One, the Buddha Vairocana, where it condensed and became one, producing the form of a great lotus flower, in size such as to pervade the Dharma-realm of empty space, which settled on the Buddha's palm.

From this form of an adamantine lotus flower there appeared the figures of Tathāgatas equal [in number] to the dust-motes of all world-systems, and they performed the play of the supernatural powers of all Buddhas, such as the *samādhi*-knowledge and supernatural faculties of All the Tathāgatas, in all world-systems. [Then] owing to their wondrous self-mastery of vision and the extreme firmness of the Vajrasattva-*samādhi,* they combined and became one, producing the figure of the Great Bodhisattva Avalokiteśvara, who settled in the heart of the World-honored One, the Buddha Vairocana, and uttered this *udāna:*

"How wonderful! I am the supreme truth, originally pure, of the spontaneous[ly born] ones,
[Whereby] the purity of the *dharmas*, which are similar to the analogy of the raft, may be obtained."[12]

Then the figure of the Great Bodhisattva Avalokiteśvara descended from the heart of the World-honored One and took up his place on a lunar disc in front of All the Tathāgatas, where he again requested instructions.

Then the World-honored One entered the adamantine *samādhi* called "Generation of the Samaya of Samādhi-Knowledge of All the Tathāgatas," and for the purification of self and complete well-being and happiness of all realms of sentient beings without exception,
211b as well as for the obtaining of the fruit of the Dharma-knowledge and supernatural faculties of All the Tathāgatas, he conferred upon the Bodhisattva and Mahāsattva Avalokiteśvara the [*samaya* of] purification of All the Tathāgatas [in the form of] the adamantine lotus flower; when he had bestowed upon him the consecration of the Dharma-body of All the Tathāgatas, [consecrating him] as the Wheel-Turning King of the True Dharma, he placed [the adamantine lotus flower] in both his hands, whereupon All the Tathāgatas consecrated him with an adamantine name, calling him "Vajranetra (Adamantine Eye), Vajranetra." Then, [holding] the adamantine lotus flower in such a manner as if to open the lotus flower, the Bodhisattva and Mahāsattva Vajranetra observed the own-nature of covetous passion, pure and without attachment, and having observed [thus], uttered this *udāna:*

> "This is that of all Buddhas which awakens [others] to the truth of desire;
> Given in the palm of my hand, Dharma is established in Dharma."

[Cb] Then the Lord again entered an adamantine *samādhi*, called "Dharma-Empowerment Born of the Samaya of the Great Bodhisattva Mañjuśrī," whereupon there came forth from his heart the heart[-mantra] of All the Tathāgatas called "Samaya of Great Knowledge-Wisdom of All the Tathāgatas":

Vajratīkṣṇa. (Adamantine Acuity!)

As soon as it had come forth from the hearts of All the Tathāgatas, he, the Lord Vajradhara, became a multitude of wisdom-swords. When they had appeared, they entered the heart of the World-honored One, the Buddha Vairocana, where they combined and became one, producing the form of an adamantine sword, which settled on the Buddha's palm.

From this form of an adamantine sword there appeared the figures of Tathāgatas equal [in number] to the dust-motes of all world-systems, and they performed the play of the supernatural powers of all Buddhas, such as the knowledge-wisdom of All the Tathāgatas. [Then] owing to their wondrous auspiciousness and the extreme firmness of the Vajrasattva-*samādhi,* they combined and became one, producing the figure of the Great Bodhisattva Mañjuśrī, who settled in the heart of the World-honored One, the Buddha Vairocana, and uttered this *udāna:*

> "How wonderful! I am called the exquisite sound of all Buddhas,
> For although wisdom is without form, its sound may be apprehended."

Then the figure of the Great Bodhisattva Mañjuśrī descended from the heart of the World-honored One and took up his place on a lunar disc to the right of All the Tathāgatas, where he again requested instructions.

Then the World-honored One entered the adamantine *samādhi* called "Samaya of Knowledge-Wisdom of All the Tathāgatas," and so that all realms of sentient beings without exception might cut off all suffering and experience complete well-being and happiness, as well as for the obtaining of the accomplishment of the fulfillment of wisdom attendant upon sound of All the Tathāgatas, he conferred upon the Great Bodhisattva and Mahāsattva Mañjuśrī the *samaya* of the severance of defilements of All the Tathāgatas [in
the form of] the adamantine sword, [placing it] in both his hands, 211c
whereupon All the Tathāgatas consecrated him with an adamantine name, calling him "Vajrabuddhi (Adamantine Sapience), Vajrabuddhi." Then the Bodhisattva and Mahāsattva Vajrabuddhi

assailed [All the Tathāgatas] with the adamantine sword and uttered this *udāna:*

> "This is the principle of the perfection of wisdom of all Buddhas,
> Which cuts down all foes and is foremost in eliminating all sins."

[Cc] Then the Lord again entered an adamantine *samādhi*, called "Dharma-Empowerment Born of the Samaya of the Bodhisattva and Mahāsattva Sahacittotpāditadharmacakrapravartin (He Who Immediately upon Generating the Intent Turns the Dharma-Wheel)," whereupon there came forth from his heart the heart[-mantra] of All the Tathāgatas called "Samaya of the Wheel of All the Tathāgatas":

> *Vajrahetu.* (Adamantine Cause!)

As soon as it had come forth from the hearts of All the Tathāgatas, he, the Lord Vajradhara, became the Great Maṇḍalas of All the Tathāgatas, forming the Great Maṇḍala of the Adamantine Realm [and so forth]. When they had appeared, they entered the heart of the World-honored One, the Buddha Vairocana, where they combined and became one, producing the form of an adamantine wheel, which settled on the Buddha's palm.

From this form of an adamantine wheel, there appeared the figures of Tathāgatas equal [in number] to the dust-motes of all world-systems, [and they performed the play of the supernatural powers of all Buddhas, such as turning the Dharma wheel immediately upon generating the intent, in all world-systems. Then][13] owing to their turning of the Dharma wheel immediately upon generating the intent and the extreme firmness of the Vajrasattva-*samādhi,* they combined and became one, producing the figure of the Bodhisattva and Mahāsattva Sahacittotpāditadharmacakrapravartin, who settled in the heart of the World-honored One, the Buddha Vairocana, and uttered this *udāna:*

"How wonderful! I am the adamantine wheel of the supreme holders of the *vajra*,
Which by merely generating the intent is able to turn the wondrous Dharma-wheel."

Then the figure of the Great Bodhisattva Sahacittotpāditadharmacakrapravartin descended from the heart of the World-honored One and took up his place on a lunar disc to the left of All the Tathāgatas, where he again requested instructions.

Then the World-honored One entered the adamantine *samādhi* called "Wheel of All the Tathāgatas," and in order to cause all realms of sentient beings without exception to enter and obtain the Dharma-wheel of non-retrogression and experience complete well-being and happiness, as well as for the supreme *siddhi* of turning the wheel of the true Dharma of All the Tathāgatas, he conferred upon the Great Bodhisattva and Mahāsattva Sahacittotpāditadharmacakrapravartin the *samaya* of the Great Maṇḍala of All the Tathāgatas [in the form of] the adamantine wheel, [placing it] in both his hands, whereupon All the Tathāgatas consecrated him with an adamantine name, calling him "Vajramaṇḍa (Adamantine Place), Vajramaṇḍa." Then, with the adamantine wheel, the Bodhisattva and Mahāsattva Vajramaṇḍa established All the Tathāgatas [in the state of] non-retrogression and uttered this *udāna:*

"This is that of all Buddhas which is able to purify all *dharma*s, 212a
For it is [the wheel of] non-retrogression, also called the 'place of enlightenment.'"

[Cd] Then the Lord again entered an adamantine *samādhi*, called "Dharma-Empowerment Born of the Samaya of the Great Bodhisattva and Mahāsattva Avāca (Speechless One)," whereupon there came forth from his heart the heart[-mantra] of All the Tathāgatas called "Samaya of Mindful Recitation of All the Tathāgatas":

Vajrabhāṣa. (Adamantine Speech!)

As soon as it had come forth from the hearts of All the Tathāgatas, he, the Lord Vajrapāṇi, became the Dharma-syllables of All the Tathāgatas. When they had appeared, they entered the heart of the World-honored One, the Buddha Vairocana, where they combined and became one, producing the form of an adamantine mindful recitation [in the shape of a tongue], which settled on the Buddha's palm.

From this form of an adamantine mindful recitation there appeared the figures of Tathāgatas equal [in number] to the dust-motes of all world-systems, and they performed the play of the supernatural powers of all Buddhas, such as the Dharma-nature of All the Tathāgatas. [Then] owing to their wondrous speech[lessness] and the extreme firmness of the Vajrasattva-*samādhi,* they combined and became one, producing the figure of the Great Bodhisattva Avāca, who settled in the heart of the World-honored One, the Buddha Vairocana, and uttered this *udāna:*

> "How wonderful! The secret of the spontaneous[ly born] ones, I am called 'secret speech,'
> For the subtle Dharma that they expound is free of frivolous arguments."

Then the figure of the Great Bodhisattva Avāca descended from the heart of the World-honored One and took up his place on a lunar disc behind All the Tathāgatas, where he again requested instructions.

Then the World-honored One entered the adamantine *samādhi* called "Secret Speech of All the Tathāgatas," and so that all realms of sentient beings without exception might have success in speech and experience complete well-being and happiness, as well as for the obtaining of the supreme *siddhi* of the essence of the secret of speech of All the Tathāgatas, he conferred upon the Great Bodhisattva and Mahāsattva Avāca the *samaya* of the knowledge of speech of All the Tathāgatas [in the form of] the adamantine mindful recitation, [placing it] in both his hands, whereupon All the

Tathāgatas consecrated him with an adamantine name, calling him "Vajravāca (Adamantine Speech), Vajravāca." Then the Bodhisattva and Mahāsattva Vajravāca conversed together with All the Tathāgatas by means of the adamantine mindful recitation and uttered this *udāna:*

> "This is that of all Buddhas which is called 'adamantine mindful recitation';
> It swiftly accomplishes the mantras of All the Tathāgatas."

Adamantine Knowledge of Dharma-Nature [Ca], Knowledge-Wisdom of All the Tathāgatas [Cb], Great Wheel-Turning Knowledge [Cc], and Knowledge of the Speech of All the Tathāgatas for Turning [Back] Frivolous Argument [Cd]: these are the Great Knowledge Sattvas of All the Tathāgatas. 212b

The Adamantine Pinnacle: The Compendium of the Truth of All the Tathāgatas and the Realization of the Great Vehicle, Being the Scripture of the Great King of Teachings, Fascicle One.

Fascicle Two

Extended Rules for the Great Maṇḍala ["Adamantine Realm"] (II)

II. *Samādhi* of the Supreme King of the *Maṇḍala (continued)*

[Da] Then the Lord again entered an adamantine *samādhi*, called "Karma-Empowerment Born of the Samaya of the Great Bodhisattva Sarvatathāgataviśvakarman (All-Doer of All the Tathāgatas)," whereupon there came forth from his heart the heart[-mantra] of All the Tathāgatas called "Samaya of Karma of All the Tathāgatas":

Vajrakarma. (Adamantine Karma!)

As soon as it had come forth from the hearts of All the Tathāgatas, he, the Lord Vajradhara, owing to full mastery, in the Vajrasattva-*samādhi,* of knowledge of the equality of karma of All the Tathāgatas, became karma light rays of All the Tathāgatas. When they had appeared, all the realms of sentient beings were illuminated by these karma light rays of All the Tathāgatas and became the karma-realm of All the Tathāgatas. This Karma-realm of All the Tathāgatas in its entirety entered the heart of the World-honored One, the Buddha Vairocana, where it condensed and became one, producing from the Karma-realm of All the Tathāgatas the form of a *karma-vajra* (i.e., double or crossed *vajra*), in size such as to pervade the entire realm of empty space, which settled on the Buddha's palm.

Then from this form of a *karma-vajra* there appeared the figures of Tathāgatas equal [in number] to the dust-motes of all world-systems, and they performed the play of the supernatural powers of all Buddhas, such as the karma of All the Tathāgatas, in all

world-systems. [Then] owing to the performance of unlimited deeds of All the Tathāgatas and the extreme firmness of the Vajrasattva-
212c *samādhi,* they combined and became one, producing the figure of the Great Bodhisattva and Mahāsattva Sarvatathāgataviśva-karman, who settled in the heart of the World-honored One, the Buddha Vairocana, and uttered this *udāna:*

> "How wonderful! I am all action of the Buddhas, great in quantity and infallible;
> Setting in motion adamantine action, I effortlessly perform the Buddha's beneficial activity."

Then the figure of the Great Bodhisattva [Sarvatathāgata]viśva-karman descended from the heart of the World-honored One and took up his place on a lunar disc in front of All the Tathāgatas, where he again requested instructions.

Then the World-honored One entered the adamantine *samādhi* called "Infallible Adamantine Samaya of All the Tathāgatas," and so that all realms of sentient beings without exception might perform all *siddhis* and experience complete well-being and happiness, as well as for the accomplishment of the fruit of the knowledge of adamantine karma-nature and the supernatural faculties of All the Tathāgatas, he conferred upon the Great Bodhisattva Sarvatathāgatavajrakarman the *samaya* of the extended rules for all immeasurable and infallible actions such as effecting all offerings [in the form of] the *karma-vajra*; when he had made him the Wheel-Turning King of Karma of All the Tathāgatas by means of the consecration of All the Tathāgatas, he placed [the *karma-vajra*] in both his hands, whereupon All the Tathāgatas consecrated him with an adamantine name, calling him "Vajraviśva (Adamantine All), Vajraviśva." Then the Bodhisattva and Mahāsattva Vajraviśva, placing the *karma-vajra* on his heart, established All the Tathāgatas [in] the state of the equality of karma and uttered this *udāna:*

> "This is that of all Buddhas which performs manifold superior action;

Given in the palm of my hand, action is placed upon action."

[Db] Then the Lord again entered an adamantine *samādhi*, called "Karma-Empowerment Born of the Samaya of the Great Bodhisattva and Mahāsattva Duryodhanavīrya (Invincible Energy)," whereupon there came forth from his heart the heart[-mantra] of All the Tathāgatas called "Samaya of Protection of All the Tathāgatas":

Vajrarakṣa. (Adamantine Protection!)

As soon as it had come forth from the hearts of All the Tathāgatas, he, the Lord Vajrapāṇi, became a multitude of firm suits of armor. When they had appeared, they entered the heart of the World-honored One, the Buddha Vairocana, where they combined and became one, producing the form of a great adamantine suit of armor, which settled on the Buddha's palm.

From this form of an adamantine suit of armor there appeared the figures of Tathāgatas equal [in number] to the dust-motes of all world-systems, and they performed the play of the supernatural powers of all Buddhas, such as the deeds of the extended rules for protection of All the Tathāgatas. [Then] owing to their invincible energy and the extreme firmness of the Vajrasattva-*samādhi*, they 213a
combined and became one, producing the figure of the Great Bodhisattva Duryodhanavīrya, who settled in the heart of the World-honored One, the Buddha Vairocana, and uttered this *udāna:*

"How wonderful! The armor of energy, I am the firm one among the firm;
Because of my firmness, I become the adamantine superior body for those without a body."

Then the figure of the Great Bodhisattva Duryodhanavīrya descended from the heart of the World-honored One and took up his place on a lunar disc to the right of All the Tathāgatas, where he again requested instructions.

Then the World-honored One entered the adamantine *samādhi* called "Firmness of All the Tathāgatas," and in order to save and protect all realms of sentient beings without exception and so that they might experience complete well-being and happiness, as well as for the obtaining of the fruit of the accomplishment of the adamantine body of All the Tathāgatas, he conferred upon the Great Bodhisattva Duryodhanavīrya the *samaya* of the *pāramitā* (perfection) of energy of All the Tathāgatas [in the form of] the adamantine armor, [placing it] in both his hands, whereupon All the Tathāgatas consecrated him with an adamantine name, calling him "Vajramitra (Adamantine Loving Friend), Vajramitra." Then the Bodhisattva and Mahāsattva Vajramitra clothed All the Tathāgatas in the adamantine armor and uttered this *udāna:*

> "This is the supreme armor of loving kindness of all Buddhas;
> The great protection of firm energy, it is called 'great loving friend.'"

[Dc] Then the Lord again entered an adamantine *samādhi,* called "Karma-Empowerment Born of the Samaya of the Great Bodhisattva and Mahāsattva Sarvamārapramardin (He Who Crushes All Mā[ras]), whereupon there came forth from his heart the heart[-mantra] of All the Tathāgatas called "Samaya of Expedient Means of All the Tathāgatas":

> *Vajrayakṣa.* (Adamantine Yakṣa!)

As soon as it had come forth from the hearts of All the Tathāgatas, he, the Lord Vajradhara, became a multitude of great tusk-weapons. When they had appeared, they entered the heart of the World-honored One, the Buddha Vairocana, where they combined and became one, producing the form of an adamantine tusk, which settled on the Buddha's palm.

From this form of an adamantine tusk there appeared the figures of Tathāgatas equal [in number] to the dust-motes of all world-systems, and they performed the play of the supernatural powers of all Buddhas, such as all [the Tathāgatas'] subjugation of violent anger. [Then] owing to their excellent destruction of all *mā*[*ras*] and the extreme firmness of the Vajrasattva-*samādhi,* they combined and became one, producing the figure of the Great

Bodhisattva Sarvamārapramardin, who settled in the heart of the World-honored One, the Buddha Vairocana, and uttered this *udāna:*

> "How wonderful! [I am] the great expedient means, the
> loving compassion of all Buddhas,
> Whereby those with a form of quietude assume a form of
> violent anger."

Then the figure of the Great Bodhisattva Sarvamārapramardin 213b
descended from the heart of the World-honored One and took up his place on a lunar disc to the left of All the Tathāgatas, where he again requested instructions.

Then the World-honored One entered the adamantine *samādhi* [called] "Extreme Anger of All the Tathāgatas," and so that all realms of sentient beings without exception might be granted fearlessness and experience complete well-being and happiness, as well as for the obtaining of the fruit of the supreme *siddhi* of the knowledge of great expedient means and the supernatural powers of All the Tathāgatas, he conferred upon the Great Bodhisattva Sarvamārapramardin the [*samaya* for] subduing those difficult to subdue of All the Tathāgatas [in the form of] the adamantine tusk-weapon, [placing it] in both his hands, whereupon All the Tathāgatas consecrated him with an adamantine name, calling him "Vajracaṇḍa (Adamantine Violent Anger), Vajracaṇḍa." Then the Bodhisattva and Mahāsattva Vajracaṇḍa placed the adamantine tusk-weapon in his mouth, terrifying All the Tathāgatas, and uttered this *udāna:*

> "This is that of all Buddhas which subdues those difficult to
> subdue,
> The adamantine tusk-weapon, the expedient means of those
> of compassion."

[Dd] Then the Lord again entered an adamantine *samādhi*, called "Karma-Empowerment Born of the Samaya of the Great Bodhisattva and Mahāsattva Sarvatathāgatamuṣṭi (Fist of All the Tathāgatas)," whereupon there came forth from his heart the heart[-mantra] of All the Tathāgatas, called "Samaya for Binding the Vajras of Body, Speech, and Mind of All the Tathāgatas":

Vajrasandhi. (Adamantine Union!)

As soon as it had come forth from the hearts of All the Tathāgatas, he, the Lord Vajradhara, became the binds of all seals of All the Tathāgatas. When they had appeared, they entered the heart of the World-honored One, the Buddha Vairocana, where they combined and became one, producing the form of an adamantine bind, which settled on the Buddha's palm.

From this form of an adamantine bind there appeared the figures of Tathāgatas equal [in number] to the dust-motes of all world-systems, and after they had appeared, they performed the play of the supernatural powers of all Buddhas, such as the knowledge of seal-binding of All the Tathāgatas, in all world-systems. [Then] owing to their excellent binding of the fist of All the Tathāgatas and the extreme firmness of the Vajrasattva-*samādhi,* they combined and became one, producing the figure of the Great Bodhisattva Sarvatathāgatamuṣṭi, who settled in the heart of the World-honored One, the Buddha Vairocana, and uttered this *udāna:*

> "How wonderful! The very firm bind, I am the *samaya* of the firm ones;
> In order to accomplish all the mind's desires [even] the liberated are bound."

Then the figure of the Great Bodhisattva Sarvatathāgatamuṣṭi
213c descended from the heart of the World-honored One and took up his place on a lunar disc behind All the Tathāgatas, where he again requested instructions.

Then the World-honored One entered the adamantine *samādhi* called "Samaya of All the Tathāgatas," and in order to cause All the Tathāgatas and divinities to appear and effectuate all *siddhi*s in all realms of sentient beings without exception, and so that [all realms of sentient beings] might experience complete well-being and happiness, as well as for the obtaining of the fruit of the supreme *siddhi* of lordship in the seal of the knowledge of the omniscient one of All the Tathāgatas, he conferred upon the Great Bodhisattva and Mahāsattva Sarvatathāgatamuṣṭi the *samaya* of the seal of All the Tathāgatas [in the form of] the adamantine bind, [placing it] in both his hands, whereupon All the Tathāgatas consecrated him with an adamantine name, calling him "Vajramuṣṭi (Adamantine Fist), Vajramuṣṭi." Then the Bodhisattva and Mahāsattva Vajramuṣṭi bound All the Tathāgatas with the adamantine bind and uttered this *udāna:*

> "This is the seal-bind of the Buddhas, great and firm;
> In order to accomplish quickly all seals, the *samaya* is not transgressed."

Action of the Extended Rules for Offering of All the Tathāgatas [Da], Firm Armor of Great Energy of All the Tathāgatas [Db], Great Expedient Means of All the Tathāgatas [Dc], and Knowledge of the Binding of All Seals of All the Tathāgatas [Dd]: these are the Great Karma Sattvas of All the Tathāgatas.

[A[1]] Then the Tathāgata Akṣobhya, having accomplished the World-honored One Vairocana's knowledge of All the Tathāgatas, entered the adamantine *samādhi* called "Adamantine Empowerment Born of the Samaya of Vajrapāramitā (Adamantine Perfection)" in order to seal the knowledge of All the Tathāgatas, whereupon there came forth from his heart the seal of All the Tathāgatas called "Adamantine Samaya of All the Tathāgatas":

> *Sattvavajri.* (Adamantine One of Being!)

As soon as it had come forth from the hearts of All the Tathāgatas, there appeared light rays [in the shape of] *vajras*. From the tips of these *vajra*[-like] light rays he, the Lord Vajradhara, became [transformed into] the figures of Tathāgatas equal [in number] to the dust-motes of all world-systems and sealed the knowledge of All the Tathāgatas. [Then] they again combined and became one, producing the form of a great *vajra* equal in size to all world-systems, which took up its place on a lunar disc in front of the

World-honored One, the Buddha Vairocana, and uttered this *udāna:*

> How wonderful! [I am] the *sattva-vajra* of all the Buddhas, and firm;
> On account of my firmness I have no body, [yet] because of that I have obtained the adamantine body."

[B¹] Then the World-honored One, the Tathāgata Ratnasaṃbhava, entered the adamantine *samādhi* called "Adamantine Empowerment of the Gem Born of the Samaya of Ratnapāramitā (Gem Perfection)" in order to seal the World-honored One Vairocana's knowledge of All the Tathāgatas, whereupon there came forth from
214a his heart his own seal called "Adamantine [Gem] Samaya":

Ratnavajri. (Adamantine One of the Gem!)

As soon as it had come forth from the hearts of All the Tathāgatas, there appeared light rays [in the shape of] gems. From these gem[-like] light rays he, the Lord Vajradhara, became [transformed into] the figures of Tathāgatas equal [in number] to the dust-motes of all world-systems and sealed the knowledge of All the Tathāgatas. [Then] they again combined and became one, producing the form of a great adamantine gem equal in size to all world-systems, which took up its place on a lunar disc to the right of the World-honored One, the Buddha Vairocana, and uttered this *udāna:*

> "How wonderful! I am called the gem-*vajra* of all Buddhas;
> For the multitude of seals [I represent] the firm guiding principle of consecration."

[C¹] Then the World-honored One, the Tathāgata Lokeśvararāja, entered the adamantine *samādhi* called "Adamantine Empowerment of the Dharma Born of the Samaya of Dharmapāramitā (Dharma Perfection)" in order to seal the World-honored One Vairocana's knowledge of All the Tathāgatas, whereupon there came forth from his heart his own seal called "Dharma Samaya":

Dharmavajri. (Adamantine One of the Dharma!)

As soon as it had come forth from the hearts of All the Tathāgatas, there appeared light rays [in the shape of] lotus flowers. From these lotus-flower[-like] light rays he, the Lord Vajradhara, became [transformed into] the figures of Tathāgatas equal [in number] to the dust-motes of all world-systems and sealed the knowledge of All the Tathāgatas. [Then] they again combined and became one, producing the form of a great adamantine lotus flower equal in size to all world-systems, which took up its place on a lunar disc behind the World-honored One, the Buddha Vairocana, and uttered this *udāna*:

> "How wonderful! I am the *dharma-vajra* of all Buddhas,
> and pure;
> Being pure by nature, I render [even] covetous passion
> taintless."

[D[1]] Then the World-honored One, the Tathāgata Amoghasiddhi, entered the adamantine *samādhi* called "Adamantine Empowerment Born of the Samaya of Sarvapāramitā (All Perfection)" in order to seal [the World-honored One] Vairocana's knowledge of All the Tathāgatas, whereupon there came forth from his heart his own seal called "[Karma] Samaya of All [the Tathāgatas]":

Karmavajri. (Adamantine One of Action!)

As soon as it had come forth from the hearts of All the Tathāgatas, there appeared light rays [in the shape of] all-*karman* (*sarva-karman* = *karma-vajra*). From these [all-]*karman*[-like] light rays of All the Tathāgatas he, the Lord Vajradhara, became [transformed into] the figures of Tathāgatas equal [in number] to the dust-motes of all world-systems and universally sealed the knowledge of 214b
All the Tathāgatas. [Then] they again combined and became one, producing the form of a great *karma-vajra,* equal in size to all world-systems and facing all directions, which took up its place on a lunar disc to the left of the World-honored One, the Buddha Vairocana, and uttered this *udāna:*

> "How wonderful! I am the action-*vajra* of all Buddhas, and many,
> For [although] one, I am skilled at performing deeds in all Buddha-realms."

Samaya of the Knowledge of All the Tathāgatas [A1], Great Consecration [B1], Adamantine Dharma-Nature [C1], and All Offering [D1]: these are the Great Pāramitās of All the Tathāgatas.

[A2] Then the World-honored One, the Buddha Vairocana, again entered an adamantine *samādhi,* called "Born of the Samaya of Delight-Offering of All the Tathāgatas," whereupon there came forth from his heart a great goddess of the family of All the Tathāgatas:

> *Vajralāsye.* (Adamantine Play!)

As soon as she had come forth from the hearts of All the Tathāgatas, there appeared *vajra*-seals. From the tips of these *vajra*-seals he, the Lord Vajradhara, became [transformed into] the figures of Tathāgatas equal [in number] to the dust-motes of all world-systems, which combined again and became one, becoming the Great Goddess Vajralāsyā (Adamantine Play), Vajrasattva's consort, who resembles Vajrasattva, [possesses] all physical features, manifold forms, colors, and modes of deportment and all articles of adornment, and embodies the family of All the Tathāgatas. She [then] took up her place on a lunar disc to the left side of the *maṇḍala* of the World-honored One, the Tathāgata Akṣobhya, and uttered this *udāna:*

> "How wonderful! Among the offerings of the Buddhas, there is none to compare [with me],
> For through the offering of covetous passion I am able to effect all offerings."

[B2] Then the World-honored One Vairocana again entered an adamantine *samādhi,* called "Born of the Samaya of Gem-Garland Consecration of All the Tathāgatas," whereupon there came forth from his heart a great goddess of the family of All the Tathāgatas:

Vajramāle. (Adamantine Garland!)

As soon as she had come forth from the hearts of All the Tathāgatas, there appeared great gem-seals. From the tips of these great gem-seals he, the Lord Vajradhara, became [transformed into] the figures of Tathāgatas equal [in number] to the dust-motes of all world-systems, which combined again and became one, becoming the Great Goddess Vajramālā (Adamantine Garland), who took up her place on a lunar disc to the left side of the *maṇḍala* of the World-honored One, the Tathāgata Ratnasaṃbhava, and uttered this *udāna:*

"How wonderful! I am incomparable, celebrated as the gem-offering, 214c
[For] those who receive [my] offering have command over supreme kingship of the three realms."

[C[2]] Then the World-honored One Vairocana again entered an adamantine *samādhi,* called "Born of the Samaya of Song-Offering of All the Tathāgatas," whereupon there came forth from his heart a great goddess of the family of All the Tathāgatas:

Vajragīte. (Adamantine Song!)

As soon as she had come forth from the hearts of All the Tathāgatas, there appeared the *dharma*-seals of All the Tathāgatas. From these *dharma*-seals of All the Tathāgatas he, the Lord Vajradhara, became [transformed into] the figures of Tathāgatas equal [in number] to the dust-motes of all world-systems, which combined again and became one, becoming the Great Goddess Vajragītā (Adamantine Song), who took up her place on a lunar disc to the left side of [the *maṇḍala* of] the World-honored One, the Tathāgata Lokeśvararāja, and uttered this *udāna:*

"How wonderful! Consisting of song, I make offerings to all seers,

> On account of which they delight in these offerings, [even though] all *dharmas* are like the response of an echo."

[D2] Then the World-honored One Vairocana again entered an adamantine *samādhi,* called "Born of the Samaya of Dance-Offering of All the Tathāgatas," whereupon there came forth from his heart a great goddess of the family of All the Tathāgatas:

Vajranṛtye. (Adamantine Dance!)

As soon as she had come forth from the hearts of All the Tathāgatas, there appeared extended rituals of dance of All the Tathāgatas. From these rituals of dance-offering of All the Tathāgatas which had appeared he, the Lord Vajradhara, became [transformed into] the figures of Tathāgatas equal [in number] to the dust-motes of all world-systems, which combined again and became one, becoming the Great Goddess Vajranṛtyā (Adamantine Dance), who took up her place on a lunar disc to the left side of [the *maṇḍala* of] the World-honored One, the Tathāgata Amoghasiddhi, and uttered this *udāna*:

> "How wonderful! [I am] a vast offering for those who perform all offerings,
> For through the ritual of the adamantine dance the Buddhas' offering is established."

Samaya of Unsurpassed Well-Being and Happiness of All the Tathāgatas [A2], Garland of All the Tathāgatas [B2], Chant of All the Tathāgatas [C2], and Unsurpassed Performance of the Act of Offering of All the Tathāgatas [D2]: these are the Secret Offerings of All the Tathāgatas.

[A3] Then the World-honored One, the Tathāgata Akṣobhya,
entered the adamantine *samādhi* called "Born of the Samaya
for Causing Joy of All the Tathāgatas" in response to the offering
215a of the Tathāgata Vairocana, whereupon there came forth from
his heart the maidservant of All the Tathāgatas:

Vajradhūpe. (Adamantine Incense!)

As soon as she had come forth from the hearts of All the Tathāgatas, he, the Lord Vajradhara, became a diverse array of clouds of incense-offering, pervading the entire Adamantine Realm. When it had appeared, there came forth from this sea of clouds of incense-offering the figures of Tathāgatas equal [in number] to the dust-motes of all world-systems, which combined again and became one, becoming the figure of the Goddess Vajradhūpā (Adamantine Incense), who took up her place on a lunar disc in a corner to the left of the World-honored One's pavilion with a pinnacle [made] of *vajras* and *maṇi*-gems and uttered this *udāna:*

"How wonderful! [I am] the great offering, possessed of joy
and graceful;
Through the entry[14] of the *sattva,* enlightenment is quickly
realized."

[B3] Then the World-honored One, the Tathāgata Ratnasaṃbhava, entered the adamantine *samādhi* called "Born of the Samaya of Gem-Adornment Offering" in response to the offering of the Tathāgata Vairocana, whereupon there came forth from his heart the great goddess and portress of All the Tathāgatas:

Vajrapuṣpe. (Adamantine Flower!)

As soon as she had come forth from the hearts of All the Tathāgatas, he, the Lord Vajradhara, became an array of offerings of all flowers, pervading the entire realm of empty space. When it had appeared, there came forth from this array of offerings of all flowers the figures of Tathāgatas equal [in number] to the dust-motes of all world-systems. When they had appeared, they combined again and became one, assuming the form of the Goddess Vajrapuṣpā (Adamantine Flower), who took up her place on a lunar disc in a corner to the left of the Tathāgata's pavilion with a pinnacle [made] of *vajras* and *maṇi*-gems and uttered this *udāna:*

"How wonderful! [I am] the flower-offering, able to perform
all adornment,

For the Tathāgatas' gem-nature is quickly obtained
[through] offering."

[C3] Then the World-honored One, the Tathāgata Lokeśvararāja, entered the adamantine *samādhi* called "Born of the Samaya of Light-Offering of All the Tathāgatas" in response to the offering of the World-honored One Vairocana, whereupon there came forth from his heart the female messenger of All the Tathāgatas:

Vajrāloke. (Adamantine Lamp!)

As soon as she had come forth from the hearts of All the Tathāgatas, he, the Lord Vajradhara, appeared as an array of offerings of all light realms, pervading the Dharma-realm in its entirety. From these decorative articles of all light realms there came forth the figures of Tathāgatas equal [in number] to the dust-motes of all
215b world-systems. When they had appeared, they combined again and became one, becoming the figure of the Goddess Vajrālokā (Adamantine Light), who took up her place on a lunar disc in a corner to the left of the World-honored One's pavilion with a pinnacle [made] of *vajras* and *maṇi*-gems and uttered this *udāna:*

"How wonderful! I am the vast offering of lamps, and
graceful;
Being quickly endowed with light, the eyes of all Buddhas
are obtained."

[D3] Then the World-honored One, the Tathāgata Amoghasiddhi, entered the adamantine *samādhi* called "Born of the Samaya of Unguent-Offering of All the Tathāgatas" in response to the offering of the Tathāgata Vairocana, whereupon there came forth from his heart the maidservant of All the Tathāgatas:

Vajragandhe. (Adamantine Unguent!)

As soon as she had come forth from the hearts of All the Tathāgatas, he, the Lord Vajradhara, appeared as an array of all unguent-offerings pervading the entire Dharma-realm. From this array of all unguent-offerings, there came forth the figures of Tathāgatas equal [in number] to the dust-motes of all world-systems. When they had appeared, they combined again and became one, becoming the figure of the Goddess Vajragandhā (Adamantine Unguent), who took up her place on a lunar disc in a corner to the left of the World-honored One's pavilion with a pinnacle [made] of *vajras* and *maṇi*-gems and uttered this *udāna:*

> "How wonderful! The unguent-offering, I am refined and pleasing to the mind,
> For the Tathāgata's perfume is thereby bestowed upon the whole body."

Entry of Knowledge of All the Tathāgatas [A^{3}], Samaya of the Factors of Great Enlightenment [B^{3}], Light of All the Tathāgatas [C^{3}], and Unguent of Morality, Meditation, Wisdom, Liberation, and Knowledge-and-Vision of Liberation [D^{3}]: these are the Executrices of Instructions of All the Tathāgatas.

[A^{4}] Then the World-honored One, the Tathāgata Vairocana, again entered an adamantine *samādhi*, called "Sattva Born of the Samaya of the Samaya-Hook of All the Tathāgatas," whereupon there came forth from his heart the master of the multitude of all seals of All the Tathāgatas:

> *Vajrāṅkuśa.* (Adamantine Hook!)

As soon as he had come forth from the hearts of All the Tathāgatas, he, the Lord Vajradhara, appeared as multitudes of all seals of All the Tathāgatas. From these multitudes of all seals of All the Tathāgatas there came forth the figures of Tathāgatas equal [in number] to the dust-motes of all world-systems, which combined again and became one, becoming the figure of the Great Bodhisattva Vajrāṅkuśa (Adamantine Hook), who took up his place on a lunar disc in the middle of the Vajra Gate of the World-honored One's pavilion with a pinnacle [made] of *vajras* and *maṇi*-gems and, summoning by hook the *samayas* of All the Tathāgatas, uttered this 215c
udāna:

"How wonderful! The hook-vow of all Buddhas, I am firm,
For those whom I universally summon by hook assemble all *maṇḍala*s."

[B4] Then the World-honored One again entered the adamantine *samādhi* called "Born of the Samaya of the Mahāsattva Induction (Praveśa) into the Samaya of All the Tathāgatas," whereupon there came forth from his heart the porter of seal-entry of All the Tathāgatas:

Vajrapāśa. (Adamantine Noose!)

As soon as he had come forth from the hearts of All the Tathāgatas, he, the Lord Vajradhara, appeared as multitudes of seals for induction into the *samaya* of All the Tathāgatas. From these multitudes of seals for induction into the *samaya* of All the Tathāgatas there came forth the figures of Tathāgatas equal [in number] to the dust-motes of all world-systems, which combined again and became one, becoming the figure of the Great Bodhisattva Vajrapāśa (Adamantine Noose), who took up his place on a lunar disc within the Gem Gate of the World-honored One's pavilion with a pinnacle [made] of *vajra*s and *maṇi*-gems and, inducting All the Tathāgatas, uttered this *udāna:*

"How wonderful! I am the firm adamantine noose of all Buddhas;
Even those who have entered all dust-motes, these I again induct."

[C4] Then the World-honored One again entered an adamantine *samādhi,* called "Born of the Samaya of the Great Sattva Chain (Sphoṭa) of the Samaya of All the Tathāgatas," whereupon there came forth from his heart the messenger of All the Tathāgatas [called] "Bind of the Samaya of All the Tathāgatas":

Vajrasphoṭa. (Adamantine Chain!)

As soon as he had come forth from the hearts of All the Tathāgatas, he, the Lord Vajradhara, appeared as multitudes of seals for binding the *samaya* of All the Tathāgatas. When they had come forth, there appeared from these multitudes of seals for binding the *samaya* of All the Tathāgatas the figures of Tathāgatas equal [in number] to the dust-motes of all world-systems, which combined again and became one, becoming the figure of the Great Bodhisattva Vajrasphoṭa (Adamantine Chain), who took up his place on a lunar disc in the middle of the Dharma Gate of the World-honored One's pavilion with a pinnacle [made] of *vajras* and *maṇi*-gems and [binding All the Tathāgatas,] uttered this *udāna:*

> "How wonderful! [I am] the great and firm adamantine chain of all Buddhas;
> I cause those liberated from all bonds to be bound for the weal of sentient beings."

[D4] Then the World-honored One again entered an adamantine *samādhi*, called "Born of the Samaya of the Great Bodhisattva Entry (Āveśa) of All the Tathāgatas," whereupon there came forth from his heart the servant of all seals of All the Tathāgatas: 216a

> *Vajrāveśa.* (Adamantine Entry!)

As soon as he had come forth from the hearts of All the Tathāgatas, he, the Lord Vajradhara, became the masters of seals of All the Tathāgatas. When they had come forth, there appeared from these masters of seals of All the Tathāgatas the figures of Tathāgatas equal [in number] to the dust-motes of all world-systems, which combined again and became one, becoming the figure of the Great Bodhisattva Vajrāveśa (Adamantine Entry), who took up his place on a lunar disc in the middle of the Karma Gate of the World-honored One's pavilion with a pinnacle [made] of *vajras* and *maṇi*-gems and [causing All the Tathāgatas to enter,] uttered this *udāna:*

> "How wonderful! I am the firm adamantine entry of all Buddhas;
> I become lord over all, and then again I also become a servant."

Hook-Summoning of the Samaya of All the Tathāgatas [A^4], Induction [B^4], Bind [C^4], and Subduing [D^4]: these are the [Executants of] Instructions of All the Tathāgatas.

III. *Samādhi* of the Supreme King of Action *(Karmarājāgrī-nāma-samādhi)*

Then, in order to assemble All the Tathāgatas, the World-honored One made the gesture of the adamantine finger-snap and uttered this heart[-mantra called] "Empowerment of the Assembly of All the Tathāgatas":

Vajrasamāja. (Adamantine assembly!)

In a fraction of a second, and having been aroused by the gesture of the finger-snap of All the Tathāgatas, Tathāgatas throughout the oceanlike clouds of all world-systems and equal [in number] to the dust-motes of all world-systems gathered, together with *maṇḍala*s of bodhisattva assemblies; having [gathered], they betook themselves to where the World-honored One, the Tathāgata Vairocana, was in the pavilion with a pinnacle [made] of *vajra*s and *maṇi*-gems, and upon arriving they uttered the heart[-mantra called] "Obeisance to the Feet of All the Tathāgatas":

Oṃ sarvatathāgatapādavandanāṃ karomi. (*Oṃ,* I make obeisance to the feet of All the Tathāgatas.)

After having made obeisance to All the Tathāgatas by mindfully reciting at will this mantra which is effective by nature, they uttered this *udāna:*

"How wonderful is the rite of homage to the Bodhisattva
Great Samantabhadra!
This is the circular altar of the Tathāgatas which illumes
the Tathāgata."

Then after having uttered [this *udāna*], the Tathāgatas who had assembled from all world-systems in the ten directions entered

the heart of the Buddha Vairocana through the empowerment of All the Tathāgatas [and together with] all the *maṇḍala*s of bodhisattva assemblies. [Then] from the hearts of All the Tathāgatas there appeared the *maṇḍala*s of their respective hosts of bodhisattvas, which formed an altar (*maṇḍala*) around the pavilion with a pinnacle [made] of *vajra*s and *maṇi*-gems of the World-honored One, the Buddha Vairocana, where, abiding in *samādhi*, 216b
they uttered this *udāna:*

"How wonderful is the vast one of all Buddhas, born without beginning!
For [Buddhas equal in] number to all dust[-motes] obtain the single nature of the Buddha [Vairocana]."

IV. Initiation Rites

1. Eulogy of One Hundred and Eight Names

Thereupon the Lords, [namely,] All the Tathāgatas, again assembled, and for the empowerment of the Great Maṇḍala of the Adamantine Realm and so that all realms of sentient beings without exception might obtain salvation and all benefits and well-being, as well as for the supreme accomplishment of the knowledge of equality, the supernatural faculties, and the *saṃbodhi* of All the Tathāgatas, they entreated the Lord—lord of All the Tathāgatas, Vajrasattva, without beginning or end, the Great Vajradhara—invoking him with these "One Hundred and Eight Praises":[15]

Adamantine Hero (Vajrasattva)! Great mind! *Vajra!* All-Tathāgata!
Universally Good (Samantabhadra)! First among the adamantine ones! We pay homage to Vajra-in-Hand (Vajrapāṇi)! [Aa]
Adamantine King (Vajrarāja)! Well-awakened one! Adamantine hook! Tathāgata!

Infallible King (Amogharāja)! [Supreme among] adamantine ones! We pay homage to Adamantine [Hook-]Summons (Vajrākarṣa)! [Ab]

Adamantine Passion (Vajrarāga)! Great bliss! Adamantine arrow! Subjugator!

Mā[ra]-Desire (Mārakāma)! Great *vajra!* We pay homage to Adamantine Bow (Vajracāpa)! [Ac]

Adamantine Applause (Vajrasādhu)! *Sattva!* Adamantine play! Great pleasure!

King of Joy (Prāmodyarāja)! [Supreme among] adamantine ones! We pay homage to Adamantine Joy (Vajraharṣa)! [Ad]

Adamantine Gem (Vajraratna)! *Vajra!* Adamantine space! Great gem!

Gem Matrix! Adamantine opulent one! We pay homage to Adamantine Matrix (Vajragarbha)! [Ba]

Adamantine Splendor (Vajrateja)! Great flame! Adamantine sun! Buddha-light!

Adamantine light [ray]! Great Splendor (Mahāteja)! We pay homage to Adamantine Light (Vajraprabha)! [Bb]

Adamantine Banner (Vajraketu)! Good benefit! Adamantine pennant! Well-pleasing one!

Gemmed Banner (Ratnaketu)! Great *vajra!* We pay homage to Adamantine Staff (Vajrayaṣṭi)! [Bc]

Adamantine Laughter (Vajrahāsa)! Great laughter! Adamantine smile! Great marvel!

Loving Joy (Prītiprāmodya)! Supreme among adamantine ones! We pay homage to Adamantine Love (Vajraprīti)! [Bd]

Adamantine Dharma (Vajradharma)! Good benefit! Adamantine lotus! Well-purifying one!

World-Prized One (Lokeśvara)! Adamantine eye! We pay homage to Adamantine Eye (Vajranetra)! [Ca]

Adamantine Acuity (Vajratīkṣṇa)! Great Vehicle! Adamantine sword! Great weapon!

Wondrously Auspicious (Mañjuśrī)! Adamantine depth! We pay homage to Adamantine Wisdom (Vajrabuddhi)! [Cb]
Adamantine Cause (Vajrahetu)! Great place! Adamantine wheel! Guiding principle! 216c
Turning [of the Dharma-Wheel] (Supravartana)! Arisen from the *vajra!* We pay homage to Adamantine Place (Vajramaṇḍa)! [Cc]
Adamantine Speech (Vajrabhāṣa)! Wondrous knowledge! Adamantine recitation! Wondrous accomplishment!
Speechless One (Avāca)! Adamantine accomplishment! We pay homage to Adamantine Speech (Vajravāca)! [Cd]
Adamantine Action (Vajrakarma)! Instruction! Adamantine extensive one! Infallible one!
Action-*vajra!* Universal goer! We pay homage to Adamantine Skill (Vajraviśva)! [Da]
Adamantine Protection (Vajrarakṣa)! Great hero! Adamantine armor! Great firm one!
Invincible One (Duryodhana)! Wondrous energy! We pay homage to Adamantine Energy (Vajravīrya)! [Db]
Adamantine All[-Devouring One] (Vajrayakṣa)! Expedient means! Adamantine tusk! Great fear!
Destroyer of Mā[ra] (Mārapramardin)! Adamantine severe one! We pay homage to Adamantine Anger (Vajracaṇḍa)! [Dc]
Adamantine Union[16] (Vajrasandhi)! Majesty! Adamantine binder! Liberator!
Adamantine Fist (Vajramuṣṭi)! Supreme vow! We pay homage to Adamantine Fist! [Dd]
If anyone should keep [in mind] these names, the one hundred and eight serene praises,
Consecrated with an adamantine name, he too will obtain the like.
If anyone should praise the Great Vajradhara with these names
And chant them with upright mind, he will be like Vajradhara.

We praise you with these names, these one hundred and eight names,
And beseech you to disseminate the great guiding principle, *The Realization of the Great Vehicle.*
We entreat you, O Honorable One, we beseech you to expound the supreme rules,
The great circle of all Buddhas, the supreme Great Maṇḍala.

2. Exposition of the Great Maṇḍala

Thereupon the Lord, the Great Vajradhara, having listened to the words of entreaty of All the Tathāgatas, entered the adamantine *samādhi* [called] "Empowerment Born of the Samaya of All the Tathāgatas" and expounded the Great Maṇḍala of the Adamantine Realm.

Next I shall fully explain the supreme Great Maṇḍala:
Since it is similar to the Adamantine Realm,[17] it is called "Adamantine Realm."
In accordance with the teachings one should sit at ease in the center of the *maṇḍala,*
And contemplating the great seal[18] of the Great Sattva, one should empower [oneself].
Abiding in the seal, one should arise, and scanning all directions,
One proceeds with haughty air, chanting "Vajrasattva."
217a With a new cord, twisted well together, of proper measurements, and fine-looking—
With [such] a cord the wise person should mark out the *maṇḍala* to the best of his ability.
It is four-sided, with four entrances and adorned with four arches;
It has four [directional] cords that intersect and is decorated with colored silken banners and garlands;

The boundary [of the *maṇḍala*] between all the corner sectors and the entranceways
Is studded with *vajras* and gems: [in this fashion] one should mark out the outer circular altar (*maṇḍala*).
One should enter the central sanctuary thereof, circular in shape,
Marked out completely with a string of *vajras* and decorated with eight pillars.
[The area] within the supreme adamantine pillars should be adorned with five [lunar] discs;
In the central *maṇḍala* install an image of the Buddha [Vairocana] [X].
Within *maṇḍalas* surrounding on all sides [the central *maṇḍala* of] the Buddha [Vairocana]
Draw in succession the four foremost Samayas [A^1–D^1].
Proceeding with adamantine pace to the four *maṇḍalas* [in the four quarters],
Install all the Buddhas, [namely,] the foursome of Akṣobhya and so forth:
One should construct the altar of Akṣobhya [A] together with Vajradhara and so forth [Aa–Ad];
The *maṇḍala* of Ratnasaṃbhava [B] is filled with Vajragarbha and so forth [Ba–Bd];
The circular altar of Amitāyus (Immeasurable Life) [C] is pure with Vajranetra and so forth [Ca–Cd];
One should draw the altar of Amoghasiddhi [D] together with Vajraviśva and so forth [Da–Dd].
One should draw the Adamantine Women [A^2–D^2], installing them in the intermediate spaces of the [central] circle;
One should draw the Buddhas' Offerings [A^3–D^3] in the corners of the outer altar;
In the middle of each of the entrances is [one of] the host of Four Gatekeepers [A^4–D^4];
One should draw the Mahāsattvas [of the Good Eon (*bhadra-kalpa*)],[19] installing them in the outer altar.

3. Teacher's Rites in the *Maṇḍala*

Then, having bound the supreme *samaya* seal[20] in accordance with the rules,
The Adamantine Teacher enters [the *maṇḍala*], after which he breaks the seal and [effects] the entry (*āveśa*) [of the deities into the *maṇḍala*].
This is the heart[-mantra] for all entry: *Aḥ*.
Requesting instructions in accordance with the basic teaching, he performs self-empowerment and so forth,
After which he announces his own name and should perform acts of accomplishment with the *vajra*.
Then the Adamantine Teacher binds the *sattva-vajra* hook (*sattva-vajrāṅkuśī*),
And by summoning with a snap of his fingers, he should invoke all the Buddhas.
217b In a moment all the Buddhas together with Vajrasattva
Will assemble in the *maṇḍala*, filling all the altars.
Then he quickly visualizes the great seal of Vajrasattva
And recites once the "One Hundred and Eight [Names]."
Pleased with the assembly, the Tathāgatas are all firm;
Vajrasattva himself having been accomplished, he stands at ease as a loving friend.
In all the entrances [the Teacher] performs [ritual] acts with the [seals of the] hook and so forth;
With the great *karma* seals he establishes the *samayas*.
With the [supreme] *samaya* seals [and the seals] *sattva-vajra* and so forth
He should accomplish the Great Sattvas, reciting *"Jaḥ hūṃ vaṃ hoḥ."*[21]
Thus he summons the Buddhas and all the Great Sattvas,
Summoning them by hook and inducting them, after which he binds and subdues them.
Then with secret offerings he causes those of great awe-inspiring excellence to rejoice

[And entreats them, saying,] "For the sake of sentient beings, I beseech you to bring about success in everything!"
Such are the deeds of the Adamantine Teacher in all the altars.

The Adamantine Pinnacle: The Compendium of the Truth of All the Tathāgatas and the Realization of the Great Vehicle, Being the Scripture of the Great King of Teachings, Fascicle Two.

Fascicle Three

Extended Rules for the Great Maṇḍala ["Adamantine Realm"] (III)

IV. Initiation Rites *(continued)*

4. Initiation of the Disciple

Next, I shall explain in detail the rules for introducing an Adamantine Disciple into the Great Maṇḍala of the Adamantine [Realm]. Among these [rules] I shall first explain the introduction [into the *maṇḍala*], which is for the sake of the supreme *siddhi* of the salvation, benefit, and well-being of all realms of sentient beings without exception.[22]

When introducing [the disciple] into this Great Maṇḍala, one should not choose between worthy vessels and unworthy vessels. 217c
Why is this?

There are, World-honored Ones, sentient beings who commit great sins. If they enter this Great Maṇḍala of the Adamantine Realm, after having seen and entered it, they will be freed from all evil destinies.

[Then again] there are, World-honored Ones, sentient beings who cling to all kinds of profit, food and drink, and lustful desires, who loathe the *samaya,* and [are incapable of] performing the preliminary practices and so forth. [But even] such beings will, if they enter [this *maṇḍala*] in accordance with their mental inclinations, attain the fulfillment of all their wishes.

[Then again] there are, World-honored Ones, sentient beings who delight in singing, dancing, fun, games, food and drink, and amusements, and who, because they do not clearly understand the Dharma-nature of the realization of the Great Vehicle of All the Tathāgatas, enter the *maṇḍala*s of other families of deities; fearing the prohibitory precepts, they do not enter the *maṇḍala*s of the family of All the Tathāgatas, which encompass the fulfillment of all wishes and are able to produce unsurpassed pleasure and joy. Accordingly, these who face the path of entry to the altars (*maṇḍala*s) of evil destinies should enter this Great Maṇḍala of the Adamantine Realm in order to experience all delight, supreme *siddhi,* well-being and happiness, and to transmute the path whereby all evil destinies appear.

[Then] again there are, World-honored Ones, sentient beings abiding in the true Dharma who, because they have for the sake of all beings been seeking the Buddha's enlightenment by expedient means for the supreme *siddhi* of the morality, meditation, and wisdom of All the Tathāgatas, have been long cultivating the [four] concentrations, [eight] liberations, [ten] stages, and so forth, and have become weary of their exertions.[23] If they enter this Great Maṇḍala of the Adamantine Realm, as soon as they have entered, the fruit of [the state of] All the Tathāgatas will be not at all difficult [for them to attain], let alone other kinds of *siddhi*.

Next, [the disciple] should first of all make obeisance to All the Tathāgatas by means of the "four obeisances." [First] he makes obeisance to the eastern quarter with the whole body, stretching out his arms in the "adamantine clasp" (*vajrāñjali*) [with the palms pressed together and the fingers interlaced] and touching the ground with his chest. The mantra is:

> *Oṃ sarvatathāgatapūjopasthānāyātmānaṃ niryātayāmi, sarvatathāgatavajrasattvādhitiṣṭhasva mām.* (*Oṃ,* I offer myself for service in worship of All the Tathāgatas. O Vajrasattva of All the Tathāgatas, empower me!)

Then, placing the foregoing adamantine clasp level with his heart, he makes obeisance to the southern quarter, [touching the ground] with his forehead. The mantra is:

> *Oṃ sarvatathāgatapūjābhiṣekāyātmānaṃ niryātayāmi, sarvatathāgatavajraratnābhiṣiñca mām.* (*Oṃ,* I offer myself

for consecration through worship of All the Tathāgatas. O Vajraratna of All the Tathāgatas, consecrate me!)

Then, placing the foregoing adamantine clasp on his head, he makes obeisance to the western quarter, touching the ground with his mouth. The mantra is:

Oṃ sarvatathāgatapūjāpravartanāyātmānaṃ niryātayāmi, sarvatathāgatavajradharma pravartaya mām. (*Oṃ*, I offer myself for the incitement of worship of All the Tathāgatas. O Vajradharma of All the Tathāgatas, incite me!) 218a

Then, bringing the foregoing adamantine clasp to his heart, he makes obeisance to the northern quarter, touching the ground with the crown [of his head]. The mantra is:

Oṃ sarvatathāgatapūjākarmaṇe[24] *ātmānaṃ niryātayāmi, sarvatathāgatavajrakarma kuru mām.* (*Oṃ*, I offer myself for the act of worship of All the Tathāgatas. O Vajrakarma of All the Tathāgatas, activate me!)

Then, with [the disciple] wearing a garment of red silken fabric and his face covered with a red cloth, [the Teacher] makes the disciple bind the *sattva-vajrī*[25] seal with this mantra:

Samayas tvam. (You are the pledge.)

Then he makes him hold a garland of flowers with his two middle fingers and introduces him [into the *maṇḍala*] with this heart-mantra:

Samaya hūṃ. (Pledge! *hūṃ!*)

Having introduced him, [the Teacher] makes the following pronouncement:

Adya tvaṃ sarvatathāgatakulapraviṣṭaḥ. Tad ahaṃ te vajrajñānam utpādayiṣyāmi, yena jñānena tvaṃ sarvatathāgatasiddhim api prāpsyasi, kim utānyāḥ siddhiḥ. Na ca tvayādṛṣṭamahāmaṇḍalasya vaktavyaṃ, mā te samayo

> *vyathet.*[26] (Today you are entering the family of All the Tathāgatas. I shall generate in you that adamantine knowledge by means of which you will obtain even the accomplishment of All the Tathāgatas, not to mention other accomplishments as well. Nor should you speak [of this] to anybody who has not seen the Great Maṇḍala, lest the pledge come to naught for you.)

[Then] the Adamantine Ācārya (Teacher) should himself bind the *sattva-vajrī* seal, which he places facing downward on the disciple's head, making the following pronouncement: "This is the *samaya-vajra* (pledge-*vajra*). It will split your head [if you talk about this to others, so] you must not speak of it."

Having empowered the oath-water once, [the Teacher] makes the disciple drink it. The "oath-water" mantra is:

> *Vajrasattvaḥ svayaṃ te 'dya hṛdaye samavasthitaḥ,*
> *Nirbhidya*[27] *tatkṣaṇaṃ yāyād yadi brūyād idaṃ nayam.*
> *Vajrodaka ṭhaḥ.*
> (Vajrasattva himself has now settled in your heart.
> If you should divulge this procedure, he will at that very
> moment burst [your heart] asunder and depart.
> Adamantine water! *ṭhaḥ!*)

Then [the Teacher] addresses the disciple [saying], "Henceforth you will look upon me as Vajrapāṇi. You must do as I say, and you must not treat me with contempt. Do not bring calamity upon yourself such that you die and then fall into hell!"

218b After having spoken thus, [the Teacher says to the disciple, "Say these words:] I beseech All the Tathāgatas to empower me; I beseech Vajrasattva to enter upon me."

[Then] the Adamantine Ācārya should bind the *sattva-vajrī* seal and make this pronouncement:

> *Ayaṃ tat samayo vajraṃ vajrasattvam iti smṛtam,*
> *Āveśayatu te 'dyaiva vajrajñānam anuttaram.*
> *Vajrāveśa aḥ.*
> (This is the pledge, the *vajra* known as Vajrasattva;

May it cause unsurpassed adamantine knowledge to enter upon you this very day!
Adamantine entry! *aḥ!*)

Then [the Teacher] binds the wrath-fist (*krodha-muṣṭi*), breaking the *sattva-vajrī* seal, and [makes the disciple] recite at will the one-hundred-syllable mantra of the realization of the Great Vehicle[28] with adamantine speech. Then the *āveśa* (entry [of Vajrasattva]) takes place, and as soon as the *āveśa* has taken place, he generates subtle knowledge. Through this [knowledge] he knows the minds of others, comprehends the minds of others, and knows the three ages with respect to all matters; his mind becomes firm in the teaching of All the Tathāgatas; he totally eliminates all suffering, is freed from all evil destinies, and is invulnerable among all sentient beings; All the Tathāgatas empower him; all *siddhis* manifest before him; and he obtains the birth of unprecedented joy, well-being, and happiness. Because of this well-being and so forth, he may accomplish either *samādhi* or the *dhāraṇī*-gates,[29] or all his wishes may be completely fulfilled, or he may even accomplish the quintessence of All the Tathāgatas.

Then [the Teacher] binds the [*sattva-vajrī*] seal and, releasing it on the disciple's heart, he recites this heart-mantra:

Tiṣṭha vajra, dṛḍho me bhava, śāśvato me bhava, hṛdayaṃ me 'dhitiṣṭha, sarvasiddhiṃ ca me prayaccha, hūṃ ha ha ha ha hoḥ. (Abide, O *vajra!* be firm for me! be eternal for me! empower my heart and grant me all success! *hūṃ ha ha ha ha hoḥ!*)

Then [the Teacher] makes the disciple throw the garland of flowers onto the Great Maṇḍala with this heart-mantra:

Pratīccha vajra, hoḥ (Receive, O *vajra! hoḥ!*)

Wherever the [garland of] flowers should happen to fall, that deity is effective for him. Then [the Teacher] takes the garland of flowers and fastens it on the disciple's head with this heart-mantra:

Oṃ pratigṛhṇa tvam imaṃ sattva[ṃ] mahābala.[30] (*Oṃ,* accept this being, O you of great power!)

With this the Great Sattva accepts [the disciple], and he quickly gains success. After entry has been accomplished, [the Teacher] uncovers the [disciple's] face with this heart-mantra:

218c *Oṃ vajrasattvaḥ svayaṃ te 'dya cakṣūdghāṭanatatparaḥ,*
Udghāṭayati sarvākṣo vajracakṣur anuttaram.
(*Oṃ,* Vajrasattva himself is intent upon opening your eyes today;
The All-Eyed One opens the unsurpassed adamantine eye.)

Then [the Teacher] recites the "vision" mantra:

He vajra paśya. (Hey, *vajra,* look!)

Then he makes the disciple look at the Great Maṇḍala in regular order. As soon as he has seen [it, the disciple] is empowered and protected by All the Tathāgatas and Vajrasattva abides in the disciple's heart, whereupon he sees the play of supernatural powers [such as] various shining figures. As a result of having seen the *maṇḍala,* he will, through the Tathāgatas' empowerment, either see the Lord, the Great Vajradhara, manifesting his original form, or else he will see a Tathāgata. Henceforth [he will achieve] all objectives, all things that his mind desires, and all *siddhi*s, up to attaining [the state of] Vajradhara or a Tathāgata.

219a After having shown [the disciple] the Great Maṇḍala, [the Teacher] empowers a flask of scented water with a *vajra* and anoints the disciple's head with this heart-mantra:

Vajrābhiṣiñca. (O *vajra,* consecrate [him]!)

Then with a particular seal and fastening a garland [to the disciple], he places his own insignia in the palms of the [disciple's] two hands, reciting [this] heart-mantra:

Adyābhiṣiktas tvam asi buddhair vajrābhiṣekataḥ.
Idaṃ te sarvabuddhatvaṃ gṛhṇa vajra[ṃ] susiddhaye.

Oṃ vajrādhipatitvam abhiṣiñcāmi.[31] *Tiṣṭha vajra. Samayas tvam.*
(You have now been consecrated by the Buddhas with the adamantine consecration.
Take for good success this *vajra,* [which represents] for you complete Buddhahood!
Oṃ, I consecrate [you] as adamantine lord. Abide, *vajra!* You are the pledge.)

Then [the Teacher] consecrates [the disciple] with an adamantine name with this heart-mantra:

Oṃ vajrasattva tvām abhiṣiñcāmi vajranāmābhiṣekataḥ, he vajranāma. (*Oṃ,* O Vajrasattva, I consecrate you with the consecration of the adamantine name. Hey, adamantine name!) Adamantine So-and-so!

When [the Teacher] confers a name on the disciple, he should add *"he"* and use this when calling him.

Here ends the detailed explanation of the rules for entry into all *maṇḍalas*.

V. Knowledge for Achieving Success (*Siddhi*)

1. Four Varieties of *Siddhi*-Knowledge

Then [the Teacher] should question the disciple, saying, "Do you prefer the knowledge of the *siddhi* of generation [of material objectives], the knowledge of the *siddhi* of supernatural powers, the knowledge of the *siddhi* of the *vidyādhara,*[32] or the knowledge of the supreme *siddhi* of the knowledge of All the Tathāgatas?" He should explain that which accords with his [disciple's] wishes.

(i) Thereupon [the Teacher] teaches [the disciple] the seal-knowledge (*mudrā-jñāna*) for achieving the *siddhi* of [material] objectives.[33]

One should visualize in one's heart the form of a *vajra* resting on treasure;

Having visualized [this], one will then see hidden treasure lying in the ground.
Having visualized the form of a *vajra,* one visualizes it in the sky;
Wherever one should see it fall, that is [the site of] hidden treasure.
The form of a *vajra* on the tongue—this the wise person should visualize;
If he himself says, "It is here," after he has spoken, [his words] will come true.
One should visualize one's own body as being completely in the form of a *vajra;*
Wherever he who has been entered upon [by the *vajra*] falls, that is [the site of] hidden treasure.

The heart-mantras for these are:

Vajranidhi. (Adamantine treasure!)

Ratnanidhi. (Gem treasure!)

Dharmanidhi. (Dharma treasure!)

Karmanidhi. (Action treasure!)[34]

(ii) Next [the Teacher] should teach [the disciple] the seal-knowledge for achieving the *siddhi* of adamantine [supernatural powers].

219b The entry of the *vajra* having been effected, water assumes the form of a *vajra;*
Through [this] visualization, one quickly succeeds in walking about on water.
Having again effected the entry of the *vajra,* one's physical form assumes one's [desired] figure;
Repeatedly practicing in this manner, one spontaneously assumes the figure of [even] a Buddha.
[The *vajra*] having entered upon oneself, one visualizes oneself as being like the sky;

After having repeatedly practiced as one pleases, one will then obtain *antardhā* (invisibility).
If, when the *vajra* has entered upon oneself, one visualizes oneself as being like a *vajra,*
Then to the extent that one jumps up [in the air], one will obtain [the ability to] move through empty space.

The mantras for these are:

Vajrajala. (Adamantine water!)

Vajrarūpa. (Adamantine form!)

Vajrākāśa. (Adamantine space!)

Vajram aham. (I am a *vajra.*)

(iii) Next [the Teacher] teaches [the disciple] the seal-knowledge for achieving the *siddhi* of the adamantine *vidyādhara.*

One should visualize the figure of the moon, and one will soar up into empty space;
Grasping a *vajra* in one's hand, one will obtain [the state of] an adamantine *vidyādhara.*
Ascending up onto a lunar disc, one should visualize an adamantine gem;
He of pure body will succeed in soaring up into the sky as he wishes in a moment.
After having ascended up onto a lunar disc, [one visualizes] an adamantine lotus held in the hand;
One should visualize Vajranetra, whereupon one will attain the stage of a *vidyādhara.*
Abiding in the middle of a lunar disc, one should visualize a *karma-vajra;*
By quickly obtaining adamantine skill (*vajra-viśva = karma-vajra*), one will then attain the [state of the] all-*vidyādhara.*

The heart-mantras for these are:

Vajradhara. (Vajra-holder!)

Ratnadhara. (Gem-holder!)

Padmadhara. (Lotus-holder!)

Karmadhara. (Action-holder!)

(iv) Next [the Teacher] teaches [the disciple] the seal-knowledge for achieving the supreme *siddhi* of All the Tathāgatas.

Abiding in the meditation of all-*vajra* (*sarva-vajra* = *karma-vajra*), one contemplates in the realm of empty space;
He of adamantine body will succeed in soaring up into the sky as he pleases in a moment.
Abiding in the mental equipoise of all-purity, one repeatedly practices what is supreme;
He in whom knowledge is accomplished quickly obtains the five supernatural faculties.[35]
If one visualizes Vajrasattva throughout all space,
Then when one's thought has become firm, one will quickly become Vajradhara.
If one visualizes everything as composed of the Buddha's form in empty space,
219c Then through the mental equipoise of all Buddhas one will attain the accomplishment of perfect enlightenment.

The mantras for these are:

Vajra vajra. (*Vajra! vajra!*)

Śuddha śuddha. (Pure! pure!)

Sattva sattva. (Being! being!)

Buddha buddha. (Buddha! Buddha!)[36]

The above represents the achievement of the knowledge of all *siddhi*s.

2. Secret Practices

Next [the Teacher] should make the disciple observe the practice for competence in secrets. First of all he should recite the "oath" heart-mantra:

> *Oṃ vajrasattvaḥ svayaṃ te 'dya hṛdaye samavasthitaḥ,*
> *Nirbhidya tatkṣaṇaṃ yāyād yadi brūyād idaṃ nayam.*[37]

Then [the Teacher] addresses [the disciple] with the following words: "You must not transgress this 'oath' heart-mantra. Do not bring calamity upon yourself such that you die prematurely and fall into hell with this body!" Then [the Teacher] should teach him the secret seal-knowledge.

> Having effected the entry of the *vajra,* one claps the hands while in mental equipoise,
> With the palms in the adamantine [clasp] and softly; even mountain stones[38] will show respect.

This is the seal of the "adamantine clap" (*vajra-tāla*).

> The rite of entry of the *vajra* completed, one strikes with the palms in adamantine bind;
> By means of the method of softly [clapping] the hands, even mountain stones will enter upon one.
> By means of the above rite of entry and with the [fingers of the] adamantine bind stretched out, 220a
> The forefingers should be burst open in unison, whereupon one will destroy the one hundred families[39] in a moment.
> With all the fingers placed together in the rite of subtle entry,
> The adamantine bind is released, whereupon one is able to remove and overcome all suffering.

Next [the Teacher] should explain the secret accomplishment.

One enters via the *bhaga* (orifice) the body of either a woman or a man;
Having entered, one mentally pervades that whole body.

The heart-mantras for this are:

Vajravaśa. (Adamantine control!)

Vajraviśa.[40] (Adamantine entry!)

Vajrahana. (Adamantine destruction!)

Vajrahara. (Adamantine elimination!)

VI. Four Varieties of Seal-Knowledge

Then, having conferred the heart-mantras, [the Teacher] should teach [the disciple] the four knowledge-seals of his own chief deity. He addresses the disciple in the following manner, saying, "Be discreet toward other people, and do not show even one of these seals to those as yet unacquainted with them. Why is this? Whenever sentient beings who have not seen the Great Maṇḍala bind these [seals], none of them will be successful. Then they will engender doubt and bring calamity upon themselves, dying quickly and falling into the Great Hell of Immediate [Retribution] (Avīci), or falling into the evil destinies."

1. Knowledge of the Great Seals

Next [the Teacher] should explain the knowledge of the great seal (*mahā-mudrā*) for accomplishing All the Tathāgatas and the [Great] Sattvas.

Starting from knowledge of the mind, one should visualize an adamantine sun;
Visualizing oneself in the form of a Buddha, one should recite "Adamantine Realm."

By merely accomplishing this, one will obtain knowledge, longevity, strength, and youth;
One will be able to go anywhere, and even the state of a Buddha will not be difficult [to attain].

This is the seal for the realization of the enlightenment of All the Tathāgatas.

Next [the Teacher] should explain the binding of the great seal for accomplishing Vajrasattva.

Brandishing the [*vajra*-]pestle with haughty air and maintaining adamantine pride,
With the *vajras* of body, speech, and mind one becomes Vajrasattva.
Thereby one's seal for going everywhere, lordship over all desires, well-being,
[Supernatural] powers, longevity, strength, and superior form become similar to Vajrasattva.
Through the rite of the three *vajras* [of body, speech, and mind], and practicing in sequence as drawn [in the *maṇḍala*],
One accomplishes the Great Sattvas, each associated with [their respective] insignia and seals.
I shall now explain of all the teachings that which accomplishes (*sādhana*), that which is accomplished (*siddhi*),
And the great action of the accomplished ones (*siddha*): I shall now explain them in order.
Every day, having first performed self-empowerment and so forth at the proper time,
One accomplishes as at the beginning, after which one should follow one's inclinations [in practice]. 220b

Next [the Teacher] should explain in detail the rules for accomplishing the great seals.

Having made the *vajra* enter, one should bind according to the rules

The great seal and contemplate the Great Sattva in front.
Seeing the knowledge-*sattva,* one should visualize him in oneself;
Summoning by hook, inducting, binding, and delighting, one gains success.

The mantras for these are:

Vajrasattva āḥ (Vajrasattva! *āḥ!*): this is the heart[-mantra] for entry of the *vajra*.

Vajrasattva dṛśya (Vajrasattva, appear!): this is the heart[-mantra] for meditating on the Great Sattva.

Jaḥ hūṃ vaṃ hoḥ: this is the heart[-mantra] for summoning by hook, inducting, binding, and delighting the Great Sattva.

Reciting *"Samayas tvam* (You are the pledge)," one enters a lunar disc behind [one],
Wherein one should visualize [oneself as] the [knowledge-]*sattva,* [reciting] "I, *samayas tvam."*
Practicing in accordance with the seal of that *sattva,* one visualizes oneself [as that *sattva*];
With adamantine speech one is able to accomplish all seals.
Reciting *"Jaḥ hūṃ vaṃ hoḥ,"* one brings all the Buddhas into one's body;
One should perform good contemplation and effect the accomplishment of the great seals.
Now I shall explain the deeds, the unsurpassed adamantine action.
By achieving visualization of the Buddhas, one quickly obtains the own-nature of a Buddha. [X, A–D]
Accomplishing Sattvavajrī, one becomes lord of all Buddhas. [A^1]
By binding [the seal of] Ratnavajrī, one becomes lord of all gems. [B^1]
If one accomplishes Dharmavajrī, then one is able to uphold the Buddha's Dharma. [C^1]

By means of the seal of Karmavajrī one performs adamantine action. [D[1]]
One accomplishes Vajrasattva by binding [Vajra]sattva's seal. [Aa]
One is able to summon the *vajra*-holders through union with Vajrākarṣa. [Ab]
The great seal of Vajrarāga is able to enrapture all Buddhas. [Ac]
One delights all Buddhas through [union with] Vajrasādhu. [Ad]
One grants the consecrations of the Buddhas through the rite of the gem seal. [Ba]
One quickly becomes adamantine light through the rite of Vajrateja. [Bb]
If one cultivates Vajraketu, then one fulfills all wishes. [Bc] 220c
Through the rite of Vajrahāsa one playfully laughs together with all Buddhas. [Bd]
One upholds the adamantine Dharma through the rite of Vajradharma. [Ca]
One obtains the superior wisdom of all Buddhas through the rite of Vajratīkṣṇa. [Cb]
If one cultivates Vajracakra, then one is able to turn the Dharma-wheel. [Cc]
One accomplishes the Buddha's speech through the rite of Vajrabhāṣa. [Cd]
One quickly attains adamantine action by performing [the rite of] Vajrakarma. [Da]
Putting on adamantine armor, one obtains an adamantine body. [Db]
Accomplishing Vajrayakṣa, one becomes like Vajrayakṣa. [Dc]
All seals are successful by binding the adamantine fist. [Dd]
By means of Vajralāsyā one obtains great adamantine delight. [A[2]]

By binding [the seal of] Vajramālā, one obtains consecration from the Buddhas. [B²]
In union with Vajragītā, one obtains adamantine song. [C²]
By binding [the seal of] Vajranṛtyā, one makes offerings to all Buddhas. [D²]
One delights all and everything through [the rite of] Vajradhūpā. [A³]
In union with Vajrapuṣpā, one causes the various kinds [of beings] to show respect. [B³]
By making offerings with the seal of Vajrālokā, one obtains vision. [C³]
One is able to eliminate all suffering through the rite of Vajragandhā. [D³]
By summoning with Vajrāṅkuśa, one is able to perform all superior action. [A⁴]
One is able to induct everything through the rite of Vajrapāśa. [B⁴]
In union with Vajrasphoṭa, one becomes competent at binding all. [C⁴]
Through the rite of Vajrāveśa one is able to accomplish all entry. [D⁴]

2. Knowledge of the *Samaya* Seals

Next [the Teacher] should explain the knowledge of the adamantine *samaya* seals (*samaya-mudrā*) of All the Tathāgatas.

Joining the palms firmly together with all the fingers interlaced
Is called the "adamantine clasp" (*vajrāñjali*); [the same gesture with the fingers] tightly bound is the "adamantine bind" (*vajra-bandha*).
The *samaya* seals are all born from the adamantine bind.
I shall now explain the rules for binding [the *samaya* seals]: the adamantine bind is unsurpassed.

With the *sattva-vajrā* [seal][41] made firm, the middle fingers are raised erect like a shoot [A];
With the thumbs and middle [fingers] like the shape of a gem, the middle fingers are bent [B];
The [middle] fingers are altered to resemble lotus petals [C]; 221a
the middle fingers are interlocked [within] [D];
The forefingers touch the middle fingers: this is called the [seal of the] fifth Buddha [X].
I shall now fully explain the superior seals of the *samaya*s of the Tathāgata family, by the binding of which one gains success.
With the two hands [joined together] in the shape of the moon,[42] the middle fingers are [raised erect] like a *vajra*
And the finger pads of the remaining [thumbs and little] fingers do not touch: [this is] the seal of Vajrasattva [Aa];
The fore[fingers like] hooks [Ab], the forefingers crossed [Ac], and with a gesture as if to snap the fingers [Ad]:
This is the group of seals of the foursome of Vajrasattva [etc.].
[The seal] "gem *vajra*": the forefingers are bent with the finger pads joined [Ba];
The middle, ring, and little fingers are stretched out and [the hands] are rotated and placed level with the heart [Bb];
The ring fingers, [raised erect] like a banner, are joined to the little fingers [Bc];
Then [the previous seal] rests in the place of laughter (i.e., mouth) [Bd]: these are designated as their seals (i.e., the seals of Vajraratna, etc.).
Raising the two thumbs equally erect, the forefingers are bent like a lotus [Ca];
Then [the seal] "adamantine sword": the middle [fingers] are joined with the upper phalanges bent [Cb];
Then both ring fingers are [raised] together and the little fingers are crossed like a wheel [Cc];

Then releasing the bind of the thumbs, [the seal] is stretched out and raised from the mouth [Cd].
The finger pads of the little fingers and thumbs are joined and brought together: [this is the seal] *"karma-vajra"* [Da];
Then both forefingers together, placed level with the heart, are stretched out [Db];
The forefingers are bent like tusks, as are the little fingers too [Dc];
With the thumbs and little fingers [touching] in between, the forefingers are bent down onto [the thumbs] [Dd].
The thumbs are [raised] together at the heart [A^2]; stretching the forearm is called the "garland" [seal] [B^2];
The superior palms [in adamantine clasp] are dispersed from the mouth [C^2]; having performed [the gestures of] dance, [the palms] are joined above the head [D^2].
The adamantine bind is bestowed downward [A^3]; one's own palms are offered upward [B^3];
The forefingers are both pressed together [C^3]; [the hands are] stretched out as if in the gesture of applying [unguent] [D^3];
One forefinger is bent [A^4]; the two forefingers are bound in a knot [B^4];
The tips of the thumbs and fore[fingers] resemble a chain [C^4]; [the palms are] joined as in the adamantine fist [D^4].
I shall now explain that which accomplishes, the supreme [rite of] adamantine accomplishment:
One's own seal is placed level with the heart in the concentration of the *sattva-vajra*.
Next I shall explain the performance of deeds, the unsurpassed adamantine action.
By assembling the Tathāgatas with the seals of the
221b Adamantine Realm and so forth,
The master of the altar accomplishes the empowerment of the disciple in a moment.
If one binds the *sattva-vajrī* [seal], then one becomes [like] Vajradhara. [Aa]

Merely binding [the seal] "adamantine hook," one is able to summon all Buddhas. [Ab]
Through the rite of Desire-Vajra (Rāgavajra = Vajrarāga), one enraptures even the enlightened ones. [Ac]
Through [the seal] "adamantine joy," all [Buddhas] rejoice with voices of applause. [Ad]
By binding [the seal] "gem *vajra,*" one obtains consecration from the Buddhas. [Ba]
By binding [the seal] "adamantine sun," one obtains a halo of light like the Buddha. [Bb]
Having held the adamantine banner, one then fulfills all wishes. [Bc]
Through the rite of Vajrahāsa one laughs together with all Buddhas. [Bd]
Displaying the seal *"dharma-vajra,"* one is identical with Dharmavajra (= Vajradharma). [Ca]
Displaying everywhere [the seal] "adamantine sword," one obtains wisdom [and becomes] savior of the world. [Cb]
Cultivating [the seal] "adamantine wheel," one is then able to turn the Dharma-wheel. [Cc]
Through [the rite of] Vajrabhāṣa adamantine speech is accomplished. [Cd]
Displaying everywhere [the seal] *"karma-vajra,"* one is identical with Vajrakarma. [Da]
Firmly making [the seal] "adamantine protection," one achieves a body like a *vajra.* [Db]
With the superior seal "adamantine tusk," one is able to destroy wicked demons. [Dc]
Firmly binding the "adamantine fist," one controls all seals. [Dd]
Through the "play" [seal] one obtains joy [A^2]; through the "garland" [seal] one obtains adornments [B^2];
Through the "speech" [seal] one's speech becomes awe-inspiring [C^2]; one obtains offerings by means of the "dance" [seal] [D^2].

With the "incense" [seal] one delights the world [A^{3}]; through the "flower" [seal] one becomes graceful in form [B^{3}];
Through the "lamp" [seal] the world is purified [C^{3}]; through the "unguent" [seal] one obtains wonderful fragrance [D^{3}].
[The seal] "adamantine hook" achieves summoning [A^{4}]; [the seal] "adamantine noose" achieves induction [B^{4}];
[The seal] "adamantine chain" is able to bind [C^{4}]; [the seal] "adamantine bell" [effects] entry [D^{4}].

3. Knowledge of the *Dharma* Seals

I shall now explain the *dharma* seals (*dharma-mudrā*):

[The mantra] *"Vajrajñānam"* (Adamantine knowledge) is common to the [Five] Buddhas and is able to make firm the Adamantine Realm. [X, A–D]
Next I shall now fully explain the superior pledges of the *dharma* seals in accordance with the basic rules.
Reciting *"Samayas tvam"* (You are the pledge), one becomes lord of all seals. [Aa]
Having recited *"Ānayasva"* (Lead hither!), one is then able to summon by hook all Buddhas. [Ab]
Having chanted *"Aho sukha"* (Oh, bliss),[43] one enraptures all Buddhas. [Ac]
221c *"Sādhu sādhu"* (Well done! well done!): having said this, with applause one causes all to rejoice. [Ad]
Having recited *"Sumahās tvam"* (You are very great), one then obtains the consecration of all Buddhas. [Ba]
Having said *"Rūpoddyota"* (Shining in form!), one then obtains the majestic splendor of the true Dharma. [Bb]
Reciting *"Arthaprāpti"* (Acquisition of objectives), one is able to fulfill all most excellent wishes. [Bc]
"Ha ha hūṃ he": laughing thus, one obtains the Tathāgata's subtle smile. [Bd]

"Sarvakāri" (All-doer): having recited this, one is able to purify what is contrary to the Dharma, making everything pure. [Ca]

Having recited *"Duḥkhaccheda"* (Terminator of suffering), one is able to cut off all action [producing] the sensation of suffering. [Cb]

"Buddhabodhi" (Buddha's enlightenment): having said this, one becomes lord in the *maṇḍala*. [Cc]

Having recited *"Pratiśabda"* (Echo), one converses together with the Buddhas. [Cd]

Having recited *"Suvaśitvam"* (Fine subduing), one is master of everything everywhere. [Da]

Having said *"Nirbhaya[s] tvam"* (You are fearless), one then obtains fearlessness in a moment. [Db]

Reciting *"Śatrubhakṣa"* (Devourer of enemies), one is able to devour all foes. [Dc]

"Sarvasiddhi" (All accomplishment): having recited this, one obtains all wondrous *siddhis*. [Dd]

"Mahārati" (Great joy!): one obtains delight [A^2]; *"Rūpaśobhe"* (Beautiful in form!): likewise [B^2];

"Śrotrasaukhyā" (Pleasant to the ear): one obtains pleasure [C^2]; *"Sarvapūje"* (All offering!): one obtains offerings [D^2].

"Prahlādini" (Delighting one!): [one obtains] delight [A^3]; *"Phalāgāmi"* (Bringer of fruits!): one obtains fruits [B^3].

"Sutejāgri" (Magnificently splendid one!): one obtains splendor [C^3]; *"Sugandhāṅgi"* (Fragrantly limbed one!): one obtains fragrance [D^3].

"Āyāhi jaḥ" (Come hither, *jaḥ!*): one accomplishes hook-summoning [A^4]; *"Āhi hūṃ hūṃ"* (Come hither, *hūṃ hūṃ!*): one is able to induct [B^4].

"He sphoṭa vaṃ" (Hey, chain! *vaṃ!*): one gains much [C^4]; *"Ghaṇṭa aḥ aḥ"* (Bell! *aḥ aḥ!*): one causes to tremble [D^4].

I shall now explain the [rite of] accomplishment of the *dharma* seals, which renders pure:

Visualizing a *vajra* on the tongue, one is able to perform all deeds.

4. Knowledge of the *Karma* Seals

Next the *karma* seals (*karma-mudrā*) are explained.

One should bind the adamantine fist[44] and in mental equipoise divide it in two:
This produces two adamantine seals; next the binding [of the *karma* seals] is explained.
Holding the adamantine [fore]finger, the right hand is placed on the left:
This seal is called "supreme awakening" and is able to confer the Buddha's enlightenment. [X]
[The seal of] the Buddha Akṣobhya is called "earth-touching" [A], [that of] Ratnasaṃbhava "wish-granting seal" [B];
[The seal of] Amitāyus is [called] "supreme concentration"
222a [C], and [that of] Amogha[siddhi] "granting fearlessness" [D].
Next I shall now fully explain in sequence the *karma* seals
Of Vajrasattva and so forth, which are able to effect adamantine action.
The left [fist indicates] pride, and the right brandishes [a *vajra*] [Aa]; [the two fists] rest in the gesture of holding hooks [Ab];
One applies oneself as in archery [Ac]; [the gesture of] applause is placed level with the heart [Ad].
The two adamantine [fists are placed on the place of] consecration (i.e., forehead) [Ba]; one shows the form of a sun level with the heart [Bb];
The right elbow rests on the left fist [Bc]; the two palms reach toward the mouth [Bd].

The right [fist] makes as if to open the lotus in the left [fist] [Ca]; the left [fist rests level with] the heart and the [right fist holding a] sword kills [Cb];

[The two fists are] rotated like a fire-wheel [Cc]; the two adamantine [fists] are dispersed at the mouth [Cd].

Having rotated in adamantine dance, [the fists released pass] both cheeks and rest on the crown [of the head] [Da];

Armor [Db]; the little fingers [are made to represent] tusks [Dc]; the two fists are joined together [Dd].

With adamantine pride one should make homage with mind atremble [A^2];

One fastens a garland [B^2]; one brings [the fists] below the mouth [C^2]; one rotates [the fists] in adamantine dance [D^2].

With the rite of the adamantine fists, one should make offerings of incense and so forth:

The offerings to all Buddhas, they are differentiated as the offering seals. [A^3–D^3]

The little fingers are interlocked and the forefingers resemble large hooks [A^4];

[The hands] resemble a noose [B^4]; the two [forefingers] resemble a chain [C^4]; the backs of the hands are pressed together [D^4].

I shall now explain the [rite of] accomplishment equivalent to the performance of adamantine action:

One should cultivate [visualization of] a *karma-vajra* in the heart.

Next the various adamantine actions of the *karma* seals will be explained.

By binding the "knowledge fist," one is able to make Buddha-knowledge enter. [X]

By binding [the seal of] Akṣobhya, one obtains immobility [of mind]. [A]

By binding the seal of Ratnasaṃbhava, one is able to embrace and receive others. [B]

By binding the seal "Dharma-wheel," one is then able to turn the Dharma-wheel. [C]

Through [the seal] "supreme fearlessness" one quickly bestows fearlessness upon sentient beings. [D]

Firmly making [the seal] "adamantine pride," [one obtains] the bliss of Vajrasattva. [Aa]

Through [the seal] "adamantine hook-summons" one assembles all Buddhas in a moment. [Ab]

With adamantine arrows one enraptures even the adamantine wife. [Ac]

[With the seal] "adamantine joy" the Buddhas all accord voices of applause. [Ad]

222b Binding [the seal] "great adamantine gem," one receives consecration from the masters. [Ba]

Displaying everywhere [the seal] "adamantine sun," one becomes like Adamantine Sun (Vajrasūrya = Vajrateja). [Bb]

If one raises erect [the seal] "adamantine banner," then one causes a shower of gems to rain down. [Bc]

Displaying everywhere [the seal] "adamantine laughter," one quickly laughs on a par with Buddhas. [Bd]

If one displays everywhere [the seal] "adamantine flower," then one sees Vajradharma. [Ca]

Firmly binding [the seal] "adamantine sword," one is able to cut off all suffering. [Cb]

Displaying everywhere [the seal] "adamantine wheel," one is able to turn the Dharma-wheel. [Cc]

All the speech of the Buddhas is accomplished by [the seal] "adamantine speech." [Cd]

The offering of the "adamantine dance" brings even the Buddhas to submission. [Da]

By putting on "adamantine armor," one obtains an adamantine core. [Db]

Displaying everywhere [the seal] "adamantine tusk," one is
able to destroy even *vajras*. [Dc]
[With the seal] "adamantine fist" one is able to carry off
[everything] and one gains success with seals. [Dd]
[With the seal] "adamantine joy" one obtains delight [A^2],
[with the seal] "adamantine garland" exquisite form [B^2],
[With the seal] "adamantine song" wondrous speech [C^2], and
[the seal] "adamantine dance" renders submissive [D^2].
With the "incense" [seal] the mind rejoices [A^3], with the
"flower" [seal] one carries off everything [B^3],
The "lamp-offering" [seal brings] great effulgence [C^3], and
[the seal] "adamantine unguent" fragrance [D^3].
[The seal] "adamantine hook" is able to summon [A^4], [the
seal] "adamantine noose" is able to induct [B^4],
[The seal] "adamantine chain" causes to be bound [C^4], and
[the seal] "adamantine bell" causes to tremble [D^4].

VII. Miscellaneous Rules

I shall now explain in detail the rules for [seal-]binding common to all [four varieties of] seals. First one should break the "adamantine bind" with a clap level with the heart, reciting the following heart-mantra:

Vajrabandha traṭ. (Adamantine bind! *traṭ!*)

Thereupon one gains mastery of all seal-binding in the *vajras* of one's body, speech, and mind. Then one binds the *samaya* seal for entry of the *vajra*, reciting this heart-mantra:

Aḥ.

Thereupon one will achieve complete *āveśa* (entry), as if empowered by a close friend. Then with the *samaya* seal one contemplates the Great Sattva, reciting this heart adamantine mantra:

Mahāsamayasattvo 'ham. (I am the great pledge-being.)

Through this mantra all seals will be successful. The above are the extended rules for success in all seals.

I shall [now] explain the extended rules common [to this scripture]. First one binds one's own [deity's] seal; having bound it, one visualizes oneself as the *sattva* of one's seal with this heart-
222c mantra:

Samayo 'ham. (I am the pledge.)

Then having visualized oneself as the *sattva* of one's seal, one empowers [oneself] with this mantra:

Samayasattvādhitiṣṭhasva mām. (O pledge-being, empower me!)

Thereafter one will be successful. The above are the rules for accomplishment.

Next [I] shall explain first the case when one desires the accomplishment of [material] objectives, with this mantra:

Arthasiddhi. (Accomplishment of objectives!)

Through this mantra one gains adamantine accomplishment at will.

Next [I] shall explain the accomplishment of adamantine *siddhi,* with this heart-mantra:

Vajrasiddhi. (Adamantine accomplishment!)[45]

Next [I] shall explain the accomplishment of the *vidyādhara,* with this heart-mantra:

Vajravidyādhara. (Adamantine *vidyādhara!*)

Through this one will obtain the accomplishment of the *vidyādhara* at will.

If one desires the supreme accomplishment, one should seek accomplishment with the mantra of one's own [deity's] seal.

I shall now explain the rules common to all [seals] for making oneself become [firm] like a *vajra* in the *vajra*s of one's body, speech, and mind. If the seal empowerment should become lax or if one's mind should wish to release [the seal], then one should make firm with this heart-mantra. The mantra is:

> *Oṃ vajrasattva samayam anupālaya, vajrasattvatvenopatiṣṭha, dṛḍho me bhava, sutoṣyo me bhava, anurakto me bhava, supoṣyo me bhava, sarvasiddhiṃ me prayaccha, sarvakarmasu ca me cittaśreyaḥ kuru, hūṃ ha ha ha ha ho, bhagavan sarvatathāgatavajra mā me muñca, vajrībhava, mahāsamayasattva āḥ.* (*Oṃ,* O Vajrasattva, keep [your] pledge! be close at hand as Vajrasattva! be firm for me! be well-pleased in me! be attached to me! be well-nurturing for me! grant me all success and bring about happiness of mind for me in all actions! *hūṃ ha ha ha ha ho!* O Lord, Vajra of All the Tathāgatas, do not abandon me! be like a *vajra!* great pledge-being! *āḥ!*)

By means of this mantra, even if one commits the [five] sins that 223a
bring immediate [retribution],[46] slanders All the Tathāgatas and the true Dharma of the vast Great Vehicle, or [performs] all manner of misdeeds, one will still obtain success. Owing to the firm state of Vajrasattva, he who [practices] the seals of All the Tathāgatas will obtain in this present lifetime quickly and at his pleasure all supreme accomplishments, including the attainment of the supreme *siddhi* of the Tathāgata—thus spoke the Lord Vajrasattva of All the Tathāgatas.

I shall now explain the rules for release common to all seals. From wherever they may have arisen, all seals are to be released in that same place with this heart-mantra:

> *Vajra muḥ.*

Raising the "adamantine gem" seal from one's heart and resting it on the place of consecration (i.e., forehead), one consecrates oneself with the forefingers and parts the hands [as if] to tie a garland around one's head. Next one fastens on armor with this heart-mantra:

Oṃ vajraratnābhiṣiñca māṃ, sarvamudrā[ṃ] me dṛḍhīkuru varakavacena vaṃ. (*Oṃ,* O Adamantine Gem, consecrate me! make every seal firm for me with this excellent armor! *vaṃ!*)

Having put on the armor, one claps with the palms at the same level and causes joy with this heart-mantra:

Vajra tuṣya hoḥ. (O *vajra,* rejoice! *hoḥ!*)

Releasing the bound [seals] with this heart-mantra, one obtains joy;
One [also] attains an adamantine state just like Vajrasattva.
If one recites "Vajrasattva" just once, one will abide in well-being in accordance with one's mind's desires;
By merely reciting, everything is quickly accomplished, as has been taught by Vajrapāṇi.

Thus spoke the Lord Samantabhadra.

The actions for performing all the accomplishments of Vajrasattva and other *sattva*s
Are all successful in all deeds when one recites mindfully at will in this [scripture].
Mantras, heart[-mantras], seals, and spells (*vidyā*): cultivating as one pleases the guiding principles [for these]
Either expounded in the teachings or undertaken by oneself, they will all bring success everywhere.

Next the four varieties of secret offering will be explained. They should be performed with this mantra of the "adamantine song":

Oṃ vajrasattvasaṃgrahād vajraratnam anuttaram,
Vajradharmagāyanai[ś ca] vajrakarmakaro bhava.
(*Oṃ,* through the protection of the adamantine being [Vajrasattva], the adamantine jewel [Vajraratna] is unsurpassed,
[And] with the chantings of the adamantine teaching [Vajradharma], be a doer of adamantine action [Vajrakarma]!)

Within the [inner] *maṇḍala* one makes offerings, singing with this adamantine song of praise, [dancing] with the adamantine dance using the two palms, and offering flowers and so forth. In the outer 223b *maṇḍala,* having made offerings [with the seals] "adamantine incense" and so forth, one places [the offerings] in their proper place. All [the disciples] should make offerings according to their means.

[The Teacher] announces [the disciples' objectives] to All the Tathāgatas, and the needs of those who, having made offerings of incense and so forth at will, have entered the *maṇḍala* he satisfies with every article of all nourishment, food and drink, comfort, and so forth already offered to the Great Maṇḍala according to their means. [Then the Teacher] should confer [upon them] the "prohibitory precept of the *vajra* for the accomplishment of All the Tathāgatas":

> "This [*vajra*] represents the quintessence of all Buddhas
> resting in Vajrasattva's hand;
> You [too] should always uphold the firm prohibitory [precept] of Vajrasattva."

> *Oṃ sarvatathāgatasiddhivajrasamaya tiṣṭha, eṣa tvāṃ dhārayāmi,*[47] *vajrasattva hi hi hi hi hūṃ.* (*Oṃ,* O pledge of the *vajra* for the accomplishment of All the Tathāgatas, abide! I hold you. Vajrasattva, *hi hi hi hi hūṃ!*)

Then [the Teacher] should address each, saying, "Do not speak of this to others!" whereupon they recite the "oath" heart-mantra.[48] [Then] he announces [the names of] those who earlier entered [the *maṇḍala*] to All the Tathāgatas. Binding the *sattva-vajrī* seal, he releases it upward from below with this heart-mantra:

> *Oṃ kṛto vaḥ sarvasattvārthaḥ siddhi[r] dattā yathānugā.*
> *Gacchadhvaṃ buddhaviṣayaṃ punar āgamanāya tu.*
> *Vajrasattva muḥ.*
> (*Oṃ,* benefit has been brought by you to all sentient beings
> and success has been given accordingly.
> Return to the Buddha's realm, but to come again!
> Vajrasattva, *muḥ!*)

In this manner [should it be performed] in all *maṇḍala*s, and so is the release of the supreme seals of the *samaya*s performed.

The Adamantine Pinnacle: The Compendium of the Truth of All the Tathāgatas and the Realization of the Great Vehicle, Being the Scripture of the Great King of Teachings, Fascicle Three.

Notes

1 The title of the text and the list of Amoghavajra's official titles are repeated at the start of the second and third fascicles, but they have been omitted in the translation. For further details on Amoghavajra's titles, reference may be made to Giebel 1995: 125–7.

2 Sanskrit *sarva-tathāgata*. In the *Sarvatathāgatatattvasaṃgraha* this term does not simply refer to "all Tathāgatas" in some vague, ill-defined sense but has a more specific meaning. When used in the singular, it refers to Vairocana, while in the plural it may refer either to literally all the Tathāgatas throughout the universe (i.e., the "Adamantine Realm" [*vajradhātu*], symbolically represented by the Vajradhātu Maṇḍala) or to the Five Buddhas who, as representatives of all the other Tathāgatas, figure in the Vajradhātu Maṇḍala (and in some cases *sarva-tathāgata* in the singular can also be construed in this latter sense). In an attempt to hint at these more specific connotations of *sarva-tathāgata*, it has been translated throughout as "All the Tathāgatas" (or occasionally "All-Tathāgata") rather than "all (the) Tathāgatas."

3 The above section describes Mahāvairocana in his aspect as the Four Pāramitās or, according to Śākyamitra and Ānandagarbha, as the four "wheel-turning" bodhisattvas Vajrasattva, Vajraratna, Vajradharma, and Vajrakarma. It should be borne in mind that Mahāvairocana described in the "Supplementary Introduction" and Vairocana referred to in the "General Introduction" are not the same—in terms of the traditional three-body (*tri-kāya*) theory, Vairocana corresponds to the *saṃbhoga-kāya* and Mahāvairocana to the *dharma-kāya*.

4 The above section describes Mahāvairocana in his aspect as the Sixteen Bodhisattvas of the *dharma-maṇḍala* (type of *maṇḍala* in which the deities are usually represented by their seed-syllables [*bīja*]).

5 The above verses describe Mahāvairocana in his aspect as the Sixteen Bodhisattvas of the *mahā-maṇḍala* (type of *maṇḍala* in which the deities are represented by their physical forms).

6 The above verses describe Mahāvairocana in his aspect as the Sixteen Bodhisattvas of the *samaya-maṇḍala* (type of *maṇḍala* in which the deities are represented by objects symbolizing their vows or functions).

7 The above verses describe Mahāvairocana in his aspect as the essence of the Dharma-realm.

8 The exact meaning of *āsphānaka* is obscure, but *āsphānaka-samādhi* seems to refer to a deep state of meditation characterized by a complete absence of mental activity. It also represents a further point of contact between the historical Śākyamuni and Sarvārthasiddhi: in the case of

Śākyamuni it is said to have constituted the final stage of his six years of austerities, and in the case of Sarvārthasiddhi it would also appear to represent the last of his ascetic practices. But whereas in Śākyamuni's case it was succeeded by "unsurpassed perfect enlightenment," in the latter's case it is followed by initiation into a distinctively esoteric five-stage process of enlightenment (*pañcākārābhisaṃbodhikrama*).

9 The Sanskrit is clearer in meaning: "That [which had the] appearance of a lunar disc, I see it really as a lunar disc." The difference between the "appearance of a lunar disc" (*candra-maṇḍalākāra*) of the previous stage and the "lunar disc" (*candra-maṇḍala*) of this stage is explained in various ways in the secondary literature, but the implication is that the former is in some way defective or incomplete when compared with the latter.

10 The remainder of this section describes the generation of the thirty-two deities who, together with the Five Tathāgatas (or Buddhas), constitute the thirty-seven main deities of the Vajradhātu Maṇḍala.

11 The five factors of "morality" (*śīla*), "meditation" (*samādhi*), "wisdom" (*prajñā*), "liberation" (*vimukti*), and "knowledge-and-vision of liberation" (*vimukti-jñāna-darśana*) are collectively known as the "five aggregates of the Dharma," and a Buddha is said to be endowed with these five qualities.

12 The Buddhist teachings (Dharma) are sometimes likened to a raft, which is abandoned once it has served its purpose of ferrying people across a river; similarly, the teachings are deemed to be only a means and not an end in themselves.

13 The passage in brackets is also missing in both Sanskrit manuscripts, but it occurs in the Tibetan translation and Dānapāla's Chinese translation.

14 On "entry" (*āveśa*), see below (e.g., p. 76–7). It refers to the "descent" of a deity into the person of a practitioner and plays an important role in the practices described in the *Sarvatathāgatatattvasaṃgraha*.

15 Sanskrit *nāmāṣṭaśata,* "one hundred and eight names." There are in fact one hundred and twelve names, i.e., seven each for each of the Sixteen Bodhisattvas.

16 Read *ho,* "union," for *ling,* "command."

17 Sanskrit *vajradhātu*. Here it signifies the world of reality as envisioned by the author(s) of the *Sarvatathāgatatattvasaṃgraha,* and the Vajradhātu Maṇḍala described below is a symbolic representation of this reality. Since the *maṇḍala* is described only summarily, reference should also be made to the diagram on page 12.

18 Sanskrit *mahā-mudrā*. Here it refers to a diety's physical form; cf. p. 85.

19 Usually sixteen in number.

[20] This refers to the seal of Vajrasattva described on p. 89 ([Aa]); it is also referred to below as the *sattva-vajrī* seal (*sattva-vajri-mudrā,* a.k.a. *sattva-vajrī*).

[21] On *karma* seals, see p. 94ff; on *samaya* seals and the *sattva-vajrī* seal, etc., see p. 88ff. The mantra *Jaḥ hūṃ vaṃ hoḥ* consists of the seed-syllables of the Four Gatekeepers, who represent the four stages in the introduction of the deities into the *maṇḍala* (alluded to immediately below); cf. p. 86.

[22] The Sanskrit text does not have personal verbs here, but "I" presumably refers to the expositor of the *maṇḍala,* etc., above (i.e., Vajradhara = Vairocana).

[23] This represents a negation of traditional forms of Buddhist practice, here encapsulated as the four states of meditation (*dhyāna*), eight kinds of meditation for attaining liberation (*vimokṣa*) from mental defilements, and ten stages (*bhūmi*) in the career of a bodhisattva.

[24] According to the rules of *sandhi,* this should read *-karmaṇa,* but Amoghavajra has *-karmaṇe.*

[25] See n. 20.

[26] Amoghavajra's transliteration is problematic in parts, and for simplicity's sake the version given here follows that of the Sanskrit text; Amoghavajra's transliteration (which is essentially identical in meaning) appears to read as follows: *Adyas tvaṃ sarvatathāgatakūle praviṣṭas. Tad ahaṃ te vajrajñānam utpādayiṣyāmi, yena jñānena tvaṃ sarvatathāgatasiddhir api prāptāsi, kiṃ punar anyāḥ siddhayaḥ <??>. Na ca tvayādṛṣṭamahāmaṇḍalasya vaktavyaṃ, mā te samayo vyathed iti.*

[27] Amoghavajra has *nirbhidyas.*

[28] I.e., the mantra beginning *"Oṃ vajrasattva..."* on p. 99.

[29] The Sanskrit text has simply *"dhāraṇīs,"* and here they probably refer to the ability to comprehend and retain the Buddhist teachings and devices toward that end rather than to mystical formulae.

[30] The Sanskrit text has *mahābalaḥ.*

[31] The Sanskrit text has *vajrādhipati tvām abhiṣiñcāmi* ("O Adamantine Lord, I consecrate you"), and Amoghavajra's transliteration could also be interpreted thus.

[32] Literally, "knowledge/spell-holder." The primary meaning of *vidyā* is "knowledge" or "science," but it also came to mean "magical power" or "spell." *Vidyādhara* thus refers to a being, either human or supernatural, possessed of magical power.

[33] Sanskrit *artha-siddhi,* i.e., the acquisition of wealth.

[34] Although *-nidhi* is not the regular vocative ending, it has been provisionally translated in a vocative sense.

35 Sanskrit *pañcābhijñā:* supernatural vision, supernatural hearing, ability to know others' thoughts, ability to know former lives, and ability to perform miracles such as appearing anywhere at will.

36 In Horiuchi's Sanskrit edition these mantras are given as compounds, i.e., *vajra-vajra,* etc.

37 See p. 76 for an English translation.

38 The Sanskrit text has simply "mountain" (*parvata*). The implication is that if even an inanimate mountain shows respect (or, according to the Sanskrit, falls under one's power), then animate beings are even more likely to do so.

39 According to Ānandagarbha, this refers to various kinds of mental defilements (*kleśa* and *upakleśa*).

40 Or possibly *vajrāveśa* (Sanskrit text has *vajraviśa*).

41 The Tibetan translation makes it clear that this refers to the "adamantine bind" (*vajra-bandha*), which, as is noted in the text, is the basic seal underlying all the *samaya* seals.

42 This again refers to the "adamantine bind."

43 Sanskrit *aho sukha iti...* indicates that *sukha* is nominative, not vocative. The differentiation between nominative and vocative case endings (the latter indicated by an exclamation mark) in the English translations of the following mantras is generally based on the Sanskrit text, unless Amoghavajra's transliteration clearly precludes such an interpretation.

44 Sanskrit *vajra-muṣṭi.* Corresponding to the *samaya* seal of Vajramuṣṭi described on p. 90 ([Dd]), it is formed by grasping the thumb with the middle, ring, and little fingers while the tip of the forefinger presses down on the thumb joint, and it forms the basis of the *karma* seals.

45 Again, *-siddhi* in this and the preceding mantra is not the regular vocative ending, but it has been provisionally translated in a vocative sense.

46 The five cardinal sins of killing one's father, killing one's mother, killing an arhat, causing the Buddha's body to bleed, and causing disunity in the Sangha.

47 The Sanskrit text has *eṣa tv ādhārayāmi* ("I receive [you]").

48 I.e., the "oath-water" mantra on p. 76.

Bibliography

Giebel, Rolf W. "The *Chin-kang-ting ching yü-ch'ieh shih-pa-hui chih-kuei:* An Annotated Translation." *Naritasan Bukkyō Kenkyūjo Kiyō* (*Journal of Naritasan Institute for Buddhist Studies*), No. 18, 1995. Translation of Taishō No. 869.

Horiuchi, Kanjin. *Bon-Zō-Kan taishō Shoe Kongōchō-gyō no kenkyū, bonpon kōtei hen*, Vol. 1. Kōyasan: Mikkyō Bunka Kenkyūjo, 1983.

Lokesh Chandra, editor. *Sarva-tathāgata-tattva-saṅgraha*. Delhi: Motilal Banarsidass, 1987.

Lokesh Chandra and David L. Snellgrove. *Sarva-tathāgata-tattva-saṅgraha: Facsimile Reproduction of a Tenth Century Sanskrit Manuscript from Nepal*. Śata-piṭaka Series, Vol. 269. New Delhi: International Academy of Indian Culture, 1981.

Nasu, Seiryū. *Kongōchō-gyō kōden*. Narita: Naritasan Shinshōji, 1976.

Snellgrove, David. *Indo-Tibetan Buddhism: Indian Buddhists and Their Tibetan Successors*. Vol. 1. Boston: Shambhala Publications, 1987. Includes translations of several passages from the Sanskrit text of the *Sarvatathāgatatattvasaṃgraha*.

Todaro, Dale. "An Annotated Translation of the *Pañcābhisaṃbodhi* Practice of the *Tattvasaṃgraha*." *Mikkyō Bunka*, Vol. 159, 1987.

Tsuda, Shiníchi. "A Critical Tantrism." *Memoirs of the Research Department of the Toyo Bunko*, No. 36, 1978.

Yamada, Isshi, editor. *Sarva-tathāgata-tattva-saṅgraha nāma mahāyāna-sūtra*. Śata-piṭaka Series, Vol. 262. New Delhi: Jayyed Press, 1981.

THE SUSIDDHIKARA SUTRA

Translated from the Chinese of Śubhākarasiṃha
(Taishō Volume 18, Number 893)

by

Rolf W. Giebel

Contents

Translator's Introduction

The Text

The *Susiddhikara-sūtra* is a Buddhist Tantric scripture belonging to the so-called Kriyā Tantras, or "Action Tantras," which represent the first category of what was to become in Tibet the standard fourfold classification of Buddhist tantras and which, as may be inferred from their designation, place particular emphasis on ritual. Among the many Kriyā Tantras, the *Susiddhikara-sūtra* is classified as a general tantra, along with the *Subāhuparipṛcchā-nāma-tantra, Sarvamaṇḍalasāmānyavidhi-guhyatantra,* and *Dhyānottara-paṭalakrama,* and it provides perhaps the most comprehensive description of the basic practices associated with the Kriyā Tantras. In the Esoteric branch of the Japanese Tendai sect, moreover, where it is regarded as one of the three basic scriptures of Esoteric Buddhism along with the *Vairocanābhisaṃbodhi-sūtra* and *Sarvatathāgata-tattvasaṃgraha,* it is defined as a "nondual" scripture unifying the teachings of the other two basic scriptures.

To date no manuscript of the Sanskrit original of the *Susiddhikara-sūtra* has been discovered (although a number of Sanskrit verses have been preserved in Chinese transliteration), but it was translated into Tibetan (Peking No. 431) and Chinese (Taishō No. 893). The Sanskrit title preserved in the Tibetan translation is *Susiddhikara-mahātantra-sādhanopāyika-paṭala* ("Section on Expedient Means for Rites of Accomplishment" in the *Susiddhikara Great Tantra*), thus suggesting that, properly speaking, the *Susiddhikara* was a larger work of which the Tibetan and Chinese translations represent but one part. There is in fact both internal and external evidence pointing toward this possibility, but it remains conjectural at present, and here the term *Susiddhikara-sūtra* is used to denote the text as preserved in the Tibetan and Chinese translations.

The Chinese translation of the *Susiddhikara-sūtra* was produced in 726 by Śubhākarasiṃha (637–735), and the Taishō Edition gives three separate recensions, all divided into three fascicles: the Koryŏ edition, the (Southern) Sung edition, and a version based on a Japanese manuscript, the earliest copy of which has since been found to date from the mid-eighth century. In addition to minor differences in wording and meaning, there are several more conspicuous differences between these three recensions—the order of the second and third fascicles has been reversed in the Japanese manuscript version; Chapters 13–15 of the Koryŏ edition are missing in the other two recensions; chapters have been divided differently, with the Koryŏ edition having thirty-seven chapters, the Sung edition thirty-five chapters, and the Japanese manuscript version thirty-four chapters; there are noticeable differences in content between Chapters 2 and 7 of the Koryŏ and Sung editions on the one hand and the corresponding chapters of the Japanese manuscript version on the other; and, perhaps because of an accidental reversal in the order of two consecutive folios, a section of Chapter 8 has been mistakenly transposed to partway through Chapter 9 in the Sung edition.

Whereas the Tibetan translation is in verse, the Chinese translation has for the most part been rendered in prose, often elaborating on points left unexplained in the Tibetan translation. If one ignores these differences, however, it is the Koryŏ edition among the three Chinese recensions that tallies most closely with the Tibetan translation (which is divided into forty chapters and is presumably more faithful to the original Sanskrit), and the fact that it contains three chapters missing in the Japanese manuscript version (perhaps because of a defective Sanskrit manuscript) and in the Sung edition suggests that the text of the Koryŏ edition had been revised at some stage after Śubhākarasiṃha's translation with reference to a Sanskrit manuscript (these revisions being also reflected in the first seven chapters of the Sung edition). Therefore, although the Japanese manuscript version represents the earliest of the three recensions and is presumably identical or closest to Śubhāharasiṃha's own translation, the English translation has been based on the Koryŏ edition since among the three Chinese recensions it appears to provide the fullest rendition of what may be assumed to have become the established Sanskrit text.

The only commentary on the *Susiddhikara-sūtra* is the *Soshitsujikara-kyō ryakusho* (seven fascicles; Taishō No. 2227) by the Japanese scholar-monk Ennin (794–864) of the Tendai sect. For further details on some of the rites covered only cursorily in the *Susiddhikara-sūtra,* reference may also be made to a manual translated (or perhaps composed) by Śubhākarasiṃha (Taishō No. 894), and a similar manual, entitled *Susiddhikarasādhanasaṃgraha* and attributed to Varabodhi, is preserved in Tibetan (Peking No. 3890). A representative Japanese rendition of the Japanese manuscript version of the *Susiddhikara-sūtra* in pseudoclassical *kundoku* style may be found in the *Kokuyaku Issaikyō* series ("Mikkyō-bu" 5), but modern research on the *Susiddhikara-sūtra* is virtually nonexistent.

Contents

The *Susiddhikara-sūtra* opens rather abruptly with the Bodhisattva Wrathful Kuṇḍalin asking Vajradhara a series of questions on the procedures for reciting mantras "in order to quickly gain success" (Chapter 1), and the rest of the work represents Vajradhara's reply to these questions (Chapters 2–37). The word *susiddhikara* in the title means in fact "good at producing success," and the *Susiddhikara-sūtra* could thus in essence be said to set forth the general rules for creating conditions conducive to "success" (*siddhi;* Chinese *ch'eng-chiu*) in any rites that a practitioner may wish to perform. These rules range from guidelines for chosing one's teacher or disciple and the ritual site to detailed lists of offerings and directions for invoking deities, performing *homa* ("burnt offering"), constructing *maṇḍalas*, and conducting other rites. "Success" is of course a very broad term, and sometimes it refers to more specific "accomplishments" or "attainments," a conspectus of which is provided in Chapter 16, and even more particularly to the act of magically charging or empowering some object, in which case the same Chinese term *ch'eng-chiu* (or simply *ch'eng*) has been rendered as "effectuation." These connotative distinctions are by no means always clearcut, but for the sake of clarity an attempt has been made to differentiate them in the English translation.

In addition to this preoccupation with "success," another salient feature of the *Susiddhikara-sūtra* is its underlying ternary system. Not only are the deities divided into three families or groups (Buddha, Lotus, and Vajra), but rites are broadly divided into three types (*śāntika* [pacification], *pauṣṭika* [prosperity], and *ābhicāruka* [subjugation]), while success is measured in terms of three grades (higher, middling, and lower), with each grade being subdivided into three further grades, and the three families of deities and three types of rites are sometimes similarly ranked in three grades. This ternary system is also applied to other situations as well, and it is important to keep it in mind, for it provides an underlying strand of logic throughout much of the text.

All in all, the *Susiddhikara-sūtra* is thus little concerned with doctrinal matters, and it focuses almost exclusively on the ritual practices characteristic of early Tantric Buddhism. There now follows a brief summary of the contents of the Koryŏ edition chapter by chapter.

Chapter 1. Questions. In this opening chapter the Bodhisattva Wrathful Kuṇḍalin poses a series of questions to Vajradhara.

Chapter 2. The Characteristics of Mantras. Vajradhara begins his reply to Kuṇḍalin's questions by describing the chief distinguishing features of the *Susiddhikara-sūtra,* and then, following a mantra, briefly explains the ternary system noted above. This is followed by the three main mantras of the three families (i.e., the mantras of the mother, *vidyārāja,* and *mahākrodha* of each family) and guidelines for determining to which family a mantra belongs, as well as miscellaneous instructions on the use of mantras. (In the

Japanese manuscript version and Tibetan translation Chapters 1 and 2 constitute a single chapter.)

Chapter 3. Distinguishing the Characteristics of an *Ācārya;* Chapter 4. Distinguishing the Characteristics of One Who Recites Mantras; Chapter 5. Distinguishing [the Characteristics of] an Associate; Chapter 6. Selection of the Site. These four chapters describe the characteristics of the teacher (*ācārya*), his prospective disciples (*mantrin*), his associates or assistants, and the places suitable for performing rites of accomplishment.

Chapter 7. Observation of the Precepts. This chapter first outlines the code of conduct to which the practitioner must adhere, with somewhat detailed instructions on ablutions. It then gives brief directions for making several articles with which the practitioner should be equipped (*vajra,* bead circlet, cogongrass ring, and protective waist-cord), and closes with further admonitions.

Chapter 8. Offering Flowers; Chapter 9. Unguents; Chapter 10. Distinguishing Incense; Chapter 11. Distinguishing the Rules for Burning Lamps; Chapter 12. Offering Food. These five chapters describe the flowers, unguents, incense, lamps, and food that serve as the five main types of offerings.

Chapter 13. The *Śāntika* Rite; Chapter 14. The *Pauṣṭika* Rite; Chapter 15. The *Ābhicāruka* Rite. These three chapters (which are missing in the other two Chinese recensions and constitute a single chapter in the Tibetan translation) provide basic instructions on how to perform *homa* for the *śāntika, pauṣṭika,* and *ābhicāruka* rites respectively. Chapter 15 also gives justificatory reasons for performing the *ābhicāruka* rite, which would at first sight seem to run counter to the spirit of Buddhism.

Chapter 16. Distinguishing the Rites of Accomplishment. As is indicated by its alternative title ("The Characteristics of *Siddhi*"), this chapter describes the various accomplishments (*siddhi*) to be attained by the practitioner, as well as explaining the relationship between the different types of mantras and the three grades of accomplishment.

Chapter 17. Invoking the Deity. This chapter first explains how to prepare offerings for receiving the deity (*argha*) and then gives instructions on how to invoke one's own and other deities.

Chapter 18. Rules for Worship Procedures. This, the longest chapter, describes how to worship the deities once they have been invoked and also provides information on other sundry matters, which include directions for making offerings, protecting the ritual site, protecting oneself, and dismissing the deities; instructions on the type of seat to be used by the practitioner; verses of homage to the Three Jewels, Avalokiteśvara, and Vajradhara, followed by formulas for the confession of sins, taking refuge in the Three Jewels, generating the mind of enlightenment (*bodhicitta*), transferring merit, and making vows; instructions on the making and use of rosaries, as well as miscellaneous rules pertaining to the recitation of mantras; signs of success in recitation; and instructions on the ingesting of the five cow products (i.e., milk, curds, ghee, dung, and urine). (This chapter is divided into three chapters in the Tibetan translation.)

Chapter 19. Rites for Irradiating [the Deity]. The title of this chapter is a misnomer, for rather than dealing with "irradiation" (on which see Chapter 32), it describes how to increase the majesty or potency of deities and the mantras over which they preside by means of rites such as *homa*.

Chapter 20. Rites for Consecrating the Deity. This chapter explains how to consecrate the deity by pouring scented water from a decorated flask over an effigy of the deity, again in order to increase the deity's potency.

Chapter 21. Signs of the Efficacy of One's Prayers. This chapter describes the types of dreams that are indicative of success and the procedures to be followed for obtaining such dreams.

Chapter 22. Rites for Receiving Mantras. This chapter explains the procedures to be followed when a teacher wishes to confer a mantra on his disciple.

Chapter 23. The Rite for Making Mantras Complete. The practitioner may have cause to suspect that his mantra is in some way defective, and this chapter explains how to remedy this situation.

Chapter 24. Increasing [a Mantra's] Majesty. This chapter describes several rites for increasing the majesty or potency of a mantra.

Chapter 25. Rules for *Homa*. This chapter explains the general rules for performing *homa*.

Chapter 26. Preparing the Appurtenances for Recitation. This chapter lists the implements and other articles necessary for performing various rites.

Chapter 27. The Characteristics of Articles for Effectuation. This chapter describes the characteristics of articles that may be ritually empowered or effectuated for use in rites of accomplishment.

Chapter 28. Taking [Possession of] Articles for Effectuation; Chapter 29. Cleansing Articles [for Effectuation]. These two chapters explain how to go about acquiring and then washing and purifying the articles to be effectuated.

Chapter 30. The Measurements and Quantities of Articles [for Effectuation]. This chapter gives the measurements and quantities to be observed when wishing to effectuate different articles.

Chapter 31. Rites in the Great Consecration Maṇḍala for Eliminating All Obstructions. This chapter explains the procedures to be followed when consecrating an initiand, including the construction of the *maṇḍala,* the performance of *homa,* and the actual consecration.

Chapter 32. Irradiating Articles [for Effectuation]. This chapter explains several methods for "irradiating" articles for effectuation, or causing them to generate radiant energy or magical power (*tejas*), thereby increasing their efficacy.

Chapter 33. Differentiating the Times for *Siddhi*. This chapter sets forth the most propitious months of the year, days of the month, and times of the day for performing different rites.

Chapter 34. Completing the Preparations for [Rites of]

Accomplishment. This chapter provides some additional instructions on the use of the protective waist-cord and on the preparation of eye ointment to relieve fatigue, and it then describes auspicious signs indicative of success.

Chapter 35. Inviting Deities to Empower the [Article for] Effectuation. This chapter explains the procedures for invoking deities to effectuate the article to be effectuated, and it covers the selection of the site, construction of the *maṇḍala,* and rites of effectuation.

Chapter 36. Rites for Redressing Deficiencies. This chapter first explains some simple procedures for redressing any deficiencies that may have occurred in one's practice, and it then describes three *maṇḍala*s, for the Buddha, Lotus, and Vajra Families respectively, to be used when these simple procedures prove to be inadequate. This is followed by instructions for a special *homa* rite called *saṃpāta-homa* ("contact *homa*"), which is performed to help effectuate an article. Next, three *maṇḍala*s for effectuating articles are described, again for the Buddha, Lotus, and Vajra Families, and these are followed by a single *maṇḍala* common to all three families. When performing these rites, various hindrances may arise, and accordingly methods for dispelling these are also explained. The chapter closes with instructions for completing effectuation. (This chapter is divided into four chapters in the Tibetan translation.)

Chapter 37. Rites for Retrieving an Article for Effectuation That Has Been Stolen. This chapter begins by describing a *maṇḍala* and accompanying rites to which one should have recourse if an article is stolen immediately after it has been effectuated or while it is still being effectuated. This is followed by instructions for a *maṇḍala* and accompanying rites to be used if some time has elapsed since the theft. Once the article has been retrieved, it is divided and shared in the prescribed manner, and the practitioner enjoys the fruits of success. In some instances he may, however, be unsuccessful in his endeavors, and this final chapter closes with several rites to be performed in such circumstances. (This chapter is divided into two chapters in both the Tibetan translation and the other two Chinese recensions, but the point of division differs.)

A Note on the Translation

The English translation presented here follows the Koryŏ edition as reproduced in the Taishō Edition (No. 893), although scribal and/or typographical errors have been corrected where necessary, and in some problematic passages I have followed the Japanese manuscript version. My aim has been to be as faithful as possible to Śubhākarasiṃha's Chinese translation, which means that when Śubhākarasiṃha translates, I generally also translate, and when he transliterates, I generally also transliterate. There are several exceptions to this, one being the treatment of proper names, for which I give the Sanskrit when known, followed on first appearance by a translation conforming with Śubhākarasiṃha's Chinese rendering (which may in some instances appear to deviate somewhat from the Sanskrit).

In accordance with the editorial policy of this translation series, the notes have in the main been confined to points having a direct bearing on the interpretation of the text. However, in view of the existence of three Chinese recensions, I have also provided in the notes translations of several passages from the Japanese manuscript version that differ markedly from the Koryŏ edition, and because of the important role played by mantras in Tantric Buddhism I have also noted their variant forms as found in the other two Chinese recensions and the Tibetan translation. (It should perhaps be pointed out here that I have been able to refer only to the sDe-dge, Peking, and sTog Palace editions of the Tibetan translation.) The mantras have, moreover, been assigned serial numbers (given in brackets) to facilitate cross-referencing and are provisionally translated on first appearance.

No attempt has been made to give the scientific names of the dozens of plant names (mostly transliterated) that appear in the text, partly because the dictionaries often list more than one equivalent, but whenever possible the common English name has been given in parentheses. The identification of these plant names is an area requiring further research, and although the improvisation resorted to here is not wholly satisfactory, the reader of the English translation should still be in a better position than earlier readers of the Chinese, for whom the transliterated plant names would have been even less penetrable. When the Sanskrit reconstruction of a transliterated term is uncertain, this has been indicated by a parenthesized question mark, while angle brackets (< >) either indicate explanatory interpolations in the Chinese or, when they enclose parts of Sanskrit reconstructions of transliterated terms, mark superfluous syllables in Śubhākarasiṃha's transliteration.

The Susiddhikara Sutra

Translated by Śubhākarasiṃha, the Tripiṭaka Master from Central India, during the Greater T'ang

Fascicle One

Chapter One 603a

Questions

Then the Bodhisattva Wrathful Kuṇḍalin joined his palms together in reverence and prostrated himself at the feet of the Honored One, Vajradhara (Vajra-Holder), and asked the following question: "Once in former times I heard from Your Honored Self the rites and procedures for the *maṇḍala*s of all the *vidyārājas*;[1] I also heard of the virtues of the divine efficacy of the *vidyārāja*s and their retainers. For the sake of future sentient beings I beg you, O Honored One, to please explain them in detail. By what rules should one recite mantras in order to quickly gain success? Although the syllables of these mantras are of one essence, the rites that they accomplish are countless in number." He then asked [the following questions] in verse:

"What are the characteristics of mantras? (v. Chap. 2)[2] And
the characteristics of an *ācārya* (teacher)? (v. Chap. 3)
What are [the characteristics of] an adept? (v. Chap. 4) And
explain the characteristics of an associate! (v. Chap. 5)
Which localities are excellent [for perfoming rites]? In which
places is it easy to succeed quickly ? (v. Chap. 6)
What are the characteristics of [self-]control? And what is it
proper and improper to do? (v. Chap. 7)
What are the expedient means and procedures for reciting
mantras? (v. Chap. 7)
Which flowers bring success easily? (v. Chap. 8) How does
one use unguents? (v. Chap. 9)
How does one make offerings of food? (v. Chap. 12) And
which incense does one burn? (v. Chap. 10)

What are the characteristics of burning lamps? (v. Chap. 11)
What is *śāntika* (pacification)? (v. Chap. 13)
What are the characteristics of [the rites for] increasing prosperity? (v. Chap. 14) How does one subjugate one's enemies? (v. Chap. 15)
What sorts of things does one accomplish in each of these three kinds [of rites]? (v. Chap. 16)
What are the characteristics of success in the higher, middling, and lower procedures? (v. Chap. 16)
By which rites does one summon [deities]? (v. Chap. 17) How does one worship them? (v. Chap. 18)
How does one protect oneself? (v. Chap. 18) What are the details of recitation? (v. Chap. 18)
What are the characteristics of reciting mantras? (v. Chap. 19) How does one perform consecration? (v. Chap. 20)
What are the characteristics of testing mantras? (v. Chap. 21) How should one receive them? (v. Chap. 22)
How are the syllables [of mantras] made complete? (v. Chap. 23) How does one increase [the potency of mantras]? (v. Chap. 24)
603b How does one perform *homa* (burnt offering) and the rites of procedure? (v. Chap. 25)
And what articles does one use to bring about quick success? (v. Chap. 26)
What are the characteristics of effectuating drugs? (v. Chap. 27) What are the characteristics of receiving drugs? (v. Chap. 28)
What are the methods for purifying drugs? (v. Chap. 29) What are the measurements and quantities for drugs? (v. Chap. 30)
Those drugs and their appearance—I beg you, O Honored One, endowed with compassion,
To explain each to me clearly! How does one protect articles for effectuation? (v. Chap. 32)

And how does one differentiate how to divide them? (v. Chap. 37) How does one make use of articles for effectuation? (v. Chap. 37)
Please deign to explain their characteristics separately! How does one cause articles that have been lost to be returned? (v. Chap. 37)
When one is harmed [by a hindrance (?)], how does one return it to him [who caused it]? (v. Chap. 36) What are the characteristics of knowing obstructors in advance? (v. Chap. 36)
What are the *maṇḍalas* of effectuation? (v. Chap. 36) What is the *maṇḍala* for accomplishing [all] deeds? (v. Chap. 36)
What is the consecration *maṇḍala?* (v. Chap. 31)
For the sake of sentient beings I beg you to discourse in detail
On the above questions and in accordance with what is important!"

Chapter Two

The Characteristics of Mantras

Thereupon Vajradhara, auspiciously adorned, worthy of worship by all *vidyādharas*,[3] and a bodhisattva of great compassion, addressed Adamantine Wrathful Kuṇḍalin of Great Energy, saying, "Well spoken, well spoken, Great Wrathful One! You have done well to ask of me such questions. Be sure to listen single-mindedly and attentively to these supreme and sublime rules. This *Susiddhikara*[*-sūtra*] has five kinds of adornment: the first is called 'great energy'; the second is called '*vidyārāja*'; the third is 'eliminating obstructions'; the fourth is 'accomplishing all valiant deeds'; and the fifth is 'effectuating all mantras.' This *Susiddhi*[*kara*]*-sūtra* is such that if you are unsuccessful when observing other mantra rites, you should also recite the basic mantra of this scripture, in which case you will be quickly successful.[4] Among the three families[5] [of Buddha, Lotus, and Vajra] this scripture is king. It is also able to accomplish all manner of deeds, namely, deeds of self-protection, boundary-binding (i.e., delimiting and protecting the ritual site), and invocation, as well as deeds of worship, assistance, punishment, and instruction, and all mantras are successful.

"Next, among the heart-mantras, that with three *hūṃ* syllables is also able to accomplish all ritual deeds such as described above. The heart-mantra with three *hūṃ* [syllables is]:

> *Namo ratnatrayāya, namaś caṇḍavajrapāṇaye mahāyakṣasenāpataye, oṃ susidhya sidhya sādhaya susiddhikara hūṃ* 603c
> *hūṃ hūṃ phaṭ phaṭ*. (Homage to the Three Jewels! Homage to Violent Vajrapāṇi, great general of the *yakṣas*! *Oṃ*, be well successful! be successful! bring success! O you who are good at bringing success! *hūṃ hūṃ hūṃ phaṭ phaṭ!*) [1][6]

"Next, the rites for higher, middling, and lower accomplishments are as have been explained in other scriptures. He who is desirous of success must understand the higher, middling, and lower rites of mantras. This scripture embraces the *maṇḍala* rites performed in all three families. The mantras of the Buddha Family are for *śāntika* (pacification) [rites], the mantras of Avalokiteśvara (Sound-Observer; i.e., the Lotus Family) are for *pauṣṭika* (prosperity) [rites], and the mantras of the Vajra [Family] are for *ābhicāruka* (subjugation) [rites]. From the armpits to the crown [of the head] corresponds to the higher grade [of accomplishments], from the navel to the armpits corresponds to the middling grade, and from the feet to the navel corresponds to the lower grade. Among the mantras you should also differentiate the three kinds of accomplishments, and the three families are each divided into three [grades]: this you must fully understand. Among the mantras of the three families, those of the *vidyārāja*s are for higher accomplishments, the mantras of sundry messengers, *ceṭa*s (male servants), *ceṭī*s (female servants), and so forth are for lower accomplishments, and the mantras expounded by other deities [are for middling accomplishments]. The rites for the three kinds of deeds are firstly the *śāntika* rite, secondly the *pauṣṭika* rite, and thirdly the *ābhicāruka* rite. All of these three deeds are to be found in each of the three familes: you should be fully acquainted with how to differentiate their procedures.

"Within the Buddha Family use the Buddha-Mother, who is called Buddhalocanā (Buddha-Eye): use her mantra for the *śāntika* [rite]. The mantra of the Buddha-Mother is:

> *Namo bhagavatoṣṇīṣāya, oṃ ruru sphuru jvala tiṣṭha siddhalocani sarvārthasādhani svāhā.* (Homage to the Blessed One, to the Protuberance [on the crown of the Buddha's head]! *Oṃ,* roar! flash! blaze! abide! O you with perfected vision! you who accomplish all objectives! *svāhā!*) [2][7]

To be recited three times.

"Within the Lotus Family use the Avalokiteśvara-Mother, who is called Pāṇḍaravāsinī: use her mantra for the *śāntika* [rite]. The mantra of the Avalokiteśvara-Mother is:

Darśanasparśanābhyavaśrāvasmaraṇena ca syām ahaṃ sarvasattvānāṃ sarvavyādhicikitsaka, tad yathā, oṃ kaṭe vikaṭe kaṭa vikaṭa kaṭaṃkaṭe bhagavati vijaye svāhā. (By observing, touching, hearing, and remembering, may I become a healer of all diseases for all beings! Namely: *Oṃ,* O Kaṭā! Vikaṭā! Kaṭā! Vikaṭā! Kaṭaṃkaṭā! Blessed One! victorious one! *svāhā!*) [3][8]

[To be recited] three times.

"Within the Vajra Family use the Vajradhara-Mother, who is called Māmakī: use her mantra for the *śāntika* [rite]. The mantra of the Vajra-Mother is:

Namo ratnatrayāya, namaś caṇḍavajrapāṇaye mahāyakṣa- 604a
senāpataye, oṃ kulaṃdhari bandha bandha hūṃ <in a loud voice>*phaṭ.* (Homage to the Three Jewels! Homage to Violent Vajrapāṇi, great general of the *yakṣas*! *Oṃ,* O family-holder! bind, bind! *hūṃ phaṭ!*) [4][9]

[To be recited] three times.

"Next, within the Buddha Family, when using the mantras of *vidyārājas*, the *vidyārāja* is called Vijayoṣṇīṣa (Victorious Buddha-Crown): use his mantra for the *pauṣṭika* [rite]. The mantra of [this] *vidyārāja* is:

Namaḥ samantabuddhānāṃ, oṃ bhrūṃ namaḥ. (Homage to all Buddhas! *Oṃ, bhrūṃ,* homage!) [5][10]

"Within the Lotus Family also use a *vidyārāja,* called Hayagrīva: use his mantra for the *pauṣṭika* [rite]. The mantra of [this] *vidyārāja* is:

Oṃ amṛtodbhava namaḥ svāhā. (*Oṃ,* O you who are born of ambrosia! homage! *svāhā!*) [6][11]

"Within the Vajra Family also use a *vidyārāja,* called Sumbha: use his mantra for the *pauṣṭika* [rite]. The mantra [of this *vidyārāja*] is:

Namo ratnatrayāya, namaś caṇḍavajrapāṇaye mahāyakṣa-

senāpataye, oṃ sumbha nisumbha hūṃ gṛhṇa gṛhṇa hūṃ ānaya hūṃ bhagavan vidyārāja hūṃ phaṭ namaḥ. (Homage to the Three Jewels! Homage to Violent Vajrapāṇi, great general of the *yakṣas*! *Oṃ,* O Sumbha, Nisumbha, *hūṃ!* seize, seize, *hūṃ!* bring hither, *hūṃ!* O Lord Vidyārāja! *hūṃ phaṭ,* homage!) [7][12]

"Next, within the Buddha Family, use the *mahākrodha* ('great wrathful one') called Aparājita: use his mantra for the *ābhicāruka* [rite]. The mantra is:

Hūṃ phaṭ vak vak (?) *cinasicik* (?) *hūṃ phaṭ.* [8][13]

"Within the Lotus Family the *mahākrodha* is called Śivāvaha: use his mantra for the *ābhicāruka* [rite]. The mantra is:

Hūṃ phaṭ hri (or *hrī / hrīḥ*?) *hūṃ phaṭ.* [9][14]

"Within the Vajra Family the *mahākrodha* is called Kuṇḍalin (= Amṛtakuṇḍalin): use his mantra for the *ābhicāruka* [rite]. The mantra is:

Namo ratnatrayāya, namaś caṇḍavajrapāṇaye mahāyakṣa-
604b *senāpataye, oṃ amṛtakuṇḍali kha kha kha kha khāhi khāhi tiṣṭha tiṣṭha bandha bandha hana hana garja vigarja visphoṭaya sphoṭaya sarvavighnavināyakā[n] mahā[ga]ṇapatijīvitāntakarāya hūṃ phaṭ.* (Homage to the Three Jewels! Homage to Violent Vajrapāṇi, great general of the *yakṣas*! *Oṃ,* O Amṛtakuṇḍalin! devour, devour, devour, devour! devour, devour! abide, abide! bind, bind! slay, slay! roar, roar out! rend asunder, rend all obstructions and obstructive demons! For you who put an end to the life of the Great Lord of [Śiva's] Hosts! *hūṃ phaṭ!*) [10][15]

"Then again, there may be mantras that do not fall under the three families. [In such cases] one differentiates the three kinds of ritual deeds—*śāntika* and so forth—according to the wording of the mantra.[16] If the mantra has the word *'śānti-kuru'* <render auspicious>, the word *'śama'* <remove>, the word *'praśama'* <very

pure>, the word *'upaśama'* <further remove>, or the word *'svāhā'* (all hail!), you should realize that it is a mantra for the *śāntika* [rite]. If it has the word *'puṣṭi'* <increased benefit>, the words *'lakṣmin'* <endowed with a [good] sign>, *'dada'* <give> or *'ūrja'* <majesty> or the words *'bala'* <strength>, *'vṛddhi'* <increase>, *'rūpa'* [<form>], *'medhā'* <intelligence>, *'dhana'* <property>, *'dhanya'* <storehouse>, *'hiraṇya'* <gold>, *'grāma'* <village>, *'nagara'* <town>, *'rāṣṭ[r]a'* <district>, *'rājya'* <lord> or *'dada'* <give>, you should realize that it is a mantra for the *pauṣṭika* [rite]. If it has the word *'hūṃ'* or the words *'hana'* <strike>, *'phaṭ'* <break>, *'matha'* <destroy>, *'bhañja'* <shatter>, *'uccāṭaya'* <punish>, *'utsāhaya'* (?) <do not release with force>, *'śoṣaya'* <parch>, *'māraya'* <kill>, *'khādaya'* <devour>, *'kīlaya'* <impale>, *'chedaya'* <sunder>, *'bhasmi'* <almsbowl> or *'kuru'* [<do>],[17] you should realize that it is a mantra for the *ābhicāruka* [rite].

"Next, if there is a mantra the meaning of which is 'compassion' or 'good,' you should realize that it is for using in the *śāntika* [rite]; if there is a mantra the meaning of which is 'violence' or 'anger,' you should realize that it is for using in the *ābhicāruka* [rite]; and if there is a mantra that is neither compassionate nor violent [in meaning], you should realize that it is for using in the *pauṣṭika* [rite].

"Then again, if you wish to quickly accomplish the *śāntika* [rite], you should use mantras of the Buddha Family; if you wish to quickly accomplish the *pauṣṭika* [rite], you should use mantras of the Lotus Family; and if you wish to quickly accomplish the *ābhicāruka* [rite], you should use mantras of the Vajra Family.

"Next, this scripture is profound and wondrous, just like the [most] heavenly among the heavenly, and it has the best among the best mantras. If you abide by its rules, there will be no deeds that you cannot accomplish. Although this scripture belongs to the lower Vajra Family, because by upholding the decrees of the Buddha's teachings it accomplishes everything, it is also able to accomplish the rites of the two higher families. It is, for example, like a monarch who acts in accordance with [his own] decrees; its

rules are the same and should be understood in accordance with
604c the meaning [of this analogy].

"If there are mantras which, although their words are few in number, have the word *'oṃ'* at the beginning and have the word *'svāhā'* at the end, you should realize that [these] mantras are quickly able to accomplish the *śāntika* rite. Or if there are mantras that have the word *'hūṃ'* at the beginning and have the word *'phaṭ'* at the end, or have the letter *repha* ('r')—this is the sound of reproof—any mantras with these words will quickly bring success in the *ābhicāruka* rite. Or if there are mantras without the word *'oṃ'* at the beginning and without the word *'svāhā'* [at the end], or without the word *'hūṃ,'* without the word *'phaṭ'* or without letters such as *repha,* you should realize that these mantras are quickly able to accomplish the *pauṣṭika* rite.

"Next, if someone should wish to subdue various demons and *āveśa*s,[18] he should use the mantras expounded by messengers, *ceṭaka*s (servants), and so forth, for he will quickly gain success. Again, should there be mantras in other families that are said to be able to accomplish everything, they are only able to accomplish what is taught for that particular family and do not apply to other families. Still, there are scriptures in which it is stated that a certain mantra was expounded in order to remove poison or illness but is also able to remove other afflictions; [in such a case] you should realize that that [mantra] is suitable for all uses.

"You should be fully acquainted with the family [to which a mantra belongs], you should be fully familiar with the circumstances in which a mantra is to be used, you must also know the mantra's efficacy, and you must fully understand how to practice the mantra rites. The characteristics of the mantras of a particular rite should accord with what you seek, and if you recite those mantras, then you will gain success."

Chapter Three

Distinguishing the Characteristics of an *Ācārya*

"Next, I shall now explain the characteristics of an *ācārya* (teacher). Since all mantras are obtained through him, know that an [*ā*]*cārya* is the very basis [of all practice].

"What are his characteristics? His limbs are sound, and he is adorned with merit; he must fully comprehend matters mundane and supramundane; he always abides by the Dharma and does not do anything that is contrary to the Dharma; he is endowed with great compassion and takes pity on sentient beings; he has been born and raised in a noble family; he is disciplined in nature and gentle; all who dwell together with him obtain happiness; he is intelligent and wise, and unimpeded in eloquence; he has forbearance and is without self-conceit; he always wishes for the Great Vehicle and understands the subtle meanings [of its teachings]; he has deep faith in the gateway to the secrets [of the esoteric teachings]; even if [he commits only] a minor offense, he is still overcome with great fear; he is quite pliant in his physical, verbal, and mental actions; he always enjoys reading the scriptures of the Great Vehicle and abides by the Dharma teachings; he assiduously recites mantras without interruption; the *siddhi* [rites] that he performs are all successful; he must also fully understand how to draw a *maṇḍala;* he is always equipped with the four [means of] conversion (i.e., giving, kindly speech, beneficial action, and cooperation); because he seeks the grand [objective of enlightenment], he does not wish for any minor objectives; he is forever free of parsimony; he has previously entered a Great Maṇḍala[19] and received consecration; moreover, his virtue has been extolled by his teacher [with these words]: 'You may go now, having proven yourself fit to be conferred initiation and become an *ācārya*';[20] and, having obtained this authorization, he is qualified to construct a *maṇḍala* with his

605a own hands in accordance with the [proper] procedures and also qualified to confer mantras on disciples—if you rely on such a person, the mantras received [from him] will quickly bring success: of this you should not have any doubts. [But] if you recite mantras on your own authority without [their having been conferred] by an *upādhyāya* (preceptor) or *ācārya,* you will be exerting yourself in vain and will never obtain any result.

"As for the disciple, he should look upon the *ācārya* just as he would the Three Jewels or bodhisattvas and so forth, for he is a place of refuge able to confer [the teachings], and of all good things he is the primary cause; [therefore] your present life will be happy and you will obtain the [desired] result in future lives. By relying on the *ācārya,* it will not be long before you obtain that which is unsurpassed and excellent, namely, enlightenment (*bodhi*). For this reason he is comparable to a Buddha, and you therefore become his disciple. If, in serving the [*ā*]*cārya,* you are without remiss and apply yourself faultlessly, then [the mantras of] the *vidyārāja*s and *vidyārāja*s' consorts (*vidyārājñī*) that you have been conferred will bring *siddhi*—of this there is no doubt whatsoever."

Chapter Four

Distinguishing the Characteristics of One Who Recites Mantras

"Next, I shall now expound the characteristics of the methods of practice whereby he who recites mantras quickly obtains success. He is pure in the three activities [of body, speech, and mind]; his mind is not confused; formerly he has uninterruptedly been always cultivating wisdom; able to perform one rite, he accomplishes all manner of things; he is also free of parsimony; the words that he utters are without impediment; he is without fear in a crowd; his deeds are quickly accomplished; he always practices forbearance; he is free of all sycophancy; he is without any illness; he always practices truthful speech; he fully understands ritual matters; he is of youthful age; his sense organs and limbs are all sound; he always has faith in the Three Jewels; he practices [the teachings of] the sublime scriptures of the Great Vehicle; and he does not entertain thoughts of falling back from the merits of good [deeds]—such a person will quickly gain success. He always has respect for bodhisattvas and mantras, and he generates great compassion toward sentient beings—such a person will quickly gain success. He always enjoys tranquility and does not desire noisy crowds; he constantly practices truthful speech and mentally applies himself to the maintenance of purity—such a person will quickly gain success. If he hears of the majestic power and sovereignty of the Bodhisattva Vajradhara, he will upon hearing of it have true faith and rejoice in his heart—such a person will quickly gain success. If someone who has few desires and knows contentment recites mantras and keeps in mind unceasingly day and night what he seeks, such a person will quickly gain success. If, on hearing of mantra rites for the first time, a person's hair should all stand on end and his heart dance for joy, such a person is a Dharma-vessel for [the fruits of] success. If someone should personally see *siddhi*

in a dream as it is described in the scriptures, and if his mind loves tranquility and he does not dwell together with others, such a person will quickly gain success. If, moreover, someone reveres his *ācārya* like a Buddha, such a person will quickly gain success. If
605b someone has been reciting a mantra for a long time without any effect, yet does not abandon it, redoubles his vast vow, and further increases his efforts until he is successful, such a person will quickly gain success."

Chapter Five

Distinguishing [the Characteristics of] an Associate

"Next, I shall explain the characteristics of his associate. He is adorned with merit; he is born of a noble family; he always wishes for the true Dharma and does not do anything that is contrary to the Dharma; he also has deep faith and is free of all fears; he does not fall back in his efforts; he respectfully practices the venerable teachings; he always practices truthful speech; his sense organs and limbs are all sound, and he has no physical illnesses; he is neither too tall, nor too short, nor too fat, nor too thin, nor should he be very dark or very light [in complexion]—he is free of all these faults: [such is] a meritorious associate. He is able to endure suffering; he fully understands mantras, the procedures for *maṇḍala* worship, and other rules; he always cultivates pure conduct; he bears with all things; the words that he utters are gentle and make people want to listen to him; he is free of all self-conceit; he has a good memory and does not forget anything; he respectfully practices any teaching and does not make excuses [for not doing so]; he is of great learning and wisdom, has a compassionate mind, and does not become angry; he is always thinking of making donations; he fully understands how to differentiate the mantras of *vidyārājas*; he should always be reciting [mantras], and the mantras that he recites are the same as those of the venerable [officiant's] practice; and he is also versed in the rites of boundary-binding, self-protection, and so forth—if you obtain such an associate, you will be quickly successful. He is well-disciplined in the three activities [of body, speech, and mind]; he has previously entered a *maṇḍala* under a teacher; he has taken refuge in the Buddha's teachings and does not cultivate evil practices; he is familiar with the procedures required by the venerable [officiant] and does not wait for words of instruction, but knows the [right] time for whatever is sought and acts accordingly—one thus endowed is an excellent associate. He is of wholesome body and mind, without mental anguish, determined and resolute, and to the last he has no thoughts of falling back—if you obtain such an associate, you will be quickly successful. He does not engender greedy attachment toward great profit—one who is endowed with such virtue is described as an excellent associate. Toward the [officiating] practitioner his mind is also without [thoughts of] abandonment—if you wish to effectuate sundry drugs and so forth, he will act as a powerful aide, and he will not abandon the spontaneous holy precepts: one who is endowed with such virtue is described as an excellent associate. He does not desire anything from the practitioner; so long as he does not attain the accomplishment of *siddhi,* he will never give up; even if years should pass by without [his obtaining] *siddhi,* he will never entertain thoughts of giving up; even if there should be great suffering and other difficulties that torment his body and mind, he will still not give up—one who is endowed with such virtue is described as an excellent associate.

"If he is possessed of various [modes of] virtuous conduct such as those [described] above, he will be fit to accomplish supreme and excellent deeds. But even if he is without the above virtues and is only versed in the rules for success with mantras and also fully understands *maṇḍalas*, has wisdom lofty and bright as well as additional merits, and excels in reciting [mantras], such an associate is also able to accomplish supreme and excellent deeds. On account
605c of his desire to accomplish supreme and excellent deeds, this meritorious associate will perform together with the [officiating] reciter for half a month at a time consecration, *homa,* [offerings of] aromatics, flowers, and lamps prepared according to the occasion, and other procedures for the protection and selection [of the site]: he must assist as the need arises. Not only does he assist in performing deeds such as the above; if the reciter should make an omission, the meritorious associate will admonish him with reason on the basis of scriptural teachings to the effect that there must be no omissions, and he will also reveal to him in detail the reasons for this—one

thus endowed is a most excellent associate. If at the time of his daily recitation, or when performing [ritual] deeds, the practitioner should on occasion happen to forget something, his meritorious associate will help him to do it as he sees fit and have everything in complete readiness. When [the practitioner] wishes to accomplish a drug rite, [his associate] should always hold the drug in his hands or use grass stalks to hold it. Even though the tasks in rites of recitation may be many, [the associate] will never be negligent. When the practitioner wishes to finish reciting, his associate should stand beside him, looking to see whether the practitioner has already wearied of recitation or fearful that he may forget to perform the rite for dismissing the deities, the rite for placing the rosary, or some other rites, and if he sees him forget something, he should help him to do it. The associate should always be reciting and worshiping, and the deeds that he performs generate merit, all of which he transfers to those who recite mantras, fulfilling their wishes. If instructions are to be given, [the practitioner] speaks only with the associate, while in order to accomplish supreme deeds one more associate is allowed, [in which case the associates] speak with one another to ensure that there are no discrepancies between them. The associates' food is the same as that of the practitioner, and the practitioner's food conforms with the prescribed rules. Those thus endowed are fit to become associates for supreme and excellent deeds. The merits of the third associate[21] are also the same as those described above."

Chapter Six

Selection of the Site

"Next, I shall explain the site for reciting mantras and [gaining] success. In which localities are you to dwell in order to quickly gain success? The place where the Buddha attained enlightenment and vanquished the armies of the four demons (i.e., the five aggregates, mental afflictions, death, and the king of demons in the Paranirmitavaśavartin Heaven) is the very best, and you will quickly gain success [there]. Because there are no hindrances on the banks of the Nairañjanā River [where the Buddha bathed before attaining enlightenment], you will quickly obtain *siddhi* in that locality; even if there should be a host of demons [there], they will be unable to effect any obstruction, and among the things that you seek there will be none that you do not accomplish—in such a place you will quickly obtain *siddhi*. Alternatively [you will gain success] at the place where the Buddha turned the Dharma-wheel, or at the town of Kuśina[garī], the site of the Buddha's nirvana, or at the town of Kapila[vastu], where the Buddha was born. The above four sites[22] are the very best, and because there are no disturbing obstructions, you will definitely gain success in the three kinds of *siddhi*.

"Alternatively [you will gain success] in the excellent sites described by Buddhas or the excellent sites described by bodhisattvas, [namely,] the Buddha's Eight Great Stupas or famous 606a
mountains with many trees, abundant fruit, and flowing springs: such places are described as excellent sites; or in an [*a*]*raṇya* (forest or hermitage) with many flowers and fruits, with flowing water, and beloved of people: such a place is described as an excellent site; or there may be an [*a*]*raṇya* with many deer that are not hunted by people and without any beasts of prey such as bears, tigers, and wolves: such a place is described as an excellent site; or a place that is neither too cold nor too hot, is agreeable to people, and is pleasing to their minds: such a place is described as an excellent site; or beside a mountain, on top of a mountain peak, on a

solitary eminence, or on a mountainside that also has water: such places are described as excellent sites. There are also [other] excellent sites, where green grass covers the ground and there are many trees and flowers, including [trees whose] wood is suitable for performing *homa:* such places are described as excellent sites. Or in front of a stupa enshrining a *śarī[ra]* (relic), or in a place in the mountains enshrining a *śarī[ra]*, or beside the four [great] rivers (i.e., Gaṅgā [Ganges], Sindhu [Indus], Vakṣu [Oxus], and Sītā), or a place where there is an *[a]raṇya* embellished with various trees and there are not many people, or in a cemetery where smoke never ceases, or on the banks of a large river, or beside a large pond, or a place where there were formerly many cows, or at the foot of a large solitary tree where a divine spirit abides and which is always in the shade, or the single shrine of many villages, or beside a large crossroads, or beside the pond of a *nāga* (serpent or dragon): such places are described as excellent sites. Or lands visited by the Buddha during his peregrinations: in such localities you will quickly gain success. If there is a country where the four categories of people (i.e., monks, nuns, laymen, and laywomen) have deep faith in the Three Jewels and spread and uphold the true Dharma, in such a place you will quickly gain success. Again, if there is a country with multitudes of many good people all endowed with compassion, in such a place you will quickly gain success.

"Once you have obtained one of these outstanding sites, you must remove refuse, potsherds, pebbles, and other objects from the ground: it is all explained in detail in the chapter on the *maṇḍala*.[23] In accordance with the rites for *siddhi* you must properly differentiate the sites for the three families, and you must also differentiate between the *śāntika* rite, the *pauṣṭika* [rite], and the *ābhicāruka* [rite]; as with these three rites, you must also differentiate between higher, middling, and lower accomplishments. In such a place, following what seems right to your mind, you should then smear [the ground with cow dung], sprinkle [it with scented water], sweep it, and perform the various [ritual] deeds, whereupon you will quickly gain success in the rites for *siddhi*."

Chapter Seven

Observation of the Precepts

"Next, I shall explain in detail the rules that govern the reciting of mantras; if you abide by these precepts, it will not be long before you gain success.

"If a person of wisdom is to recite mantras, he should first renounce anger; neither should he engender ire toward malevolent gods, nor should he harbor anger toward mantra-reciters of other categories. He should not differentiate between mantras on his own 606b
authority with regard to their merits and rules, and he should [instead] engender a deep respect for mantras and their rules. He must offer protection to wicked people. Why? Because they are able to impede important matters and harm him. Even if he should see faults in his *ācārya,* his three activities [of body, speech, and mind] will not produce [behavior indicative of] thoughts of arrogance, his mouth will not discuss the various rights and wrongs [of the matter], and his mind will never conceive thoughts of his [*ācārya*'s] faults. Even if [the *ācārya*] has faults, he does not discuss them, and even less so if he abides by the Dharma. Even if others bear malice [toward him], he will never retaliate, nor should he bind another's *vidyārāja* by means of his own regular mantra and cause injury or inflict bitter punishment, nor should he perform rites for vanquishing foes.

"If someone has not yet received mantras from an *ācārya,* you should not confer them on him to recite, while someone who does not have respect for the Three Jewels is a non-Buddhist [and you should not confer any mantras on him either]. If someone has received mantras from an *ācārya* but has subsequently fallen back from his original aspiration, you should also not confer [any mantras] on him, nor should you confer on him hand-seals (*mudrā*), mantras, rites of [special] efficacy, or ordinary rites. You should also not confer them on those who have not yet entered a *maṇḍala*.

"You should not leap over any sentient beings, neither two-legged creatures nor likewise many-legged [creatures]. You should also not step over insignia on the ground, namely, mallets, discs, staves, scepters, conches, *vajras*, and so forth, nor step over what is marked off with a rope. You should also not step over sundry medicinal herbs, roots, stalks, branches, leaves, or fruits, nor should you dispose of them in unclean places.

"If you wish for success in mantra rites, you must abide by the code of rules and you should not dispute the correct meaning of the Great Vehicle. If you hear of the profound, remarkable, and inconceivable practices of bodhisattvas, you should engender true faith and not entertain any thoughts of doubt. A person who recites mantras should not contest their efficacy with other reciters, nor should he perform a rite of subjugation on account of some minor offense.

"A person who wishes for success should not sing or disport himself, nor should he apply makeup or wear garlands of flowers in order to adorn himself. Again, do not go dancing about and do not playfully float in a river. In a word, you should not perform any insolent acts with the body. You should [also] not perform any unwholesome acts of speech, such as mendacious speech, speech of a defiled mind, [speech that] sunders harmony, and offensive language and abuse; when a reply is required, do not resort to verbosity, and never indulge in idle chatter. Again, do not dwell together with non-Buddhists or argue with them, do not speak with any [outcaste] *caṇḍālas* and their ilk, and do not converse with people other than
606c your associates, while at times of recitation do not speak even to your associates. At times other than when you are reciting do not speak with your associates if there is no need to do so.

"Again, do not rub your body with oil, and you should not eat the five pungent [vegetables], [such as] onions, garlic and radishes, or sesamum and vinegar, nor should you eat any other green vegetables, rice flour, bean cakes, steamed peas, sesamum cakes, or dumplings. You should not eat any food relished by *vināyakas* (class of demons) or the remains of offerings, gruel made with sesamum, nonglutinous rice, and beans, or milk gruel. Do not ride on any carriages or saddled [animals]. You should eat neither food that has been stepped over nor food that has been touched. [Do not use] any accoutrements of bodily adornment such as mirrors, flowers, powders, or parasols if there is no reason for doing so. You should not rub your hands together [when washing], nor should you rub your legs together. Do not defecate or urinate in any water or in the vicinity of water. You should not take food in your hands to eat it, and do not use brass dishes for eating; dish food out onto leaves without turning them over [on their reverse sides]. Do not sleep on large or small couches, and do not sleep together with other people. When you wish to sleep, relax the mind, making it calm and pure, and then go to sleep, reflecting on wisdom. Do not sleep with your face covered (i.e., facing downward) and do not sleep facing upward, but sleep like the king of lions on your right side. When sleeping, do not sleep with your eyes open. You should not eat again [and again] during the day, nor should you fast; you should not eat too much nor too little. If you have doubts about any food, you should not eat it. Do not look at any forms of amusement, at large congregations of people, or at women. You should not be attached in body, speech, and mind to any fine living quarters or fine food that you receive, nor should you reject any poor living quarters or poor food that you may receive. You should not wear purple garments, nor should you wear old torn robes or dirty robes; at times of recitation you should wear an undergarment.

"Moreover, do not deprecate yourself, saying, 'I have committed many wrongs, and there is no way in which I can gain success in *siddhi*.' [Even if] you should be afflicted with various illnesses on account of residual karma [from past lives], never wilfully neglect your recitation, and never abandon the mantras that you have received from your *ācārya*. A voice in your dreams or in midair may declare, 'You should not recite this mantra,' but even if you hear this frequently, do not abandon [the mantra] and do not be angry [at the voice]. Why? Because it is all due to demons. You must simply exert yourself, and you should not fall back and stop [practicing]. Do not have wicked thoughts in your mind, [do not] be distracted by [unwholesome] objects, and [do not] indulge your sense organs; always maintain purity and recite [your mantras].

"If you seek great accomplishments, you should not subjugate mountain spirits with your regular mantra, and do not protect yourself or others and do not rescue [people] from difficulties or suppress poisons [with it either]. This is not only the case with your regular mantra, and you should not perform [such deeds] with any other
607a mantras either. All your mantras, each according to its use, should not be practiced with any great frequency, and do not contest your magical powers with others.

"If you wish to seek *siddhi*, you must recite three times [daily] and wash yourself three times [daily]. When washing, do not [use] simply plain water, but mix in mantrafied water and wash yourself. The 'water' mantra is:

> *Oṃ hūṃ hana vajri vajreṇa ha* <in a frightening voice>. (*Oṃ, hūṃ,* slay! O adamantine one! with a *vajra, ha!*) [11][24]

"When bathing, you should use purified earth to rub all over your body and cleanse yourself. Use mantrafied earth, reciting [the mantra] seven times. The 'earth' mantra is:

> *Oṃ vajra hara hūṃ.* (*Oṃ,* O *vajra!* dispel! *hūṃ!*) [12]

"In the water and in the earth there are many *vināyaka*s who cause obstructions: you must first dispel them and then use [the water and earth]. Recite this mantra to drive them away. The mantra for dispelling obstructions in water and earth is:

> *Namo vajrāya, hūṃ hana dhuna matha vidhvaṃsayotsāraya phaṭ.* (Homage to the *vajra! Hūṃ!* slay! shake! destroy! crush! expel! *phaṭ!*) [13]

"Then first take some water, and when you have finished reciting the mantra while stirring [the water] with your hand, use it for bathing. The 'bathing' mantra is:

> *Namo ratnatrayāya, namaś caṇḍavajrapāṇaye mahāyakṣasenāpataye, namo dam.* (Homage to the Three Jewels! Homage

to Violent Vajrapāṇi, great general of the *yakṣas*! Homage to...) [14][25]

"Using this mantrafied water, bathe at will. When bathing you should not converse. While still bathing you must constantly mentally recite the following heart-mantra. The heart-mantra when bathing is:

Oṃ amṛte hūṃ phaṭ. (*Oṃ*, O immortal one! *hūṃ phaṭ!*) [15]

"Once you have finished bathing, you should take up a scoop of water with both hands and use the above heart-mantra to empower it; reciting it seven times, pour [the water] over your head. Do this three times.

"[Then] you should tie the hair on the crown [of your head]: reciting [the following mantra] to mantrafy it seven times, you should make a topknot on the crown [of your head]. If you are a renunciant [with a shaven head], you should make a fist with your right hand, place it on top of your head and, [reciting the mantra] the same number of times as above, similarly [make as if to] tie the hair on the crown [of your head]. The 'crown-hair' mantra is:

Oṃ susiddhikari svāhā. (*Oṃ*, O you who are good at bringing success! *svāhā!*) [16]

"Next, you should wash your hands, take some water, and rinse your mouth three times. Then bathe your deity, using his mantra 607b
and reciting it seven times. While reciting the [following] mantra for rinsing the mouth, [empower] the five places on the body (i.e., crown, both shoulders, throat, and chest).

Oṃ kīli kīli vajra hūṃ phaṭ. (*Oṃ*, O you with a stake! you with a stake! O *vajra! hūṃ phaṭ!*) [17]

"When you have completely finished bathing, imagine that you bathe your deity. Then in that [same] place you should recite your regular mantra as many times as you like: only then may you proceed to your usual site of recitation.

"On your way there do not feel greed or anger, and conform

with external circumstances, pure in body and mind; think reverently of your deity and proceed slowly, firmly observing the prohibitory precepts as laid down before: you should observe them without forgetting them. Once you have reached the site, you should perform as prescribed the various [ritual] deeds and recite [mantras], and you should construct a *maṇḍala,* constantly reciting [as you do so]. If you become tired, you should read the scriptures of the Great Vehicle or make *caitya*s (cairns), and never neglect other good deeds either.

"You must [daily] take refuge three times in the Three Jewels, repent three times of your sundry sinful deeds, generate three times the mind of enlightenment (*bodhicitta*)—if you do so, you will gain success—and make a vow three times, vowing to accomplish the excellent deed [of enlightenment]. In order to expiate your sins, you should perform good deeds in accordance with the teachings: always make charitable gifts, have great compassion, do not be parsimonious with the Dharma teachings, always have forbearance, exert yourself without falling back, have deep faith, [keep] in mind the six [objects of] mindfulness (i.e., Buddha, Dharma, Sangha, morality, charity, and gods), and think carefully on the meaning of the scriptures that you hear; you should always read the merits of mantras, and you should worship the scriptures of mantra rites.

"Carefully drawing a fine *maṇḍala* in accordance [with the scriptures], you should enter it: first induct *bhikṣu*s (monks) of true faith, and then induct *bhikṣuṇī*s (nuns), *upāsaka*s (laymen), and *upāsikā*s (laywomen) one after another, all firm in their generation of the mind of enlightenment and with determined minds and right views. Once they have entered the *maṇḍala,* you should confer [on them] the methods for binding hand-seals as well as mantras and [other] rules, and you should also properly explain in detail all the rules for mantras.

"On the fourteenth day, the eighth day, and the last day of [bright half-]months and on the [first] fifteen days of the eleventh month[26]—on such days double the offerings, recite [mantras], perform *homa,* and additionally observe the prohibitory precepts: you must always remember to double everything, and the mantras will be quickly successful.

"When performing *homa,* you must always hold a *vajra* in your hand: recite [the following mantra] to mantrafy it more than one thousand times or one hundred times. The mantra of the *vajra* for accomplishing [all] deeds is:

Oṃ dhuna vajra ha. (*Oṃ,* shake! O *vajra! ha!*) [18][27]

For the *vajra* for [accomplishing] all deeds use wood [from a tree] that has been burned by lightning or margosa wood, or take a piece of charred wood from the fire remaining after burning a corpse, or use white sandalwood or red sandalwood: take any one [of these kinds of] wood and make a *vajra,* adding three prongs. At times of *homa* and at times of recitation always hold it in your left hand. 607c
Because it is able to accomplish all deeds, it is called the '[well-accomplishing] *vajra.*' If you carry this *vajra,* all *vināyakas* and other obstructors will all take fright and flee. Rub this *vajra* with red sandalwood unguent and place it in front of your deity; using the mantra given above, you should mantrafy flowers and incense and offer them to it. The *vajra* for [accomplishing] all deeds is secret and subtle and is able to accomplish sundry deeds.

"When performing various [ritual] deeds, you must always wear a bead circlet on the right wrist which has been rubbed with unguent and mantrafied by reciting [the following mantra] one hundred times or one thousand [times]. The 'bead circlet' mantra is:

Oṃ kulaṃdhari bandha bandha hūṃ phaṭ. (*Oṃ,* O family-holder! bind, bind! *hūṃ phaṭ!*) [19; cf. No. 4][28]

This great seal of the *vidyārājas* is called Māmakī. She is able to effectuate the mantras of all *vidyārājas,* able to increase [the majesty of a deity], able to make the wording of mantras complete, and also able to accomplish other rites and deeds such as self-protection. Not only is she the mother of the *vidyārājas,* but she is also the mother of the Vajra [Family]. In the case of a bead circlet for the Vajra Family affix a *rudrākṣa* [berry], stringing it onto a cord [the ends of which are] then tied together to make a knot. It being thus in the case of the Vajra Family, the other two [families] may be known accordingly. For a bead circlet of the Buddha Family you should use the mantra of the Buddha-Mother [Buddhalocanā], while in the case of a bead circlet for the Lotus Family you should use the mantra of Pāṇḍaravāsinī, and for a bead circlet of the Vajra Family you should use the mantra of Māmakī. <The mantras of the three family mothers correspond to those given previously [in Chapter 2 (Nos. 2–4)].>[29] If you wear this bead circlet, *vināyaka*s will be unable to cause any obstruction, your body will become purified, and you will quickly succeed in fulfilling your wishes.

"When performing rites, you should also make a ring using cogongrass (*kuśa*) and put it on the ring finger of your right hand. You should recite the three-and-a-half-syllable heart-mantra of the corresponding family one hundred times or one thousand times and then place [the ring] on your finger. The [three-and-a-half-syllable] heart-mantra of the Buddha Family is:

Jinajik. [20]

The [three-and-a-half-syllable] heart-mantra of the Lotus Family is:

Ārolik. [21]

The [three-and-a-half-syllable] heart-mantra of the Vajra Family is:

Vajradhṛk. [22][30]

At times of worship, at times of recitation, and at times of *homa* you should wear [this] grass ring. On account of your wearing this grass ring, obstacles [resulting from past] sins will be eliminated, your hand will become purified, and your actions will all be successful.

608a "Next take some cotton thread and hemp fiber, have a young girl dye them red in color or saffron in color, twist them into a string, knot it, and make a mantra-cord. With each knot recite the [following] mantra seven times, making seven knots. Place it in front of your deity and mantrafy it with the mantra one thousand times. At times of recitation, at times of *homa*, and when you go to sleep—'when you go to sleep' means at dusk—you should use [the cord], tying it around your waist, for then there will be no seminal loss when asleep at night. You must always empower it; the cord mantra is:

> *Oṃ hara hara bandhani śukradhāraṇi siddhārthe svāhā.* (*Oṃ*, retain, retain! O semen-holding cord! O you who have accomplished your objective! *svāhā!*) [23]

"At times of recitation and at times of *homa* you must wear an outer garment and an undergarment with the right shoulder bared; when sleeping and when washing or bathing this rule does not apply. The outer garment that you wear should be mantrafied. When defecating and urinating you should wear wooden shoes, but when in the presence of your own deity, in the presence of an *upādhyāya* or *ācārya*, or in the presence of other venerable elders you should not wear them.

"At revered places worship with body, speech, and mind if you wish to quickly gain success in *siddhi*. If you see a *caitya* or *bhikṣu*, you should always pay your respects to them. If you encounter the image of a non-Buddhist god, you should only join your palms together or chant a *gāthā* (verse), and if you see a venerable person you should also do reverence to him. If you hear the wonderful Dharma, generate profound devotion, and if you hear of the inconceivable characteristics of a bodhisattva or hear of the things accomplished by mantras, you should rejoice in them all and your heart dance for joy. If you wish for quick success, you should always proceed valiantly onward and not engender indolence.

"You must always reflect on rules such as the above, for otherwise you will violate the code of precepts, incur very grave sins, and be unsuccessful in *siddhi*. Be ever mindful of the body and other sense organs (i.e., eyes, ears, nose, tongue, and mind) and do not be greedily attached to various desires. You must always observe rules such as the above, and do not forget them. If you commit misdeeds in the morning then repent of them when evening comes, and if you indulge in committing [mis]deeds during the night, repent of them with a sincere mind when morning comes. In addition, you must be pure in recitation as well as *homa*, worship, and so forth in accordance with your own precepts. In this manner you should spend your days, and you should always bear in mind the *vidyārāja* precepts, for then it will not be long before you dwell in *siddhi*."

Chapter Eight

Offering Flowers

"Next, I shall explain separately the three kinds of [ritual] deeds. The three kinds [of ritual deeds] are, namely, the *śāntika* rite, the *pauṣṭika* rite, and the *ābhicāruka* rite: these are the three kinds. In 608b
[each of] the three families (i.e., Buddha, Lotus, and Vajra) there are three grades of mantras, namely, those expounded by holy ones (*ārya*s), those expounded by [celestial] gods (*deva*s), and those expounded by earth-dwelling gods (*bhaumadeva*s): this applies to the three families. Those expounded by holy ones are those that have been expounded by Buddhas, bodhisattvas, listeners (*śrāvakas*), and dependently enlightened ones (*pratyekabuddha*s): theirs are the mantras of the holy ones. Those expounded by gods are those that have been expounded by gods ranging from the Gods of Pure Abode (*śuddhāvāsa*) to the Thirty-three (*trāyastriṃśa*) Gods: theirs are the mantras of the gods. Those expounded by earth-dwelling gods are those that have been expounded by *nāga*s (serpents or dragons), *yakṣa*s, *rākṣasa*s (classes of demons), *asura*s (demigods), *garuḍa*s (mythological birds), *gandharva*s (celestial musicians), *kiṃnara*s (gods of song), *mahora*[*ga*]s (mythological snakes), *bhūta*s, *piśāca*s, *kumbhāṇḍa*s (classes of demons), and so forth: [theirs] are the mantras of the earth-dwelling gods. When performing the *śāntika* rite, you should use mantras expounded by holy ones; when performing the *pauṣṭika* rite, you should use mantras expounded by gods; and when performing the *ābhicāruka* rite, you should use mantras expounded by earth-dwelling gods. If you seek higher accomplishments, you should use the mantras of holy ones; if you seek middling accomplishments, you should use the mantras of gods; and if you seek lower accomplishments, you should use the mantras of earth-dwelling gods. Seek the three grades of accomplishment and perform the three kinds of rites in the three families as [explained] earlier.

"[When doing so,] you should use various flowers growing in water and on land, and you must carefully differentiate each in accordance with the family in question. You should offer them after having empowered them with the mantra [given below], and when offering them make this supplication:

'This flower is pure,
And the place where it grew is also pure;
I now offer it up:
Please deign to accept it,
And grant me success.'

The mantra for offering flowers is:

Āhara āhara sarvavidyādharapūjite svāhā. (Take it, take it! O you who are worshiped by all *vidyādharas*! *svāhā!*) [24][31]

"You should use this mantra to mantrafy flowers and offer them to all three families. If you offer flowers to the Buddha [Family], take white flowers with a fragrance and offer them; if you offer [flowers] to the Avalokiteśvara [Family], you should take white flowers that have grown in water and offer them; if you offer [flowers] to the Vajra [Family], you should use various fine flowers and offer them; and if you offer [flowers] to the earth-dwelling gods, take any of the various kinds of flowers available at the time and offer them.

"[The flowers that should be offered are] the *mālatī* flower (type of jasmine), *pāṭala* flower (trumpet flower), lotus flower, *campa[ka]* flower (champac), 'dragon-filament' flower (*nāgakesara:* rose chestnut) <it resembles the flower of the peony>, *bakula* flower, *kumuda* flower (white water lily), *śāla* (sal) tree flower, *malli[kā]* flower (type of jasmine), *kūyaka* (?) flower, *yūthikā* flower (type of jasmine), *śaivālika* flower (duckweed), *kuruvaka* flower (red amaranth), *kadamba* flower, *madhupiṇḍikā* flower, *tṛṇa* flower (Kashmir crocus), *gandhapuṣpa* flower, *puṃnāga* flower, *nava-mālikā* flower (type of jasmine), *aśoka* flower, *mucukunda* flower,
608c *damana* flower, *cūtamañjarī* (mango) flower, *vṛkṣotpala* (mayeng)
flower, *kaṭhara* (?) flower, *kāñcanāra* (mountain ebony) flower,

sapiṇḍikā flower, *utpala* flower (blue lotus), *tagara* flower, *kunda* flower (type of jasmine), *karavī[ra]* flower (oleander), and so forth. With regard to flowers such as these above that grow in forests, towns, and *[a]raṇyas* and grow in water or on land, you should be thoroughly familiar with their use in the three families and with the three kinds [of rites] and the three grades [of accomplishment] when offering them.

"Use flowers such as the *mālatī* flower, *tagara* flower, *kunda* flower, *mallikā* flower, *yūthikā* flower, and 'dragon-filament' flower for offering to the Buddha Family. It is best to use flowers such as the *utpala* flower, *kumuda* flower, lotus flower, *śāla* tree flower, *śaivāli[ka]*, *jātika* flower, *puṃnāga* flower, and *tagara* flower for making offerings to the Avalokiteśvara Family. The blue lotus flower, *priyaṅgu* flower, branches with flowers and leaves, and others not mentioned [here] are all suitable for offering to the Vajra Family.

"Among the above flowers, those white in color are for performing the *śāntika* rite, those yellow in color are for performing the *pauṣṭika* rite, and those purple in color are for performing the *ābhicāruka* rite. Among these flowers, those sweet in taste are for performing the *śāntika* rite, those bitter in taste are for performing the *ābhicāruka* rite, and those mild in taste are for performing the *pauṣṭika* rite.

"Alternatively, you may use in accordance with their kind twigs, vines, and flowering branches that grow in pure places, reeds and grasses sprouting for the first time, or various flowers such as the flowers of small grasses, the flowers of medium-sized trees, and the flowers of large trees.

"The *jāti* flower and *sumanā* flower (types of jasmine) are only suitable for offering to the Buddha [Family], the lotus flower is only suitable for offering to the Avalokiteśvara [Family], and the blue lotus flower is [only suitable] for offering up to the Vajra [Family]: these are the best for each [family]. In the Buddha Family, use the *jāti* and *sumanā* flowers when performing the *śāntika* rite, use the lotus flower when performing the *pauṣṭika* rite, and use the blue lotus flower when performing the *ābhicāruka* rite. In the other two families perform [the rites] in a similar fashion.

"Flowers of superior color and fine fragrance, flowers of middling color and fragrance, and flowers of inferior color and fragrance are to be used separately according to the [ritual] deed [to be performed]. You may take either flowering branches or clusters of flowers and use them for offering to the consorts of the gods: these are said to be the best. The *karavīra* flower in the two colors of purple and white should be used for offering up to the chief wrathful deities and their messengers: this is said to be the best. The *kuṭaja* flower, *tilaka* flower, *śāla* flower, *karṇikārā* flower (mayeng), *asanadūrvā* flower, *bilva* (bel) flower, and *kaṭhara* (?) flower—taking any one of these, offer it, for they are suitable for all three families as well as [the rites for] higher, middling, and lower [accomplishments] and the three [rites] for the elimination of calamities (*śāntika*) and so forth. In addition, there are various flowers that you may intertwine to form garlands, or you may gather various flowers and offer them: these are suitable for all nine kinds [of rites].

609a "Among the various flowers, do not use malodorous flowers, those produced by thorny trees, or those bitter in taste, nor should you use those not named among the names of flowers listed above. You should also not use the rose of Sharon, *ketaka* flower, *atimuktaka* flower, *maṅgalā* flower, or *nīpa* flower.

"Those for offering over a long period of time and suitable for the nine kinds [of rites] are the safflower, *śamī* flower, *priyaṅgu* flower, and *kuru* grass, as well as those of a similar kind or a mixture of parched rice and sesamum: offerings of various flowers and so forth such as those mentioned above are the very best. If you do not have these kinds of various flowers, simply use [ordinary] nonglutinous white rice, selecting some that has been ground and offering it: this is also suitable for the nine kinds [of rites].

"You should not use flowers interchangeably. If, when performing a rite, you do not obtain [the flower] that you seek, you should recite the flower mantra of the corresponding family and empower whatever flower you have obtained. If you have no flowers to offer, you should use branches or leaves of *surasa* or *maruva* (marjoram) leaves, *dānta* leaves, *tamāla* leaves, *kṛṣṇamallikā* leaves (holy basil), *mātuluṅga* (citron) leaves, *arjaka* leaves (type of basil), or sweet basil [leaves] and offer these instead. If you have none of these branches or leaves, you should use the *vālaka* root, spikenard root, selaginella root, achryranthes root, or other fragrant medicinal roots and fragrant fruits, and offer them in all cases. Cloves, cardamoms, nutmegs, oranges, and all fragrant fruits can, namely, be offered instead of flowers in all cases.

"If you have none of the above flowers, leaves, roots, or fruits to offer, you should employ your mind to visualize according to your knowledge offerings that you have formerly seen, [offerings] that you have formerly heard described, or flowers that you yourself have formerly offered, and then offer these: this is the very best offering. Even if you do have flowers and fruits such as the above to offer, if you can join your palms together and raise them to your head with wholehearted devotion and [mentally] offer flowers and so forth to your deity, a mental offering such as this is supreme and unsurpassed. Acting thus, you should always make offerings in this manner, and you should not entertain any doubts."

Chapter Nine

Unguents

"Next, I shall now explain the rules for unguentary substances: those that are fit for offering with mantras are able to effect manifold blessings.

"Their names are: nut grass, *kuṭannaṭa,* costus root, *vālaka, uśīra, śārivā,* 'decocted aromatic' (*tagara*?), agallochum, saffron, the aromatic white sandalwood, the aromatic red sandalwood, *varṇa*[*ka*], *pīluparṇaka* <or *pamarāpattra* (?)>, *sarala* <called '[five-leafed] pine tree' [in China]>, *spṛkkā, padmaka* <called 'juniper'[32] [in China]>, *tailaparṇi*[*ka*] (type of sandal tree), *kāleyaka* 609b
(type of curcuma) <or, translated, called 'black aconite' (?) [in China]>, cloves, Brahman cinnamon, deodar, *priyaṅgu, arjuna* (arjun), *saurabha, deva, sailavāluka, kapittha* (wood apple), *rodhra, kramuka, paliknī, nālika, śivācampū, suvarṇa, śakala, mātuluṅga* (citron) <with its skin>, *tālīśa, bhūstṛṇa, māṃsī* <spikenard>, *damana* (mugwort), *maruva, murā, keśī* <called 'field nettle' [in China]>, *tamāla, puṃnāga, elā* (cardamom), *vyāghranakha, mocī, lāvalī* (type of myrobalan), *bāṣpīkā, dhānya* <coriander>, *śatapuṣpa* <fennel>, *haritaka* <called 'vegetable-hoof grass' (?) [in China]>, *kakkola* (Java pepper) <cluster cardamom>, *jātiphala* (nutmeg), *coraka, kaṭphala, sthauṇeya, dhyāmaka, caṇḍā, turuṣka* <storax>, *prastabhva* (?), *kesara,* and so forth, as well as gum resins such as camphor, *gandharasa, sarjarasa,* bdellium, frankincense, *śallakī, śrīvāsaka,* and other aromatics from resinous trees. These you should all mix well together in accordance with the family in question.

"Using the threesome of aromatics from grasses, aromatics from the sap of roots, and flowers, mix them to make unguents for offering to the Buddha Family. The bark of fragrant trees, heartwood aromatics such as sandalwood, agallochum, and deodar, and fragrant fruits such as were differentiated earlier are mixed to make unguents for using with the Lotus Family. Fragrant grasses, roots, flowers, fruits, and leaves are mixed to make unguents for using with the Vajra Family. Or you may have an unguent containing various roots and fruits that was previously compounded by someone else and has an excellent aroma—this is suitable for [all] three families. Alternatively, use only agallochum and mix it with a little camphor to make an unguent for offering to the Buddha Family; use only white sandalwood and mix it with a little camphor to make an unguent for using with the Lotus Family; and use only saffron and mix it with a little camphor to make an unguent for using with the Vajra Family. Red sandalwood unguent is suitable for using with Vajra[dhara] and all others. Nutmeg, *kakkola, jātisumanā,* or *<sūkṣmai>sūkṣmailā* (small cardamom), and *priyaṅgu* are suitable as unguent offerings for all messenger goddesses. Spikenard, *sūkṣmai*[*lā*], and nutmeg are used to make unguents for offering to [*vidyārājñī*s. White sandalwood, agallochum, and saffron are used to make unguents for offering to] *vidyārāja*s. The bark of fragrant trees is used to make unguents for offering to messengers. Any obtainable aromatic is used to make unguents for offering to earth-dwelling gods.

"An unguent made using only [black] agallochum is suitable
609c for using with the nine kinds of rites of the three families as well as the *vidyārāja*s and their consorts in all instances. Or if you should perform the *śāntika* rite separately, use aromatics of white color; for the *pauṣṭika* rite use aromatics of yellow color; and for the *ābhicāruka* rite use aromatics of purple color and without any aroma. If you wish to accomplish a great *siddhi,* use the earlier resinous aromatics together with fragrant fruits; in the case of a middling *siddhi,* use heartwood aromatics together with fragrant flowers; and in the case of a lower *siddhi,* use roots, bark, flowers, and fruits to make an unguent and offer this.

"When compounding aromatics, you should not use aromatics derived from sentient beings, such as onycha, musk, and lac, nor spirits or vinegar, nor aromatics that are excessively fragrant or that are not generally liked: you should not use any of these for making offerings.

"There are four kinds of aromatics, namely, unguents, powdered aromatics, [granular] aromatics, and pilular aromatics. Using any unguent, draw an altar for flowers and worship daily.[33] When you wish to offer them, say the following words:

'This aromatic is of heavenly exquisiteness.
And having kept it pure,
I now offer it up:
Please deign to accept it,
And fulfill my wishes!'

The unguent mantra is:

Āhara [ā]hara sarvavidyādharapūjite svāhā. [25 = No. 24]

First recite this mantra and mantrafy [the unguent], and then recite your regular mantra to purify it as prescribed and offer it up to the deity. If you are unable to obtain the aromatics that you seek, [take] any unguent that you can get, use the above mantra to mantrafy it in worship, and then, having mantrafied it with the unguent mantra of the family in question, offer it up to the deity."

Chapter Ten

Distinguishing Incense

"Next, I shall now explain the rules for burning incense common to the three families. Take agallochum, white sandalwood, and saffron singly and offer them in that order [to the Buddha, Lotus, and Vajra Families respectively]. Alternatively, mix [these] three kinds of aromatics together and apply them to the three families, or take one of [these] aromatics and apply it to the corresponding family.

"The names of the aromatics are: the resin *śrīveṣṭaka, sarjarasa* <that is, the gum of the *śāla* tree>, *gandharasa,* bdellium, *śallakī,* camphor, frankincense, *guḍa* (molasses), *dhyāmaka, girija,* honey, *harītakī* (chebulic myrobalan), granular sugar, nut grass, storax, agallochum, *vālaka,* white sandalwood, red sandalwood, five-leafed pine tree, deodar, *nālika, paripelava, uśīra,* barley sugar, spikenard, and fruits.

"If you wish to accomplish mantra rites, you should mix [these]
aromatics together. The resinous aromatic *śrīveṣṭaka* is suitable
for all three families and is also suitable for gods. Bdellium is suit-
able for offering to *yakṣas*, frankincense is suitable for goddesses, 610a
the aromatic *sarjarasa* is to be offered to earth-dwelling gods, the
aromatic *śallakī* is to be offered to female messengers, and the aro-
matic *gandharasa* is to be offered to male messengers.

"Camphor, *gandharasa, sarjarasa,* frankincense, bdellium, *śallakī,* and *śrīveṣṭaka:* mix these seven resinous aromatics and burn them—they are suitable for all nine kinds [of rites], and these seven aromatics are, moreover, the very best.[34] Resinous aromatics are for higher [accomplishments], heartwood aromatics are for middling [accomplishments], and other [aromatics] from flowers, leaves, and roots are for lower [accomplishments].

"The aromatics storax, agallochum, and saffron when mixed together constitute the first incense; if you add white sandalwood and also add granular sugar, this constitutes the second incense;

and if you add bdellium and frankincense, this constitutes the third incense. Use any one of these three kinds of compounded incense for all [ritual] deeds. For earth-dwelling gods and tutelary [gods] you should use *sarjarasa,* granular sugar, and *harītakī,* mixing these to make incense and offering it to them. There are again five aromatics, namely, granular sugar, *śaileyaka, sarjarasa, harītakī,* and barley sugar: when mixed together to make incense they are suitable for using in all [ritual] deeds of the three families. Alternatively, if you have [only] one aromatic, it [too] is suitable for all [ritual] deeds. Pleasing [incenses] such as the above are the finest compounded incenses prized by all people. If you do not have any of these incenses, whatever you are able to obtain is also suitable for using in sundry [ritual] deeds of the three families. The rules for compounding aromatics [to make incense] as explained above must be carefully differentiated; according to requirements, mix roots, leaves, flowers, and fruits and offer them.

"There are four kinds of incense, and you have to know them. They are, namely, natural [incense], incense pounded into pills, powdered incense, and incense molded into pills, and you must also know the circumstances in which they should be used. For the *śāntika* rite use incense pounded into pills, for the *ābhicāruka* [rite] use powdered incense, for the *pauṣṭika* [rite] use incense molded into pills, and for applying to all [rites] use natural [incense]. When mixing incense pounded into pills, add some granular sugar; when mixing powdered incense, add some resinous aromatic from a tree; when making incense molded into pills, you should use good honey, or you may substitute ghee, milk, or granular sugar for honey; and on top of natural incense you should pour a little ghee.

"If, when seeking the incense to be burned for a particular family, you are unable to obtain it, first recite the incense mantra of that family to mantrafy whatever incense you have and then recite this mantra [given below]. In the compounding of incense do not include the aromatics onycha, musk, and lac, nor should you use *madya* (liquor) and so forth for mixing incense; also do not make it excessively foul-smelling or without any aroma.

"[When offering incense, say the following words:]

> 'With these tree aromatics and resinous [aromatics] from the forests and fields
> One may satisfy the wishes of all people;
> The staple food of the gods,
> I now bring it in offering:
> Deign to accept it out of pity!'

[The incense mantra is:]

Āhara āhara sarvavidyādharapūjite svāhā. [26 = No. 24] 610b

First, using this mantra, mantrafy [the incense]; then, using your regular mantra, take the incense, mantrafy it, and use it as prescribed."

Chapter Eleven

Distinguishing the Rules for Burning Lamps

"Next, I shall now explain the rules for burning lamps. By adhering to these rules you will cause the gods and seers to rejoice and bring about success.

"Make the [lamp-]bowl with gold, or make it using silver, or using copper, [or using iron,] or using clay. If you take any one of these five kinds [of materials] and use it, your deity will rejoice.

"The rules for making the lampwick: make it using cotton, or make it with new cotton cloth, or make it with fiber from the bark of the *dukūla* tree, or make the wick with new clean cloth.

"Use fragrant oils pleasing to all or use fragrant ghee. For the *śāntika* rite use superior fragrant oil, for the *pauṣṭika* rite use secondary fragrant oil, and for the *ābhicāruka* rite use inferior fragrant oil. Oil from fragrant trees is for using in the *śāntika* [rite], sesamum oil is for using in the *pauṣṭika* [rite], and white mustard-seed oil is for using in the *ābhicāruka* [rite]; oil from the fruit of the *atasī* (flax) is for using with mantra-consorts and female seers, oil from other fruits is for using with mantra-lords, oil from the fruit of the 'bitter tree' (*tikta*) is for using with gods in the heavens such as Mahākāla, fish oil is for using with demons, animal oils are for using with *yakṣa*s, *bhallātaka* (marking nut) oil and hempseed oil are for using with lower classes of gods such as the Four Sisters and Cāmuṇḍā, and when raising a *vetāla* (corpse-dwelling demon) in a cemetery and so forth use the fat from dog's flesh.[35] Among the various oils, ghee from a blackish-yellow cow is the best and is suitable for all three families. Alternatively, ghee from a white cow is for using in the *śāntika* [rite], ghee from a yellow cow is for using in the *pauṣṭika* [rite], and ghee from a black cow is for using in the *ābhicāruka* [rite]. Or if [the oils] are differentiated in the family in question, use them accordingly. Oils produced from drugs are for using in the *pauṣṭika* [rite], oils derived from aromatics are for using in the *śāntika* [rite], and foul-smelling oils are for using in the *ābhicāruka* [rite].

"The procedures for burning lamps briefly explained above you should carefully examine for yourself, and even if something is not explained here, use it after [careful] consideration. If you have lamp oil that does not conform with the family in question, mantrafy it with the mantra of that family and [then] offer it. [When offering lamps, say the following words:]

'This lamp is able to drive away obstructions
And able to eliminate darkness;
I now hold it up in offering:
Deign to accept it out of pity!'

The mantra is:

Ālokaya ālokaya sarvavidyādharapūjite svāhā. (Behold, behold! O you who are worshiped by all *vidyādhara*s! *svāhā!*) [27]

610c Having recited this mantra, then recite the mantra of your deity to mantrafy [the lamp], and then perform the purification rites in order to remove any faults as was explained earlier."

Chapter Twelve

Offering Food

"Next, I shall now explain the rules for offering food, whereby you cause the gods and seers to all rejoice and quickly obtain success.

"I shall explain the food offerings in brief: you should use bulbous roots, long roots and fruits, cakes with ghee and cakes without ghee, other delectables such as soup, and various gruels and beverages. These four kinds of food are suitable for offering to all [three] families.

"The fruit of the *bījapūraka* (citron) is suitable for all three families, and the pomegranate and fruit of the *cūta* (mango) are also suitable for the three families: in this order each is suitable for one family. [Fruit] that is sweet in taste is for using in the *śāntika* [rite], that which is sweet and sour in taste is for using in the *pauṣṭika* [rite], and that which is bitter, acrid, or insipid in taste is [for using in] the *ābhicāruka* [rite]. The fruit of the *tāla* (palmyra) tree, the fruit of the coconut, the fruit of the *bilva,* the fruit of the *nimba* (neem), and other malodorous fruits unpleasant to all should not be offered. Then there are fruits of superior taste that are, moreover, generally abundant and also most highly prized: if you offer such fruit, you will obtain higher accomplishments. Alternatively, there are fruits whose taste is of secondary savoriness and which are also generally readily available but whose value is not prized: with such fruit you will obtain middling accomplishments. Or there are fruits whose taste is bitter, acrid, or insipid and which are also generally plentiful but whose value is most disparaged: if you offer such fruit, you will obtain lower accomplishments. Then again, if you wish to add meaning when making offerings, you should take fruits with feminine names such as persimmons, apricots, and peaches and offer them to goddesses. Fruits produced by [forest] trees and not bitter in taste are offered to mantra-consorts. The fruit of the *śrīphala* (bel) is suitable for all wrathful [deities] of the three families. The fruit of the *vaṭa* (banyan) is suitable for seeking [success with] all *yakṣas*. The fruit of the *kapittha* is for using with the god[dess] Śrī. The fruit produced by the *piyāla* tree is for using with the *praiṣika*.[36] There are many more kinds of fruit such as the above varieties, but with different names: examine their taste and use them accordingly to make offerings.

"If you take the roots of grasses to be found in the vicinity of a village or in a pure site within an [*a*]*raṇya* whose taste is sweet and delicious and offer them up, you will quickly gain success. The *vidārī* root is suitable for all uses, and if there are [any other roots of] unusually delicious taste, they are also suitable for all offerings, not only to the gods in the heavens but also for use among people. Roots that grow in the mountains and are of delicious taste are for offering to the Buddha Family. The ripened taro root is also suitable for the Buddha Family, [as are also] the *kaśeruka* root, the *vidārī* root, the *vāyasī* root, the [*ku*]*kūṭī* root, and other bulbous roots. [Roots] growing in water are for using with the Lotus Family. All medicinal bulbous roots, [roots] bitter, acrid, [or insipid] in taste, and many kinds of raw taro are for using with the Vajra
611a Family. Bulbous roots that are white in color, of [superior] fragrance, and extremely sweet and tasty with ample flavor are for offering up to the Buddha Family; bulbous roots that are yellow in color, of middling fragrance, and of middling flavor, being neither too sour nor too sweet in taste, are for using with the Lotus Family; and bulbous roots that are red in color, bitter, acrid or insipid in taste, and with a foul smell that is not sweet are for using with the Vajra Family. In this manner they are all suitable for the *śāntika* and other [rites] and the higher, middling, and lower [accomplishments] of the three families. I have explained bulbous roots in brief: use them to make offerings in due accordance with the particular family and [the distinctions between] higher, middling, and lower [accomplishments]. If you differentiate them in this manner, you will quickly gain success.

"In the above I have explained bulbous roots; the growth and use of long roots are similar to those of the varieties of bulbous roots. As for the roots of onions, garlic, and leeks, as well as other [roots] extremely malodorous and acrid or bitter in taste, they should not be offered.

"[Offer] *svasti[ka]* cakes, *ulopika* (?) cakes, *pūpa* cakes, *vaṭaka* cakes, and other flour cakes, or make various sesamum balls; there are also various cakes made with white sugar, 'joy' dumplings (*laḍḍuka*), *madhuśīr[ṣaka]* cakes, *phenaka* cakes, *piṇḍakośaka* cakes, *aśokavartaya* (?) cakes, *cicchilla* (?) cakes, pastries, *gulapiṣṭaka* cakes, *śaṣkulī* cakes, *parpaṭa* cakes, *pūpa[pūrṇa]* cakes, *māṣapūpa* cakes, *vidagdhaka* cakes, *pauṣavarta* (?) cakes, *lāvaṇikā* cakes, *garbhotkarikā* cakes, *kukkuṭī* cakes, *ramakā* cakes, *haṃsa* cakes, *sikthikā* cakes, *pṛṣañcillikā* (?) cakes, *śrīpūraka* cakes, *veṣṭikā* cakes, *chindaka* (?) cakes, *ṭadaraka* (?) cakes, *guḍapūraka* cakes, *citrapūpa* cakes, *kharjūra* cakes, *guḍaparpaṭaśṛṅgāṭa* cakes, *ghata* (?) cakes, various *garbhitapiṇḍapūpa* cakes, *rājahaṃsa* cakes, *sarjaka* cakes, *ghṛtapūraka* cakes, *kamoṭika* (?) cakes, *kosalikā* cakes, *sampuṭa* cakes, *ṣāḍava* cakes, *hariṇī* cakes, *śakuna* cakes, *mīna* cakes, various *parṇibhṛṣṭaka* cakes, *dvīpikā* cakes, *jalahāstinīya* (?) cakes, *karkapiṇḍaka* cakes, *valagarta* (?) cakes, *vaṭṭikā* cakes, *kṣiptikā* (?) cakes, and *gajakarṇikā* cakes:[37] cakes such as the above are either made with granular sugar or made by mixing in ghee or sesamum [oil]. As before, take them in accordance with the family in question and use them as offerings; if you offer them up as prescribed, you will quickly gain success.

"Cakes of rice flour and so forth are for the Buddha Family, *śāntika* [rites], and higher accomplishments; all cakes of wheat flour are for the Lotus Family, *pauṣṭika* [rites], and middling accomplishments; and cakes made with sesamum or beans are for the Vajra Family, *ābhicāruka* [rites], and lower accomplishments. Those decorated with white sugar among all the flavorings used should always be offered up among the offerings to the Buddha Family; *śrīveṣṭaka*[38] cakes are for using with the Lotus Family, and 'joy' dumplings are for using with the Vajra Family. *Pūpika*[39] cakes are to be used when seeking [success with] *yakṣas*. Cakes with feminine names are for using with mantra-consorts—cakes with femi-

611b

nine names are *kamolī* (?) cakes, *parpaṭī*[40] cakes, and so forth. Among the cakes, offer those that are most highly prized and also of delicious taste when seeking higher accomplishments; as for those of secondary taste, they are for the other two families. Any [cakes] that have been made and are not included here are for using with the eight classes [of supernatural beings (i.e., gods, *nāgas*, *yakṣas*, *gandharvas*, *asuras*, *garuḍas*, *kiṃnaras*, and *mahoragas*)].

"When offering food, first spread something like cloth or leaves for decoration. [Then] first set down the *svastika* cakes, *ulopika* (?) cakes, and *pūpa* cakes, first making in this manner [offerings] to the three families together. Then offer food as required by the family in question to the best of your ability.

"Dishes of [ordinary] nonglutinous rice (*śāli*), dishes of nonglutinous rice that ripens in sixty days (*ṣaṣṭika*), dishes of barley cooked with milk, dishes of self-sown nonglutinous rice, and dishes of Indian corn: offer as prescribed that which should be offered. Offer up unusually delicious soups with various condiments as well as pulse soups. Dishes of barley cooked with milk and dishes of self-sown nonglutinous rice are for seeking higher accomplishments, dishes of [ordinary] nonglutinous rice and dishes of nonglutinous rice that ripens in sixty days are for seeking middling accomplishments, and dishes of Indian corn and boiled rice are for [seeking] lower accomplishments.

"Use the *śāntika* rite for performing higher accomplishments, the *pauṣṭika* rite for performing middling accomplishments, and the *ābhicāruka* rite for performing lower accomplishments. When making offerings of rice dishes, roots, fruits, and rice gruels, offer them up in accordance with [the distinctions between] higher, middling, and lower [accomplishments]. The *śāntika* rite is for the highest [accomplishments] and the Buddha Family, the *pauṣṭika* rite is for middling [accomplishments] and the Lotus Family, and the *ābhicāruka* rite is for lower [accomplishments] and the Vajra Family. The highest *siddhi*, as well as middling and lower [*siddhis*], must duly conform with the rules, and they should be known according to their type.

"Among the soups, those that are sweet and tasty are for using in the *śāntika* [rite], those that are sour and sweet are for using in the *pauṣṭika* [rite], and those that are bitter, acrid, or insipid are for using in the *ābhicāruka* [rite]. Milk gruel is for using in the *śāntika* [rite], pomegranate gruel, curd gruel, and so forth are for using in the *pauṣṭika* [rite], and *kṛsara* gruel, [made,] namely, with sesamum, nonglutinous rice, and pulse, is for using in the *ābhicāruka* [rite].

"As for the flavors of the dishes briefly described above, there may be various differences according to the locality: observe [the distinctions between] higher, middling, and lower [accomplishments] and offer them up. Or if there are flavors extolled by all or which you yourself like, you should take them in offering to the Buddha [Family]. Or if there is a procedure for offering food explained for the mantras of the family in question, you should follow that; if you deviate from it, you will not gain success. Among the dishes, those 611c
that are brightly colored[41] and foul-smelling are for using with the Vajra Family.

"For using the unguents, incense, lamps, food, and so forth described above, first follow [the rules for] the family in question, and for the *śāntika* [rite] and so forth you should also follow them. Examine the nature of a mantra, whether it is joyful or wrathful; then examine it again with regard to what deeds it is able to accomplish, and then carefully consider what wishes it will fulfill. Once you have ascertained this, offer to the best of your ability the above oblatory foods.

"If among the oblation rites you see one that uses '*kāmika* (desirable) food,' you should offer *svasti[ka]* cakes, *ulopika* (?) cakes, and other dishes prepared to the best of your ability: these include [dishes with] granular sugar, boiled rice mixed with curds, roots, fruits, and milk gruel. This *kāmika* food is suitable for offering in all instances except *ābhicāruka* [rites].

"If among the oblation rites you see one that uses '*vicitra* (variegated) food,' add to the *kāmika* food two or three kinds of food different from the above: this is [*vicitra* food].

"If among the oblation rites you see one that uses '*udāra* (great) food,' double the above *kāmika* food and set out large quantities: this is [*udāra* food].

"If among the offering rites you see one that uses 'three white dishes,' you should use boiled rice with milk, with curds, and with ghee. Again, if you see one with 'three sweet dishes,' they are boiled rice with ghee, with honey, and with milk.

"If among the offering rites you see one with '*sarvabhautika* (for-all-demons) food,' [use] *sāyalika* (?) cakes, *liṅgilika* (?) cakes, *jambūliya* (?) cakes, *tilapiṣṭaka*[42] cakes, boiled rice mixed with curds, and roots and fruits, or else take one or two tasty [dishes] from among the dishes described earlier and set them down, put parched rice, flowers, and leaves in a large vessel and fill it with water, and [then] discard it far away from the site of recitation: this is [*sarvabhautika* food].

"If among the offering rites you see one with '*śāntika* food,' use *svasti*[*ka* cakes], milk gruel, parched rice, ghee, honey, and milk, dishes of barley cooked with milk, and *bījapūra* (citron): you will assuredly be able to eliminate calamities—of this you should have no doubts.

"If among the offering rites you see one with '*pauṣṭika* food,' you should use dishes such as gruel mixed with curds, 'joy' dumplings, *ulopika* (?), granular sugar, and *śrīveṣṭakā*:[43] you will assuredly be able to fulfill your wishes—of this you should have no doubts.

"If among the offering rites you see one with '*ābhicāruka* food,' you should use dishes of red nonglutinous rice or use *kodrava* (ditch millet) seeds, or boiled rice that has been colored red, or sesamum pastries, *sapūpaka*,[44] *jambūliya* (?), *kṛsara* gruel, and so forth: you will assuredly be able to vanquish your foes—of this you should have no doubts.

"If there are no rules [in your ritual] for offering food when reciting the mantras of *yakṣa*s, you should follow this method to make offerings: use dishes of red nonglutinous rice, roots and fruits, honey-water, honey, granular sugar, rice-flour pastries, and so forth: these are [the food offerings for *yakṣa*s].

"When chanting the mantras of female deities, you should offer delicacies such as soup with boiled rice, pulse soup, sweet liquids, and *parṇabhṛṣṭakā,* [that is,] baked leaves, as well as various fruits: to all female deities you should offer these dishes. 612a

"When you wish to seek higher accomplishments, follow the offering rite of the family in question to make offerings. There are foods, roots, fruits, and condiments eaten by all, delicious in taste, and also prized by many: offer up superior delicacies such as these when seeking higher accomplishments.

"The rules for offering food such as have been briefly explained above should each conform with the rite for your particular objective in the family in question, and everything has been stated in brief. In other localities foods may differ in taste: examine their color and taste and offer them accordingly.

"When you wish to offer food, first cleanse the ground, sprinkle scented water all around, spread out on [the ground] leaves that have been washed clean, [such as] lotus leaves, *palāśa* (dhak) leaves, and leaves from lactescent trees, or new cotton cloth, and then set down the oblatory dishes. Make use of these [aforementioned] leaves for the *śāntika* [rite]; use leaves growing in water and leaves from unusual trees or plantain leaves when performing the *pauṣṭika* [rite]; use leaves from the *bhallā*[*ta*]*ka* tree, leaves from the *arka* (mudar) tree, leaves from the 'bitter tree,' or [leaves] that you happen to obtain at the time for the *ābhicāruka* [rite]; use leaves from trees with feminine names, such as the first plantain leaves to sprout and lotus leaves, in the case of the mantras of female seers; for the *praiṣika* use dried tree leaves; and for earth-dwelling gods use grass.

"You must be well-acquainted with the rites for seeking higher, middling, and lower [accomplishments]. First smear and sprinkle the ground and then spread the leaves; wash your hands clean, rinse out your mouth several times, swallow some water, and then you should set down the food. First set down the *svastika* cakes, next set down the bulbous roots, long roots and fruits, then set down the gruels, then set down various [other] foods, then set down the soups and boiled rice, and then set down the milk and curds: for each follow the rite in question and set them down accordingly.

"If you construct a *maṇḍala* or undertake to accomplish various deeds, once you have obtained indications [of success], you should double [the amounts] and offer up a variety of pure food, flowers, and fruits. At the time of the initial recitation, offer up according to your means and in accordance with your own ritual whatever delicacies you have obtained. If it should be the eighth day, fourteenth day, or fifteenth day of the dark or bright two [half-]months, the time of a solar or lunar eclipse, or the time of an earthquake, then add extensively to the offerings.

"At the time of *homa* the reciter first places in preparation the necessary things in front of his deity, and when he eats he first sets aside one portion of his meal and similarly places it in front of the deity; if he first performs *homa* and then eats, he should make the food ready in advance and lay it out. Having first set out the food prepared as offering, he should then commence the recitation. In offering flowers, fruits, and various foods, you must always be mindful of this and you should not forget it while following your own ritual.

"If you wish to recite once [during the day], make offerings of
612b roots, fruits, and food once; if you wish to recite twice, make offerings twice; and if it says to recite three times, make offerings three times. If you follow the rules in this manner, you will be quickly successful. But if the reciter does not offer food and acts contrary to [the rules for] the family in question, he will then be afflicted by demonic obstructions, his body will have no luster, he will be afflicted by wind [causing his skin to become rough],[45] he will be hungry and thirsty, he will constantly have wicked thoughts, and he will be unable to effectuate his deity's mantra, all because he has not offered fruit and food to his deity.

"On the above[-mentioned] days of the dark and bright two [half-]months you should set out extensive offerings and offer them up to your deity and his retainers. At the time of the initial recitation, prepare [*sarva*]*bhautika* food on the above days and discard them in the four directions far away from the site of recitation.

"[Food] that is not explained here or is incompatible with the family in question, or, even though compatible, if you seek higher accomplishments with inferior dishes, or if the prescribed food is of a foul-smelling variety—none of these you should use. Always offer boiled rice mixed with curds. If you seek higher, middling, or lower [accomplishments] or the *śāntika* and other [rites] in the [three] families, as well as mastery of the mantras of the gods, you should make offerings in this manner. If you do not have the proper prescribed food, mantrafy whatever you obtain with the mantra of the family in question. [When offering food, say the following words:]

'These drugs, unusually fragrant and tasty,
Are fit only to offer to the Honored One;
I now bring them in offering:
Deign to accept them out of pity!'

[The mantra when offering food is:]

Āhara āhara sarvavidyādharapūjite svāhā. [28 = No. 24]

This mantra is suitable for all three families; [mantrafy the food with it,] then recite your regular mantra to mantrafy it [again and offer it up]."

The Susiddhikara Sutra, Fascicle One.

Fascicle Two

Chapter Thirteen

The *Śāntika* Rite

"Although the *śāntika* rite, the *pauṣṭika* rite, and the *ābhicāruka* rite were earlier explained in general terms, [the explanation] was still not thorough. I shall now explain them again and expand on their meaning. He who would quickly accomplish these three kinds of rites should perform them one after another as prescribed.

"If you would do *śāntika* recitation and perform the *homa* rite for the elimination of calamities, [then] take refuge in the Three Jewels, arouse deep thoughts of compassion, and at dusk on the first day of a bright [half-]month commence recitation, whereupon you will succeed in the *śāntika* rite, for at this time the Gods of Pure Abode descend and roam about among humankind, and with the assistance of the gods you will quickly obtain *siddhi*. 612c

"Don white robes, sit on *kuśa* grass facing toward the north with both body and mind calm and quiet, and perform the *śāntika* [rite]. First take some cow dung that has not yet fallen to the ground and smear the ground with it three times (i.e., in the morning, at noon, and in the evening), and [then] scatter white flowers everywhere.

"If you are going to perform *homa*, first prepare wheat, milk, curds, parched rice, sesamum, green *kuśa* grass, *priyaṅgu* flowers, boiled nonglutinous rice, dried white flowers, and dried stamens and pistils; [for firewood] use *śamī* wood, or use [wood from] trees that are resinous and fragrant, or use *yajñika* (dhak) wood, or use wood from lactescent trees—be sure to take branches from the treetops and do not discard the leaves, and cut them according to measure; also use ghee and honey. These accoutrements for *homa* are common to all [three] families. If anything else is explained in your own ritual, you should follow that.

"When performing the *śāntika* [rite], take [sticks of] wood from a lactescent tree and rub them together to get fire, or else you should bring [fire from a permanent fire]place, do *homa,* and perform the *śāntika* [rite], whereupon you will be quickly successful. Cut the branches of lactescent trees to one handspan[46] [in length], mix ghee, honey, and milk together in a vessel, [use] dried fuel sticks [dipped in the mixture of ghee, honey, and milk] to light the fire, and do *homa*.[47] Alternatively, if you produce fire with dried cow dung from the pure grounds of an [*a*]*raṇya,* that [too] will be most excellent. Make fuel for the *śāntika* [rite] from either *śamī* wood or fragrant wood.

"Make the hearth round and one cubit[48] in size; the ground for it should be a site that is white and clean, and the pit should be twelve fingers[49] deep—use [the breadth of] the thumb to measure it. Around the top of the pit make a rim, four fingers [wide] on all [sides], and inside the pit fashion a disc four inches [across] and one finger high.

"The reciter sits with crossed legs, the objects [of his meditation] follow the rite for the family in question, and he worships as prescribed. He makes offerings to Buddhamaitrī (Buddha-Compassion [= Tathāgatamaitrī]), and also to Tathāgata-ūrṇā (= Tathāgatorṇā [Tathāgata-Tuft]), the mantra-consort Aparājitā (Victorious One), Prajñāpāramitā, and Buddhalocanā; next he makes offerings to the hosts of *pratyekabuddhas* and arhats; then he makes offerings to the Gods of Pure Abode and then to the *nāga* kings Nanda and Upananda.

"Your own mantra-lord is on the Buddha's seat in the center, and to the left are Buddhamaitrī, Buddhalocanā, and bodhisattvas such as Samantabhadra (Universally Good), Maitreya, Ākāśa[garbha] ([Repository of] Empty Space), Kṣitigarbha (Earth Repository), and Sarvanīvaraṇaviṣkambhin (He Who Removes [All] Obstacles); then install the *pratyekabuddhas* and so forth, as well as the Gods of Pure Abode and so forth, and to the west of the entrance the *nāga* king Nanda; to the right are Tathāgatorṇā, Prajñā, the Great Buddha-Crown[50] Jaya, the Buddha-Crown Vijaya, and the Buddha-Crown Tejorāśi."

Chapter Fourteen

The *Pauṣṭika* Rite

"At the time of the *pauṣṭika* rite, with your mind dancing for joy, you either recite [mantras] or do *homa* in accordance with [the rites for] the family in question. Starting on the fifteenth day of a bright [half-]month and finishing on the fifteenth day of the following bright [half-]month, perform the *pauṣṭika* [rite] in accordance with [the rites for] that particular family. Moreover, start at the hour of the tiger [in the early morning] and finish before the end of the day—just follow your inclinations in this. If you start at this time, at that time the gods and heavenly hosts visit [this] world; in addi- 613a
tion, there are Śakra and other gods, as well as the gods of the various rites, who descend to inspect the world at this time, and if they see people doing good, their minds rejoice and they fulfill their wishes. [Therefore] when this time comes, the reciter should have utmost sincerity and should not be indolent.

"Don white robes, sit with half-crossed legs facing toward the east, and perform the *pauṣṭika* [rite]. Smear the ground with fine aromatics three times (i.e., in the morning, at noon, and in the evening) and scatter flowers of variegated colors all over the ground.

"If you are going to perform *homa,* do it in the following manner. Use thick milk gruel, or ghee, milk, and honey, or a mixture made of the four substances of ghee, honey, curds, and sesamum, or simply use ghee, or use plain curds, or use the *śatapuṣpa,* or use the *bilva* fruit, or use nonglutinous rice, or use *nāgakesa*[*ra*] flowers, or use lotus flowers, or use *karṇikā*[*ra*] flowers—take any one of these, dip it in ghee, and do *homa.* Alternatively, use boiled rice mixed with curds or various grains—take any one of these as well as the branches of lactescent trees and things such as [were explained] earlier [in Chapter 13] and perform the *pauṣṭika* [rite] in accordance with your own ritual.

"Take fire from the house of a *kṣatriya* or from a king's palace, or take [sticks of] wood from a forest and rub them together to produce fire, or take [fire from] a great [sacrificial] fire—if you obtain any one of these fires, it is auspicious. [Take] a bundle of thick [sticks of] wood one cubit long, dip them in ghee, milk, and curds, and perform *homa*. First take some fuel sticks to produce fire and get it alight, or else use wood from flower- and fruit-bearing trees to make fuel for producing fire.

"On black ground, or if there is no such ground, bring some black earth from elsewhere, fill a pit, and on top of it dig a hearth, which should be two cubits square and one cubit deep. Inside the pit fashion a lotus flower one two-finger [hand]span[51] in size and four fingers high. The rim [of the hearth] is one handspan wide; smear it with black earth on both the inside and the outside.

"Do this as prescribed in accordance with [the rites for] the family in question. Think clearly of your principal objective without forgetting it intermittently and perform the *pauṣṭika* [rite]. In front you should place the Bodhisattva Avalokiteśvara, to the right Mahāsthāmaprāpta (He Who Has Attained Great Strength), and to the left place the *vidyādhara* kings of the Avalokiteśvara [Family]; to the right [place] the *vidyādhara* king-seer Siddhārtha and to the left place bodhisattvas; here also place gods such as the Seven Auspicious Ones (Śrīdevī), then *vidyādhara* kings, then place the god Brahmā and the retainers of the god Brahmā. In order to seek [the fulfillment of] your wishes, also worship at will *yakṣas*, the great [female] seer Hārītī, and the hosts of gods and seers of the Lotus Family—act in each case as prescribed. First anoint yourself on the crown [of the head] and then recite [mantras] and perform the *pauṣṭika* [rite]. Seeking longevity, or asking that teeth that have fallen out be made to grow and hair that is white turn black, or seeking physical health and increased blessings and strength, or seeking various virtues and your heart's desires—if you make wishes such as these, it is called '*pauṣṭika*.'"

Chapter Fifteen 613b

The *Ābhicāruka* Rite

"In the case of the *ābhicāruka* [rite] your mind espouses anger, and angry at those to be chastised and yourself without fear, you should perform this rite. Using wrathful mantras, recite them, or else perform *homa*.

"Do not choose a [particular] time or day and do not practice abstinence—you should start when you are angry. If you do consider the time and day, [start] on the eighth day or the fifteenth day of a dark [half-]month in the middle of the day or [at midnight], for at [this] time and on [these] days hosts of *piśā*[*cas*], demons, *bhūtas*, and *rākṣasas* gather in one place or roam about in different regions. If you perform the *ābhicāruka* [rite] at this time, wrathful thoughts will arise and it will be easy to gain success; various kinds of demons will help the reciter to increase his anger, and the deeds that he performs will be quickly successful.

"Don red robes or blue-colored garments—sprinkle them with water to make them damp and then wear them. When performing an extremely ferocious deed, sprinkle them with your own blood to make them damp. Stand facing toward the south with the right foot pressing down on the left foot; your enraged eyes are not level, your brows are knitted in anger, you gnash your teeth, and you make a loud noise. You imagine that you are the lord of this family [in accordance with which the rite is being performed] and well able to endure physical and mental hardship. Following the procedures of this rite, [then] perform the *ābhicāruka* [rite].

"On three separate occasions during the day (i.e., in the morning, at noon, and in the evening) take some black earth and smear [the ground for] the *maṇḍala* with it; alternatively, use the dung of donkeys or the dung of camels, sheep, pigs, or dogs, or the ashes of burned corpses. For offerings use fragrant flowers red in color, or offer malodorous flowers or blue-colored ones, or offer the chaff of grain, wheat, and pulse. When doing *homa* use white mustard seeds or mustard-seed oil or your own blood, or else use salt, or use [black] mustard seeds or margosa leaves, or else use ashes or dirt from the soles of your feet, or use the dung of donkeys or the dung of camels, dogs, pigs, or sheep, or human feces, or use hair that has been pulverized, or use crow's feathers or birds such as cormorants, eagles, vultures, cranes, and magpies, either using their feathers or using their down, or use the fat of the above birds and animals, or use thorns or potsherds or bone powder, or use dog's flesh or pig's flesh[52] or *kovidā*[*ra*] wood or margosa wood or wood for burning corpses or wood left after burning a corpse or thorny wood or *khadira* (catechu) wood: cut [the wood] as prescribed and use it for *homa*. Anything that you use among the above kinds of things should be mixed with the three substances of poison, your own blood, and salt. With the deeds to be performed you should call out his (i.e., your foe's) name.

"Take crematory fire or fire from the cottage of a *caṇḍāla* or fire got by striking a bone or a stone. Take [wood from] the base of the trees mentioned earlier and cut it [into sticks] ten fingers [long]—
613c you should break them all off, make both ends pointed, and smear them with poison and mustard-seed oil. When lighting the fire, use the dried wood of malodorous or astringent trees or wood for lifting corpses or wood left after burning a corpse: first use these to light the fire.

"Dig a triangular hearth in black ground with one corner facing outward [away from the practitioner]. The distance between the three corners is each twenty fingers, and [the hearth] is ten fingers deep. The rim is three fingers wide: smear it with crematory ashes. In the bottom of the hearth fashion a *vajra* eight fingers [long] and three fingers high.

"Using crematory ashes or using chaff or using charcoal, or taking substances used for *homa*—namely, poison, dung, mustard seeds, and salt—fashion an effigy of your foe. [Then] cut the effigy in half and perform *homa* or tread on the heart of the effigy with your left foot and perform *homa*. *Homa* is [performed] thus: recitation is also the same. Use a knife to cut [the effigy] into pieces, or use a stick to flog it: use either the thorny Chinese honey locust or *khadira* wood to make a stick with which to beat it.

"This applies to all the families and rites as before; if your own ritual explains it [otherwise], then you should follow that. Do *homa* according to the rules as was explained before in detail. [While doing so,] your mind should not forget the objective of the deeds that you perform.

"When performing this rite, first worship the *mahākrodha* Vajra[pāṇi] and also worship all his retainers. First place the *vidyādhara* consort Vajrāṅkuśī, next place Kuliśāśani—this is the *vidyādhara* king called 'He Who Devours Thunderbolts'—then Mahāmari—this is the *vidyādhara* king called 'Great Death'—then Śatākṣi—this is the *vidyādhara* king called 'Hundred-Eyed One'[53]—then *nāgas*, *kumbhāṇḍas*, *rākṣasas*, and so forth. You should use *śāntika* mantras first to protect yourself, prepare the offerings as prescribed, and [then] perform the *ābhicāruka* [rite].

"Causing the limbs of your foes to become separated, or making them move their place of abode, or making close friends hate one another, or making [your foe] seriously ill, or causing his retainers to scatter, or stultifying him, or performing various other evil deeds—if you perform rites such as these, it is called '*ābhicāruka*.' Practicing these evil deeds, you punish wicked people who harbor wicked thoughts toward the Three Jewels; or seeking out their faults, you wish to make them suffer slightly in this world and escape the tribulations of hell [after death]. If you see sentient beings commit various sins, or violate the bodhisattva's pure code of discipline, or slander the Three Jewels, or rebel against their teachers and elders, perform the *ābhicāruka* [rite] out of pity for them.

"When performing this rite, you must follow [the rules for] the family in question, and you should not act on your own authority. Use the mantras of wrathful [deities], or use the mantras of evil *rākṣasas*, or use the mantras of *praiṣyas* (servants) and messengers to perform this *ābhicāruka* [rite]. Once you have performed this rite, punishing a person's wickedness and your wishes consummated,

if you see with eyes full of anger that he is becoming increasingly
614a critically ill and will die before long, you should quickly perform the *śāntika* [rite] and then slowly perform the *pauṣṭika* [rite]; you should not [continue to] perform this [*ābhicāruka*] rite. When you do wish to perform it, it is good to use the mantras of *rākṣasa*s and so forth, or else follow your own ritual; even if its mantras are for the Buddha Family, have no fear.

"If you perform this rite to discipline a wicked person, your mind should be without anger and resentment [toward that person], you should possess great compassion and, concerned that he has been experiencing suffering for a long time because of his evil karma and that if he constantly performs this evil it will only be the cause of long suffering, you should perform this rite out of a desire to grant him eternal happiness—[therefore] you must generate thoughts of anger. People who practice evil will descend to hell, and because the mantra-lords wish to remove the suffering of hell, they have devised this expedient means to save and protect them. When you consider the wicked conduct of such people, there will be differences in the relative gravity of their karma, and you should deal with them accordingly. You should not cause them to die for minor sins, nor should you make them suffer other excessive pain in order to chastise them.

"In order to make them rejoice, you should perform the *śāntika* rite. On such an occasion either use the hearth [used for the *ābhicāruka* rite] or make another one instead and do *homa* with milk to accomplish *śāntika*. Use *ābhicāruka* mantras, removing words such as '*hana hana*' ('slay! slay!'), '*paca paca*' ('roast! roast!'), and '*mara mara*' ('die! die!') and inserting the word '*śānti-kuru*' ('cause peace!'), whereupon you will accomplish the *śāntika* rite.

"Once someone has undergone a change of heart, he will meditate on the mind of enlightenment, generate the mind of enlightenment, and always think of benefiting sentient beings—[in such circumstances] how can it be proper to perform a rite such as this [*ābhicāruka* rite]? According to the teachings of the Buddhist scriptures, if someone harbors anger, he will create karma [that will make him descend to] hell. [Therefore] the wise should quickly generate thoughts of kindness [and perform the *śāntika* rite after having performed the *ābhicāruka* rite].

"If you wish to quickly succeed in performing the *śāntika* rite, you should do it in front of a stupa with a *śarī*[*ra*]; perform the *pauṣṭika* rite beside a pond; and perform the *ābhicāruka* rite in a cemetery: in such places you will be quickly successful."

Chapter Sixteen

Distinguishing the Rites of Accomplishment

(also called "The Characteristics of *Siddhi*")

"Next, [I shall now explain] the accomplishment of *siddhi*. Ascending into the sky and moving forward: this is the highest [accomplishment]. Concealing your form and hiding your traces: this is a middling accomplishment. Worldly deeds: these are lower *siddhi*s. There are these three kinds: higher, middling, and lower accomplishments. [These] three kinds of accomplishment—ascending into the sky, hiding your form, and worldly deeds—are further divided into higher, middling, and lower [grades].

"I shall now recapitulate the higher accomplishments of the three families: [becoming] a *vidyādhara* seer, ascending into the sky, accomplishing the five [supernatural] faculties, having many kinds [of forms], or achieving the extinction of defilements (*āśravakṣaya,* i.e., nirvana) or [becoming] a *pratyekabuddha,* or realizing the stages of a bodhisattva, or comprehending all things, or eloquence and much learning, or accomplishing [the raising of] a *vetāla*-corpse, or accomplishing [the rite of] a female *yakṣa*, or obtaining a *cintāmaṇi* (wish-fulfilling gem), or obtaining inexhaustible hidden treasure—if they comprise deeds such as the above, they are the highest among the higher accom- 614b
plishments.

"Next, I shall explain the rites for middling accomplishments in the three families: hiding your form and concealing your traces, obtaining great physical strength, being previously lethargic and then gaining assiduity, entering the [*a*]*sura*s' palace and obtaining the elixir of longevity, accomplishing [the rite of] a *praiṣika* or heavenly messenger, or being able to control demons, or being able to effectuate a *śālabhañjikā* tree spirit,[54] or achieving much learning, or understanding with depth the import of what you have not heard before, or mixing together drugs, rubbing a little on your feet and the crown [of your head], and traveling even to distant places without becoming tired—the *siddhis* described above are known as the highest of the middling accomplishments.

"Next, I shall explain the rites for lower accomplishments: causing people to look on joyfully through the power of mantras, or prevailing over people, or punishing wicked people, or vanquishing foes, or other lowly deeds—these are the lowest (= highest?) among the lower [accomplishments].

"If you wish to effectuate drugs [and other] articles, there are three kinds of [signs of] accomplishment: the arising of bright flames constitutes a higher [accomplishment], smoke constitutes a middling [accomplishment], and warmth constitutes a lower [accomplishment].

"Next, the mantras of holy ones are for higher accomplishments, those expounded by the gods are known to be for middling accomplishments, and the mantras of worldly gods are for lower accomplishments. Next, the mantras of the Buddha Family are for higher *siddhis*, the mantras of the Lotus Family are for middling *siddhis*, and those of the Vajra Family are for lower *siddhis*. If you wish to seek a lower [accomplishment] with a higher mantra, you will obtain a lower accomplishment. Or if you wish to seek a higher [accomplishment] with a lower mantra, you will obtain a higher accomplishment. Or if you use a middling mantra to achieve a higher or lower [accomplishment], it will be the same.

"Mantras are endowed with these [following] four virtues. You should realize that the higher, middling, and lower divisions of mantras are able to achieve 'great results': namely, fulfilling the stage of a *pratyekabuddha,* fulfilling the ten stages of a bodhisattva, and becoming a Buddha are great results. Next, [mantras] accomplish 'great virtuous conduct,' namely, being surrounded in front and behind by many retainers—if they fulfill a wish such as this, it is great virtuous conduct. Next, the 'stage of long life,' namely, obtaining the state of a victorious one, the state of a wheel-turning

[king] (*cakravartin*), or [the state of] a longevous seer—if [mantras] fulfill wishes such as these, it is the stage of long life. Next, an 'expansiveness of appearance and manner,' namely, radiance shining afar—this is expansiveness of appearance. If endowed with these four virtues, even though it may be a mantra of the lower grade, it is able to achieve [accomplishments of] the higher grade. [Mantras] among those of the higher grade that are not endowed with these virtues, even though they may be mantras of the higher grade, are to be used for [accomplishments of] the lower grade.

"In this manner the mantras expounded by Buddhas and bodhisattvas are variable. Many of those expounded by Buddhas and bodhisattvas, although they belong to the lower grade, are also able to accomplish deeds of the higher grade. Among the mantras expounded by deities there are [also] those only capable of one deed, namely, the *śāntika* rite, the *pauṣṭika* rite, or the *ābhicāruka* rite. Although they are capable of [only] one deed, each of them has higher, middling, and lower grades.

"How can it be that mantras of the lower grade are able to accomplish higher deeds? It is like a fine lotus flower coming forth from dark mud—of this there is certainly no doubt. How can it be 614c
that kindly mantras of the higher grade are able to achieve wrathful accomplishments of the lower grade? It is like a white sandalwood tree, which is cool by nature, but if wind strikes it and rubs [its branches] together, fire will naturally arise—it is not without cause. Although such discrepancies [between the mantra and its effect] are not in sequence, you should not have any doubts about all the other *siddhi*s.

"*Siddhi*s pertaining to the body are accomplishments of the higher grade; *siddhi*s pertaining to drugs are accomplishments of the middling grade; and *siddhi*s pertaining to wealth are accomplishments of the lower grade.

"Moreover, should there be a person who has for a long time been reciting a mantra of the lower grade, even though he himself may have no power, his own deity may instead seek a [*siddhi* of the] higher grade [from another higher deity] and together they will grant it to him. [But] if he recites and worships while his mind has doubts about a mantra of the higher grade, and if he is also without pure sincerity, then even though it may be a mantra of the higher grade, because his reciting is lighthearted, he will attract accomplishments of the lower grade. Know, therefore, that recitation is entirely dependent upon the mind.

"For instance, among the gods there are also some who are poor, and among the classes of demons there are also some who are rich and strong. Just as they are, so is it with mantras: every mantra is endowed with the three [grades of] *siddhi,* namely, higher, middling, and lower, and if you recite them with a sincere mind, you will obtain *siddhi* from them all."

Chapter Seventeen

Invoking the Deity

"Next, when you wish to enter the deity chamber, first look at the diety's face, join your ten fingers together, and bow your head slightly. Then fill a vessel with clean water, place the proper flowers for offering in accordance with the deed to be performed, then place unguents, and following your own ritual perform *argha:*[55] burn incense to cense them, and [then] you should recite the mantra seven times to empower them and, taking them [in your hands], invoke [the deity]; once you have invoked [the deity], you should worship as prescribed.

"For the vessels for holding *argha* you should use [gold or] silver or use copper or use stone to make them. Alternatively, use clay or wood or take conches to make them, or use *śukti*[56] (pearl-oyster shell), or use lotus leaves, stitching them together to make vessels, or the leaves of lactescent trees. When you come to use *argha* vessels such as those described above, you must know the procedure: in the case of the *śāntika* [rite] you should use white vessels, for the *pauṣṭika* [rite] you should use yellow vessels, and for the *ābhicāruka* [rite] you should use black vessels. For performing the accomplishment of higher, middling, and lower *siddhi*s, you should use them on analogy with what has been said [just] above.

"In the *argha* used when performing the *śāntika* [rite] include a little wheat, for the *pauṣṭika* [rite] you should add some sesamum, and for the *ābhicāruka* [rite] you should include some Indian corn. Furthermore, for the *śāntika* [rite] include some milk, for the *pauṣṭika* [rite] add some curds, and for the *ābhicāruka* [rite] you should include some cow's urine or add some of your own blood. For use in all instances you should add parched rice, unguents, flowers, sesamum, and cogongrass rings. Use copper vessels and fill them with *argha*. If you do not have these vessels, any that you happen 615a
to obtain will also be suitable for using in all instances.

"When invoking [the deities], you should use the mantra and *mudrā* of the *vidyārāja* of the corresponding family. If an invocatory mantra is already given in your ritual, you should take that and use it and not bother about any other. First invite the [chief] deity of the family, and then invite the *vidyārājñī:* it is like this for all three families. If your ritual does not have an invocatory mantra, you should use the mantras of the *vidyārāja* and so forth to invoke them. Even if your ritual does give an invocatory mantra, should it be inferior, how can it be suitable for inviting the lord of the family? If you use the mantras of your own ritual to invoke [the deities], you will be quickly successful, and no hindrances should arise.

"If your ritual has an invocatory mantra and one for dismissal, at the time of invocation the lord of these mantras goes to the place of the lord of the family and invites him, saying, 'Now So-and-so invokes you for such-and-such a deed,' and when dismissing him it is like this: 'The deed that was to be performed has been completed; I beg you, O Honored One, to agree to leave at your pleasure.'

"Use the mantra of the *vidyārājñī* to invite female seers and so forth and the mantra of the *vidyārāja* to invite mantra-lords. There may be mantra-lords who do not accept being invited [only] by the mantra of a *vidyārāja:* these must be invited by using the mantras of both the *vidyārāja* and *vidyārājñī,* as explained elsewhere.

"When setting out *argha*, you should recite the mantra once in the case of a long [mantra], three times in the case of a medium-length one, and seven times in the case of a short one; in the case of an extremely short one, recite it twenty-one times.

"The above exposition represents the rules for *argha*."

"First place both knees on the ground—you should wear a pure cogongrass ring on your hand as explained earlier [in Chapter 7. Then] take the *argha* in your hands, burn incense to cense it, and make this invocation:

'I implore you, O Honored One,
On account of your vow
To descend to [this] ritual site;

Please deign to take pity [on me]
And accept this *argha*
And [these] meager offerings.'

"There is a mantra-lord called Sole Victor over Violence and Wrath[57] who does not accept invocation by other mantras; if you use the mantra expounded by him, then he will descend upon being invited. His retainers also do not accept invitation by other mantras, and again you should use the mantras of his retainers to invoke them.

"If it is just for invocation, use the heart-mantra. Alternatively, it is explained that the root[-mantra] or the mantra expounded by the *vidyārājñī* is to be used for invocation. The family heart-mantras (Nos. 20–22) are [each] suitable for [one of] the three families: use them for invocation, and when [the deity is] about to descend, add the word '*ehi*' ('come hither!')—this is a further secret—and you will quickly fulfill your wishes.

"At this juncture, make obeisance with a sincere mind and make [this] pronouncement several times: 'Great Compassionate One, I invite you to come down to [this] ritual site on account of your vow.' If you are not sincere in mind, you will repeat much in vain. Then [recite] mantras, all of them also conscientiously.

"Hold the *argha* vessel up with both hands: raising it up to the crown [of your head] in offering is for higher *siddhis*, holding it level with your chest is for middling *siddhis*, and holding it level with your navel is for lower *siddhis*.

"First look at the painted image of your deity: if the image is 615b
standing, the reciter should also stand to invite [the deity]; if the painting or image is seated, you should also sit to invite [the deity]; and if you see that the image is standing with its body bent, then you too should imitate this and invoke him.

"At the time of invocation, first look in the direction where your deity resides and face toward him to invite him; then turn around and place the *argha* vessels in front of the deity's image. There is another secret: also look in the other directions of [those for whom] the *śāntika* [rite] and so forth are to be performed and then invoke him.

"Or at other times when you obtain flowers and fruits that are pleasing to your deity, you should invoke him and then offer them. At the time of invocation, join your hands and fingers together and, facing the proper direction, simply invoke him with thoughts of utmost sincerity, or hold up the *argha* vessel with both hands and invoke him, whereafter you should offer the things that you have obtained. If you wish to accomplish higher, middling, or lower deeds or the *śāntika* [rite] and so forth, you must in all instances add mantras and *mudrā*s to perform the invocation.

"When undertaking to accomplish sundry deeds, obstructions may occur, or demons may arise, or the sick person [for whom the rite is being performed] may increasingly suffer. At such times the matter is urgent and it is not possible then to prepare *argha* vessels, in which case you mentally invoke your deity and perform the rite for dispelling [the obstructions]. [But] if you desire success as explained above in accordance with the relative scale [of your objective], [use] *argha* to invite [the deity]. [However,] in cases of sudden trouble, [simply] invite him with a sincere mind. In addition, if someone should wish to submit to the deities of a [particular] family, he should perform [the rites according to] the rules for invocation: the reciter will quickly gain success."

Chapter Eighteen

Rules for Worship Procedures
(also called "Rules for Recitation")

"Next, once you have invoked the deity, then, depending on the family [to which the deity belongs] and the deeds [to be performed] and taking into account the relative scale [of your objective], worship [the deity] in accordance with the rules. Once you have invoked [the deity], say the following words:

> 'It is good that you have come, O Honored One!
> Out of pity for us
> Descend to [this] ritual site,
> And showing pity
> Take this seat
> And seated accept [these] meager offerings.'

Then engender thoughts of sincerity, repeatedly make obeisance, and address the deity, saying:

> 'O Great Compassionate One, taking pity [on us]
> And on account of your vow,
> You have indeed descended;
> It is not within my power
> To invoke Your Honored Self.'

"In this manner you should follow this [procedure] three times [daily], and [then] you should prepare offerings as explained earlier. First offer unguents, then give flowers, then offer incense, then offer food, and then burn lamps. Following this sequence, use the mantra of the *krodharāja* ('king of wrathful ones') [to purify them]. For each of these things, pure, wholesome, and delightful to people's minds, use the appropriate mantra to mantrafy it. After you have offered the unguents, give the name of each and offer up *argha* in the manner explained earlier. Similarly, flowers, incense,

615c food, and so forth also all follow this [procedure]. If you do not have any unguents, incense, flowers, or food to offer, then simply recite the appropriate mantra, make the [corresponding] hand-seal, and offer it in this way, declaring, 'I have been unable to obtain [any offerings]: just accept my true intent.' Then perform *argha*. Because it is done with true intent, you will quickly fulfill your wishes.

"Apart from this, there are four [methods of] offering that are suitable for all [three] families and are for using in all circumstances: (1) joining the palms together, (2) using *argha,* (3) using mantras and *mudrās*, and (4) simply employing the mind [to make mental offerings]. Among these wholesome kinds [of offerings] you should perform whatever accords with your ability. Moreover, among long-term offerings there is absolutely none that surpasses employing the mind. As was explained by the World-honored One, the mind is foremost among all things. If you are able to give expression to the mind and make offerings, you will fulfill all wishes.

"If you wish to accomplish various other deeds, you should dispel obstructors. If you do not dispel them, you will perhaps be harmed by them later. Therefore, you must first perform the rite for dispelling them. Recite the mantra of the *krodha*[*rāja*] or use the mantra 'accomplisher of [all] deeds' of the corresponding family:[58] recite this and dispel [the obstructors].

"Next, you should first recite the mantra for the deities of the family in question and empower some water. [Then] invite all [the deities], do *homa,* and make hand-seals and so forth.[59] The mantra [for the deities] of the Buddha Family is:

> *Oṃ tathāgatodbhavāya svāhā.* (*Oṃ,* for the coming forth of the Tathāgata! *svāhā!*) [29]

The mantra for the deities of the Lotus Family is:

> *Oṃ padmodbhavāya svāhā.* (*Oṃ,* for the coming forth of the Lotus! *svāhā!*) [30]

The mantra for the deities of the Vajra Family is:

> *Oṃ vajrodbhavāya svāhā.* (*Oṃ,* for the coming forth of the Vajra! *svāhā!*) [31]

"Alternatively, you may use the family heart-mantra. The heart-mantra of the Buddha Family is:

> *Jinajik.* [32 = No. 20]

The heart-mantra of the Lotus Family is:

> *Ārolik.* [33 = No. 21]

The heart-mantra of the Vajra Family is:

> *Vajradhṛk.* [34 = No. 22]

"Either using [one of] these mantras (Nos. 32–34) or using [the mantra for] the family deities (Nos. 29–31), sprinkle the flowers and so forth [with the mantrafied water]; otherwise use the mantra and seal of the *krodha* ('wrathful one') Kīlikīla. Recite the mantra, make the seal with your left hand, and seal all the unguents, incense, food, flowers, and so forth—only then will they become purified and removed of pollution.

"In order to purify your own person, take a scoop of scented water in your right hand, recite the heart-mantra while looking at the scented water with your eyes, and pour it over your head: you 616a
will be purified and removed of pollution.

"Then use the mantra '[accomplisher of] all deeds' and the mantra of the *krodha*[*rāja*]: this is in order to purify the seat. Mantrafy scented water and sprinkle [the seat] with it.

"Then recite [the following mantra] seven times [over scented water] and sprinkle [the water] all over the ground: this will remove pollution and [the ground] will become purified. The mantra of Kīlikīla is:

> *Oṃ kīli kīli vajra vajri bhūr bandha ba*[*ndha*] *hūṃ phaṭ.* (*Oṃ,* O you with a stake! you with a stake! O *vajra!* O you with a *vajra!* bind, bind the earth! *hūṃ phaṭ!*) [35][60]

"After you have protected the ground with this above mantra, for binding the sphere of empty space [above the ritual site] you should use the following Susiddhi mantra. Take some burning incense in your hand, recite the mantra, and cense the air: this will remove pollution and [the air] will become purified. The Susiddhi mantra is:

> *Oṃ susiddhikari jvalitānan[ta]mūrtaye jvala jvala bandha bandha hana hana hūṃ phaṭ.* (*Oṃ,* O you who are good at bringing success! to you who have blazing and infinite forms! blaze, blaze! bind, bind! slay, slay! *hūṃ phaṭ!*) [36]

This above [mantra] is the Susiddhi mantra of the Vajra Family; it is suitable for all deeds and is for using to bind the sphere of space.

"Next is explained the mantra of the Buddha Family for binding the sphere of space:

> *[Oṃ] jvala hūṃ.* ([*Oṃ,*] blaze! *hūṃ!*) [37]

This above [mantra] is the mantra of the Buddha Family for binding the sphere of space, and it is only suitable for that family.

"Next is explained the mantra of the Lotus Family for binding the sphere of space:

> *Oṃ padmini bhagavati mohaya mohaya jagadmohani svāhā.* (*Oṃ,* O Lotus One! O Blessed One! delude, delude! O world-deluding one! *svāhā!*) [38]

This above [mantra] is the mantra of the Lotus Family for binding the sphere of space, and it is only suitable for that family.

"Next, you should use the family heart-mantra [Nos. 32–34] to mantrafy some scented water and sprinkle it in all directions. Then take one of either the root-mantra of the *vidyārāja* or his heart-mantra or the heart-mantra of the messengers of the mantra-lord and use it to bind the surrounding area.[61] Use these heart-mantras to perform boundary-binding: it is as if you had placed a fence around the site that has been bound. The seers and gods of the corresponding family will always protect it, and none will be able to create obstructions. If there should be any obstructors to the [ritual] deeds of the [three] families, you should have recourse to the rite of Amṛtakuṇḍalin to dispel them.

"There are five kinds of protective rites, and you must always perform them inside the [recitation] chamber on the ritual site. They are, namely, [the rites of] the adamantine fence, the adamantine canopy, the adamantine stake, the *krodha* Kīlikīla, and the *krodha* Amṛtakuṇḍalin. The 'adamantine fence' mantra is: 616b

> *Oṃ sara sara vajraprākāraṃ hūṃ phaṭ.* (*Oṃ*, array, array the adamantine fence! *hūṃ phaṭ!*) [39][62]

The 'adamantine canopy' mantra is:

> *Oṃ visphura rakṣa vajrapañjara hūṃ phaṭ.* (*Oṃ*, glitter! protect! O adamantine net! *hūṃ phaṭ!*) [40][63]

The 'adamantine stake' mantra is:

> *Oṃ kīli kīli vajra vajri bhūr bandha bandha hūṃ phaṭ.* [41 = No. 35][64]

The mantra of the *krodha* Kīlikīla is:

> *Oṃ kīli kīli krodha hūṃ phaṭ.* (*Oṃ*, O you with a stake! you with a stake! O wrathful one! *hūṃ phaṭ!*) [42][65]

The mantra of the *krodha* Amṛtakuṇḍalin is:

> *Namo ratnatrayāya, namaś caṇḍavajrapāṇaye, namo vajrakrodhāya daṃṣṭrotkaṭabhayabhairavāya asimusalaparaśupāśahastā[ya], oṃ amṛtakuṇḍali kha kha khāhi khāhi tiṣṭha tiṣṭha bandha bandha hana hana garja visphoṭaya visphoṭaya sarvavighnavināyakān mahāgaṇapatijīvitāntakarāya hūṃ phaṭ svāhā.* (Homage to the Three Jewels! Homage to Violent Vajrapāṇi! Homage to the Adamantine Wrathful One, terrifying with enormous tusks and with a sword, club, axe, and noose in his hands! *Oṃ*, O Amṛtakuṇḍalin! devour, devour! devour, devour! abide, abide! bind, bind! slay, slay! roar! rend asunder, rend asunder all obstructions and obstructive demons!

> For you who put an end to the life of the Great Lord of [Śiva's] Hosts! *hūṃ phaṭ, svāhā!*) [43][66]

If your own ritual has [other] mantras for the adamantine fence and so forth such as these, you should bind [the ritual site] again [using these other mantras].

"When the [ritual] deeds [of protection] have been completed, you should next [begin] recitation. At times of recitation first recite the mantra of the mother of the corresponding family. The mantra of the mother of the Buddha Family is:

> *Namo bhagavate uṣṇīṣāya, oṃ ruru sphuru jvala tiṣṭha siddhalocani sarvārthasādhani svāhā.* [44 = No. 2][67]

The mantra of the mother of the Lotus Family is:

616c *Namo ratnatrayāya, nama āryāvalokiteśvarāya bodhisattvāya mahāsattvāya mahākāruṇikā[ya], darśanasp<ṛ>[a]rśanābhiśrāvasmaraṇena ca syām ahaṃ sarvasattvānāṃ sarvavyādhicikitsaka, tad yathā, oṃ kaṭe vikaṭe kaṭa vikaṭa kaṭaṃkaṭe bhagavati vijaye svāhā.* (Homage to the Three Jewels! Homage to the Bodhisattva and Mahāsattva Holy Avalokiteśvara of Great Compassion! By observing, touching, hearing, and remembering, may I become a healer of all diseases for all beings! Namely: *Oṃ,* O Kaṭā! Vikaṭā! Kaṭā! Vikaṭā! Kaṭaṃkaṭā! Blessed One! victorious one! *svāhā!*) [45][68]

The mantra of the mother of the Vajra Family is:

> *Namo ratnatrayāya, namaś caṇḍavajrapāṇaye mahāyakṣasenāpataye, oṃ kulaṃdhari bandha bandha hūṃ phaṭ.* [46 = No. 4][69]

"By first reciting these mantras of the [family] mothers, you will be able to protect your deity, you will also cause your sins to be extinguished, you will be able to remove obstructions, and you will be in harmony with the gate to [the attainment of] *siddhi.* If you only recite the mantra of Māmakī (i.e., the mother of the Vajra Family), it will also apply to the [other] two families, and if you recite it before and after [a rite], the gods will increase their protection. Should [other mantras] be explained in your own ritual, recite these first at times of recitation—you should recite them in accordance with your ritual. Or if your ritual has the mantra of Sole Victor (Ekavīra),[70] then you should first recite this and not bother about any other.

"The procedures for worship and [ritual] deeds such as removing pollution, protecting and purifying, and boundary-binding explained above should all be performed at times of initial recitation,[71] when performing [different] rites, and when the *śāntika* [rite] and so forth are performed.

"Either use the mantra of the lord of the family deities, or use the family heart-mantra, or use the mantra 'king of all mantras,' or use the mantra 'king of the Susiddhi rite,' or use the mantra '[accomplisher of] all deeds'—these five kinds of mantras are found in all three families. In accordance with the [ritual] deeds that you perform, you should take one of each from the family in question and use it to perform them. That is to say, for self-protection, invocation, sprinkling water, purification, binding the surrounding area, chastising by the rules, in order to increase the power of the mantra if it is not complete, in order to punish [others'] mantras, in order to incite, and for other deeds not described [here]—again take any one of the [above-mentioned] five mantras of the corresponding family and use it: you will quickly [obtain] *siddhi*.

"The family heart-mantra is able to protect your deity and pro- 617a
tect yourself. When protecting yourself, you should recite it three times or seven times and tie the hair on the crown [of your head] into a single [top]knot. If you are a renunciant [with a shaven head], tie [a knot in] a corner of your robes or tie [a knot in] your protective cord. Alternatively, chant [the mantra] directly over your fore[finger] (= thumb?) seven times and touch five places [on the body]—this will also protect you. [The five places are,] namely, the crown, both shoulders, throat, and chest. Otherwise use cow bezoar or white mustard seeds or *argha* water—take any one of these and use it to protect yourself.

"If you are performing the *ābhicāruka* rite, you should use the mantra of the lord of the family deities to protect yourself; if you are performing the *śāntika* rite, you should use the mantra of Krodhavajra (Wrathful Vajra) to protect yourself; and if you are performing the *pauṣṭika* rite, you should use the mantra of the lord of the family deities and the mantra of Krodhavajra and protect yourself with both. If the reciter is afraid when the mantra-lord appears, he should use the mantra of the lord of the family deities and protect himself with it. When performing [ritual] deeds, always protect yourself with two mantras, namely, the mantras of the lord of the family deities and of Krodha[vajra].

"When you have finished reciting, you should dismiss [the deities]. At the time of dismissal protect the mantra-lord either [with] the mantra of the lord of the family deities or with [the mantra of] the family mother or with the family heart[-mantra] and also protect yourself, doing as you please.

"If, owing to circumstances, you have to go to a polluted place or a place that is unclean and so forth, first recite the mantra of Ucchuṣma, make his seal, seal the five places [on your body], and then go at will; you should constantly recite his mantra and not forget it.[72]

"When bathing, first recite the mantra for subduing obstructions to protect yourself, and until you have finished bathing you should not forget [to continue reciting it]; the mantra for subduing obstructions is Kuṇḍalin['s mantra (cf. Nos. 13–15)]. When eating food, use the mantra of the lord of the family deities to protect yourself, and keep it [constantly] in mind. When you wish to go to sleep, use the mantra of the family mother to protect yourself. If, when performing rites, you end up forgetting to perform [the protective rites according to] the rules for protection, you will cause demons to arise, and so in order to expel the demons you should quickly recite the mantra of the *vidyārāja* of the corresponding family: this will protect you, and all demonic obstructions will be unable to achieve their purpose.[73]

"Once the self-protection, boundary-binding, and other rites explained above have been completed, then compose your mind and recite [mantras] in a relaxed manner. As for the seat used by the reciter, use green cogongrass to make the seat. The seat should be four fingers high, one handspan wide, and sixteen fingers long. Such a seat should always be used at times of initial recitation and at times of [regular] recitation. Alternatively, use *kuśa* grass or other green grasses, or else, following [the distinctions between] the rites of the [three] families, take a lactescent tree and use its wood—this is regarded as the most excellent; use [the wood] to fashion a chair, its size as explained above and well-trimmed. [Again,] either use leaves or use branches and stalks and make [a seat] as above: observing the rules for [ritual] deeds, take branches 617b
and leaves and use them to make a seat. On this seat sit with crossed legs to perform the *śāntika* [rite] and higher accomplishments, sit with half-crossed legs to perform the *pauṣṭika* [rite] and middling accomplishments, and sit with both legs hanging down to perform the *ābhicāruka* [rite] and lower accomplishments.

"When you have finished worshiping, you should arouse sincere thoughts and extol the Buddha, then praise the Dharma and Sangha, then Avalokiteśvara, and then praise the Vidyārāja Awesome Vajra[dhara]. Praise them in the following manner:

'Great compassionate one, savior of sentient beings, good guide, and omniscient one,
Who is an ocean of merit and virtue: with head bowed I now make obeisance to the Buddha.
That which purifies the poisons of greed and anger, removes evil destinies through goodness,
And is alone the principle of thusness: I now make obeisance to the Dharma.
Those who have attained the gate to liberation, who fully abide in the points of learning (i.e., precepts),
And are the supreme field of merit and [possessed of] virtue: I now make obeisance to the Sangha.

Extolled unanimously by the Buddhas, able to produce various merits,
And called Avalokiteśvara: I now bow my head in obeisance.
Having great strength and a body of wrath, the goodly *vidyādhara* king
Who vanquishes those difficult to vanquish: I now bow my head in obeisance.'

"After having sincerely extolled the Buddha and bodhisattvas in this manner, again join your fingers and palms together, arouse earnest thoughts, and praise the Buddhas' virtues and other bodhisattvas. For the text of the eulogy you should use a eulogistic text spoken by the Buddhas or hosts of bodhisattvas and so forth, and it should not be your own composition. When the eulogy is finished, arouse thoughts of utmost sincerity and repent of your sins:

> 'I now take refuge in the Buddhas, World-honored Ones, arhats, Holy Sangha, and bodhisattvas in world-systems throughout the ten directions. Take cognizance of us! From the past through to this life, mental afflictions have obscured my mind and I have long been drifting through [the realms of] life and death. Moreover, in other lives, [my mind] obscured by greed, anger, and delusion, I have committed evil acts, either toward the Buddha, Dharma, and Holy Sangha, or toward the holy hosts of arhats and bodhisattvas, or toward parents and venerable ones and other sentient beings both with virtue and without virtue—toward the above I have committed evil acts, either doing them myself, abetting others, or rejoicing in seeing them done, and the actions of my body, speech, and mind have extensively accumulated sins. With palms joined and a sincere mind, I make obeisance with head bowed before the Buddhas and bodhisattvas and repeatedly repent in this manner. Just as the sins that I have committed through unwholesome actions are known to the Buddhas,[74] I repent of them all.
>
> 'Arousing thoughts of utmost sincerity, I take refuge as long as I live in the [Three] Jewels of the Buddha, Dharma,

and Sangha and in the right path to nirvana. In order to remove the sufferings of life and death of sentient beings, I 617c
take refuge in the Three Jewels.'

"Arousing thoughts of reverence and taking refuge in this manner, make obeisance with your head [on the ground]. Then again arouse sincere thoughts and, seeking from the supreme seed the fruit of the ambrosia of liberation, you should dance [for joy], generate the mind of enlightenment, and seek the fruit of *siddhi:*

'I shall eliminate the countless sufferings of sentient beings throughout [all] world-systems and also rescue them from all evil destinies and liberate them from mental afflictions; they are variously pressed by all manner of sufferings, and so I arouse great compassion and generate the mind of enlightenment. For sentient beings who are in anguish, I shall become a refuge; for sentient beings without a leader, I shall become their leader; for sentient beings who have lost their way, I shall become their guide; for sentient beings who are afraid, I shall become [a source of] fearlessness; sentient beings who are in anguish I shall make happy; and for sentient beings who are pressured by mental afflictions, I shall eliminate [their mental afflictions].

'The merit produced by the sundry good acts that I am now performing and by my generation of the excellent mind [of enlightenment] I transfer to all sentient beings so that they may arrive at the right path [to nirvana]. [The merit] produced through the gates of the six *pāramitās* (i.e., the perfections of giving, morality, forbearance, energy, meditation, and wisdom) and other merits that I have produced I transfer to [all] sentient beings so that we may together arrive at the supreme fruit [of nirvana]. Stated in brief, the excellent [acts of] merit performed by me in the past, present, and future I transfer entirely to all sentient beings so that they may quickly accomplish the path of the Buddha and not engender indolence until they reach enlightenment. Thus I generate the mind of enlightenment, think with pity of sentient beings, and arouse thoughts of great compassion—should someone have sufferings, may I eliminate them some day!'

"In order to purify your mind, constantly keep [in mind] the six [objects of] mindfulness, and ever mindful of these six [objects of] mindfulness, concentrate on them exclusively without becoming distracted; nor should you be attached to the self. In addition, make a vow as did the Buddhas of the past—you should make the vow in this manner:

> 'The pure karma that I have produced I transfer to [all] sentient beings so that they may accomplish [various] virtues. I also ask that through the merits that I have produced all sentient beings may obtain inexhaustible wealth and that they may also be generous, increase their wisdom, achieve great forbearance, always cultivate wholesome kinds [of deeds], always have knowledge of former lives, and always espouse great compassion—wherever the [various] categories of sentient beings are born, may they be endowed with the above qualities!'

"Next, you should join your palms together, make obeisance with head bowed to the lord of the family deities, and call to mind the *vidyārāja*. Then perform various [ritual] deeds in accordance with the rules.

"First take your rosary with your right hand, place it in your left hand, join your palms together [with the rosary held between your palms], and raise them, thinking of the *vidyārāja*. [Then,] using the rosary [to count], recite [one of] the [following] mantras [to purify the rosary]. The mantra of the Vajra Family is:

> *Namo ratnatrayāya, namaś caṇḍavajrapāṇaye mahāyakṣasenāpataye, oṃ kiri kiri raudriṇi svāhā.* (Homage to the Three Jewels! Homage to Violent Vajrapāṇi, great general of the *yakṣas*! *Oṃ, kiri kiri,* O fierce one! *svāhā!*) [47][75]

The mantra of the Buddha Family is: 618a

Namo ratnatrayāya, oṃ adbhute vijaye siddhārthe svāhā. (Homage to the Three Jewels! *Oṃ,* O marvelous one! victorious one! you who have accomplished your objective! *svāhā!*) [48][76]

The mantra of the Lotus Family is:

Oṃ amṛtaṃgame śriye śrīmālini svāhā. (*Oṃ,* O going to immortality! for auspiciousness! O auspicious one with a rosary! *svāhā!*) [49][77]

"With the forefinger[78] and ring finger of both hands work [the rosary], counting the recitations with the right hand—this applies to use [of the rosary] in all instances. In the case of the *ābhicāruka* [rite], the seal is raising the thumbs (= forefingers?) and working the rosary.

"Beads of *bodhi* seeds are for recitation in the Buddha Family, beads of lotus seeds are for using with the Avalokiteśvara Family, and *rudrākṣa* berries are for beads for the Vajra Family. For general use in the three families, each is as explained above, and these rosaries are the very best: you should hold them for all recitation. Otherwise use seeds of the soapberry or *tāla* tree, or use clay to make [the beads], or make the beads with conch, or use crystal or use pearls or ivory to make the beads, or use red gems or *maṇi*[-gems], or use beads of tear grass or the seeds of other grasses, each in accordance with the family [in question]: observing their color and type, you should take them [and use them] for recitation. If you are performing the *ābhicāruka* rite, you should use bones to make the rosary, and you will quickly gain success.

"In order to protect and purify [the rosary] and increase the efficacy of the rite, you should in addition recite [the following mantras]. The mantra of the Buddha Family [for increasing efficacy] is:

Oṃ namo bhagavati, siddhe sādhaya siddhārthe svāhā. (*Oṃ,* homage to the Blessed One! O accomplished one! cause success! O you who have accomplished your objective! *svāhā!*) [50][79]

The mantra of the Lotus Family for increasing efficacy is:

> *Oṃ vasumati śriye svāhā.* (*Oṃ,* O wealth-possessing one! For auspiciousness! *svāhā!*) [51][80]

The mantra of the Vajra Family for increasing efficacy is:

> *Oṃ vajraṃ jitaṃjaye* (= *vajrājitaṃjaye*?) *svāhā.* (*Oṃ,* O *vajra!* you who are victorious over the [in]vincible! *svāhā!*) [52]

Use the earlier rosary seal when reciting these.

"At times of recitation hold the rosary level with the chest—it should be neither higher nor lower. When taking up the rosary, bow your head slightly and with determined will and sincere mind make obeisance to the Three Jewels. Then make obeisance to the Eight Great Bodhisattvas, then make obeisance to the *vidyārāja*'s retainers, and then you should commence reciting the mantra, thinking of the mantra-lord as if he were before your very eyes. Focusing your sincerity in this manner, you should not distractedly think of other things.

618b "Mantras that have the word '*oṃ*' and words of *namaskāram* (exclamation of homage; i.e., *namo,* etc.) and so forth at the beginning should be recited with a quiet mind. At times of the *śāntika* [rite] and at times of the *pauṣṭika* [rite] all [mantras] should be recited slowly or recited mentally. There are also mantras that have the word '*hūṃ*' and the word '*phaṭ*' at the end—you should realize that these all ought to be recited with a harsh voice; use them when performing the *ābhicāruka* [rite] and at other times of wrath.

"If you examine the number of syllables in a mantra, there will be some with more and some with less. If it has fifteen syllables, you should recite it fifteen *lakṣa* times (1 *lakṣa* = 100,000), and if it has thirty-three syllables,[81] you should recite it three *lakṣa* [times]. Those with more than this number [of syllables] should be recited ten thousand times or more. At the time of the initial recitation complete the above number [of recitations]. Consider the family and type [of the mantra], whether it is for higher, middling, or lower [accomplishments], or [to which of] the three kinds of deeds [it applies], or consider whether it was expounded by a holy one, expounded by a [celestial] god, or expounded by an earth-dwelling god—carefully consider its family and type and [then] you should recite it until it has been effectuated: such is the initial recitation. If you do not do the preliminary recitation and all the [requisite number of] recitations, even [the objectives of] a lower rite that you seek after will not be obtained for a long time—how much more so if you seek the accomplishment of higher or middling *siddhis*? For this reason engender most excellent thoughts and do the preliminary recitation. However, at the time of the initial recitation of mantras divide the number of recitations explained earlier into ten parts and then recite them.

"When you have completed [the requisite number of recitations], supplicate the mantra-lord for conditions [favorable to] *siddhi*. If at first there is no sign, supplicate in a similar manner from the beginning a second and a third time. If there is a sign, then you should recite the mantra as prescribed. If there is no indication [of success], abandon it and do not recite it [any more]. The rules for supplication are the same as the rules for invocation. If at times of supplication you see in your dreams the mantra-lord turn his face away and leave or not speak to you, you must recommence the recitation. After doing this several times, if you see the mantra-lord speaking to you in your dreams, then you should realize that it will not be long before you are successful. If there is no indication, you should not recite [the mantra]; if you persist in reciting it, it will cause you misfortune.

"At the time of the initial recitation, commence the recitation in a clean and secluded place. From the recitation on the first day until you become exhausted the number of times [that you recite the mantra] must consistently follow the prescriptions, and you should not add to or subtract from them.

"As regards recitation three times [daily] mentioned earlier, there are the first watch and the last (i.e., third) watch during the day, and during these two periods you should recite [mantras], while during the middle watch you additionally bathe and perform good acts. During the night there are three periods that are also the same as the above, and the duration of the middle watch is for rest and so forth. It is said to be best if you recite during the night and also perform *ābhicāruka* rites, *antardhāna* (invisibility) rites, and rites for raising [dead] bodies during these night watches.

"If you recite during the day, perform *homa* at night, and if you recite during the night, perform *homa* during the day. [Or] perform *homa* with many drugs [and other substances] before recitation,
618c and again do *homa* after having finished reciting: if you are able to do this, it is much better. With the [offerings of] dumplings [and other food] explained earlier [in Chapter 12], you should perform *homa* irrespective of whether you do it before or after [making the offerings].

"Recite and do *homa* only in accordance with these methods. Even if you only perform *homa* and [thereby] gain success in a rite, you should realize that you must also recite mantras, for if you do so, the *vidyā* [deities][82] will rejoice and it will be easy to achieve efficacy in the rite.

"The reciter does not engender anger, he does not seek sensuous pleasures, he should not deprecate himself, he does not mind hard work, he does not become frightened, he does not seek overzealously, and he does not have contempt [for others]. At times of recitation he does not make irrelevant comments; even though physically exhausted, he does not give way to [his exhaustion]; he controls his foul gases; he does not think about any worldly talk; he does not forsake his own deity; and even if he sees a strange sign, he should not be surprised at it. At times of recitation he also does not discriminate between various signs.

"When you have finished reciting, you should recite the mantra of the family lord or recite the mantra of the family mother. By reciting these mantras, you will gain protection and none will be able to obstruct you. If, after having finished reciting in accordance with your own ritual, you have exceeded the proper number [of recitations], there is no reason to be afraid. You should arouse sincere thoughts and make a supplication, saying, 'I have in accordance with this ritual completed the number of recitations. I beg you, O Honored One, to accept and bear witness to them and bestow instructions on me in my dreams.'

"If at the time of actual recitation you should suddenly cough, belch, break wind, or forget the words of a mantra, then rise and use water to perform the rite of purification by sprinkling. Even when you are counting the rosary and need [only] one [more recitation] to complete the cycle, these ailments may occur. After having finished the purification by sprinkling, recite again from the beginning. In the case of obstacles to the path such as these mentioned above, you must in every instance recite [again] from the start.

"When you are about to finish counting [one cycle of] the rosary, extend thanks, make a bow, and when you have finished start [counting] again, also making one obeisance. Be it in front of a painting [of the deity] or at the site of a statue or in front of a stupa or at the site of a [hallowed] seat—wherever you recite, for every cycle of the rosary look once at the face of the deity and make one obeisance.

"When you have finished reciting as explained above, rest your mind in quietude or meditate on the mantra and its chief [presiding] deity. Recite three times [daily], and during the first, middle, and last [watches] apply your mind with sincerity; the number of recitations [during the three watches] must all be identical, without increase or decrease.

"Bathe three times [daily] and perform all deeds such as smearing the ground, offering flowers, removing withered flowers, and various oblations three times [daily]. You should have three robes (i.e., waist-cloth, outer garment, and undergarment). Moreover, your undergarment[83] [and the two other robes] may be washed and dried, fumigated with incense, or purified by sprinkling [them with water] during the three periods [of the day]: it is permitted to perform any one [of these actions] during each of the [three] periods. Have separate sleeping robes and bathing robes—change the undergarment on these two occasions (i.e., when sleeping and bathing) and

wash it once daily. If this [under]garment is difficult to dry, it is permitted to fumigate it. Wash three times [daily] the bowls for offering to the deities and replace the withered flowers that have already been removed with fresh ones. During the three periods [of the day between sessions of recitation] always read the *Prajñā*[*-pāramitā*] and other scriptures of the Great Vehicle, make *caitya*s, and
619a paint *maṇḍala*s.

"If, after having finished the mantra's preliminary recitation and service, you have still not obtained [the objective of] your supplications, you should recite uninterruptedly for one period or two periods exclusively without stopping in between. If you are affected by demonic obstructions, the karma of illness afflicts your body, your mind is without pure sincerity, you are constantly negligent, you are physically or mentally fatigued, you miss the time or season, you do not abide by the rules, or you have not bathed at the time, and you perform recitation and *homa* in such circumstances, they should not be counted. Composing the mind, engaging in [proper] conduct, and reciting as prescribed—it is [recitation] endowed with these [qualities] that should be counted. When performing *homa*, at times of recitation, and during invocation—in these three deeds, if the number [of recitations] of all the mantras [is not as prescribed], they will all be unsuccessful; for each and every one you must complete the number as prescribed. Even if the [prescribed] number is about to be completed and one [recitation] is needed before finishing, but an obstruction then occurs, count again from the beginning.

"When making a *maṇḍala* as prescribed or at the time of a solar or lunar eclipse—if you engage in recitation on these two occasions, the merit thereof will increase immensely and it will not be long before you are successful: of this there is no doubt. Alternatively, [reciting] at the Eight Great Sacred Stupas or at places where past Buddhas practiced the bodhisattva practices are the very best, and during the [first] fifteen days of the first month [of the year][84] is also an excellent time. Or when you receive a mantra from a master, if you first go through [a period of preliminary] service and then recite [the mantra], it will not be long before you are quickly successful. Or if you see the mantra-lord giving you instructions in a dream, you will also be quickly successful if you follow his directives.

"The reciter may increase the offerings, the place may be preeminent, or at the time in question he may increase his pure sincerity, and even though the number [of recitations] may be incomplete, simply because these [other factors] are outstanding the mantra-lord will be delighted and grant success. [But] you should realize that although the *siddhi* of this rite has been quick [to manifest], it will dissipate before long [because the preliminaries have not been performed]. For this reason that which is obtained after the preliminary service has been completed is described as firm [and will not dissipate].

"At the time of the preliminary service you should make extensive offerings, and at the time of a solar or lunar eclipse and on the eighth day, fourteenth day, and fifteenth day [of each half-month] also increase the offerings to the hosts of gods and seers, as is explained elsewhere. On the above days increase your good deeds and acts of abstinence and so forth and also increase the offerings to your mantra-lord. Again, on these days [take] a flask filled with scented water and bedecked with flowers and twigs or take an *argha* vessel [filled with scented water], mantrafy it using the mantra of Amṛtakuṇḍalin, and pour it over your head—this will enable you to remove demonic obstructions. Alternatively, when you offer food, paint *maṇḍala*s, do *homa,* and burn lamps and [make] other offerings on those days, you must increase them all.

"In some rites it may be simply stated that if you recite [a mantra] the effect will appear spontaneously, and [this means that] the painting, statue, stupa with *śarī*[*ra*], and so forth will suddenly tremble or bright flames appear—you should realize that it will not be long before you quickly gain success.

"When you gain success, there is some sort of sign: namely, the body becomes lithesome, suffering from illness is forever removed, 619b
excellent wisdom is increased, the mind has no fear, the body manifests radiance, valor increases, in dreams at night you always see

things that are pure and true, the mind is always peaceful, when reciting and performing [ritual] deeds you never feel tired, the body emits unusual scents, or you make ready gifts, you respect admirable virtues, and you engender deep reverence for the mantra-lord—at times of success things such as the above appear, and you should realize that these are signs of success.

"When the preliminaries have finished, worship your deity according to the rules, and you should increase the offerings and also do *homa*. Once the rites of the preliminary service have been completed in accordance with the [requisite] number [of recitations], you must next perform recitation for *siddhi*. Moreover, first entreat [the deity, saying that] you wish for an indication [of success] in your dreams.

"You should perform recitation for *siddhi* at the [same] place where the recitations were done when you performed the rites of the preliminary service, and you should not move elsewhere. Should there be difficulties and you wish to move, when you reach the [new] location, you must again first perform [the rites according to] the rules for the [preliminary] service and then perform recitation for *siddhi*. If you do not observe the preliminary recitation, you should perform penance—you will be made to take the mantra of the lord of the family deities and recite it one thousand times or at certain times made to recite your own regular mantra one hundred thousand times. Otherwise you [must] again perform the [preliminary] service as explained earlier.

"At the time of actual recitation you may suddenly recite another mantra by mistake. Once you have realized your mistake, repent of the error with a sincere mind, [admitting that] you made the mistake through negligence, ask the deity to disregard the error, and then with bowed head make obeisance; you must [then] recite [the mantra] again from the beginning. Should you suddenly recite your mantra in a polluted place on account of mental negligence, then once you have become aware of it, you must do penance—when you reach the site of recitation, recite the mantra of the lord of the family deities seven times.

"Fast for one day each half-month and then ingest the five pure [cow products (*pañcagavya:* milk, curds, ghee, dung, and urine)]; recite the mantra for the five pure [cow products] eight hundred times and then ingest them. If you ingest these five pure [cow products], the contaminated food that you have consumed during the [previous] half-month will be purified and the mantras [that you recite] will increase their power. The mantra of the Buddha Family for the five pure [cow products] is:

> *Namo bhagavate uṣṇīṣāya, viśuddhe viraje śive śāntikari svāhā.* (Homage to the Blessed One, to the Protuberance [on the crown of the Buddha's head]! O you who are purified, unsoiled, auspicious, and cause peace! *svāhā!*) [53][85]

The mantra of the Lotus Family for the five pure [cow products] is:

> *Oṃ yaśoje svāhā.* (*Oṃ,* O you who are born of glory! *svāhā!*) [54][86]

The mantra of the Vajra Family for the five pure [cow products] is:

> *Namo ratnatrayāya, namaś caṇḍavajrapāṇaye mahāyakṣa-senāpataye, oṃ śikhi śikhi nirmale prabhe prabhāsvare teje* 619c
> *tejovati pra[bhā]vati svāhā.* (Homage to the Three Jewels! Homage to Violent Vajrapāṇi, great general of the *yakṣas*! *Oṃ,* O you who have a topknot! you who have a topknot! untainted one! light! radiant one! splendor! splendorous one! luminous one! *svāhā!*)[55][87]

"Take some milk, curds, ghee, dung, and urine from a yellow cow, mantrafy them each separately eight hundred times, place them [together] in one spot, and again [mantrafy them all together] eight hundred times. Place them on a *palāśa* (leaf) or on the leaves of lactescent trees or in an *argha* vessel, then stir them with cogongrass and recite the mantra one hundred times. Then, facing toward the east, squat down and drink three *ho* (1 *ho* = 180 ml) all at once. Do this three times as when using liquid measures for medicine. When taking this, you should not speak.

"Should the image [of the deity] emit a voice and speak while you are reciting, you should first examine [the voice]. Recite the mantra of the lord of the family deities and [make] his seal at once: if it is the work of a demon, it will withdraw of its own accord. Or if it makes statements that differ from your own ritual, you should realize that it is the work of a demon. Likewise, if it makes statements urging you to perform wicked deeds, you will also know that it is a demon.

"If you have a bad dream, then you must first recite the mantra of the family mother one hundred times. If you do not first recite the mantra of the family mother [to counteract the bad dream], you must not recite [any other mantras during the following day].

"When reciting, if the number [of completed recitations] is less [than prescribed], you should not stop, but if it is more, you have committed no error.

"The procedures for recitation explained above must all be adhered to. If you act contrary to these rules and [still] wish to seek *siddhi,* it will be unobtainable."

Chapter Nineteen

Rites for Irradiating [the Deity]

"Next, I shall now explain how to increase the majesty of the gods and cause them to rejoice so that your mantras [over which they preside] will be quickly successful.

"First, using scented water, bathe the body and head [of the divine image] on days of important seasonal junctures and increase the offerings. Then take one hundred *sumanā* flowers and, taking one flower at a time, recite the mantra twenty-one times or seven times or sometimes three times—first examine the number of syllables in the mantra and then recite it; [then] offer up [the flowers] to your deity. Next, offer unguents and incense of unusual fragrance and then offer food as was explained earlier [in Chapter 12], adding granular sugar and curds.

"Next, perform *homa*. [First,] simply using [fuel] sticks, take them and burn them—the sticks should not exceed the [proper] measurements; burn one hundred and eight of them. Next, use milk and curds mixed with honey and do *homa* one hundred and eight times. Next, use ghee and curds mixed with boiled nonglutinous rice and perform *homa* one hundred and eight times. [Do this] for twenty-one days or seven days or again on three mornings. When this three[fold *homa*] has been completed, you should take some milk gruel, mix it with cow's ghee, and again perform *homa* one hundred and eight times. When this has been completed, take an *argha* vessel, recite with the mantra one hundred and eight times, pour out a little water, and perform *homa*.

"If you perform these rites, your mantra will be energized. For example, it will curtail the majesty of other mantras and gain increased [majesty]. Or it will impair [other] mantras and gain increased 620a
[majesty]. Or the mantra may be incapacitated and not function, or it may be fettered [and unable to function], or other mantras may cross with it, or the mantra may be missing some syllables, or the

syllables of the mantra may have increased—troubles such as the above will all be eliminated and [the mantra] will gain increased majesty.

"If you take any one of the medicinal herbs mentioned in *homa* [rites] and perform *homa* with it for one day and night, the mantra [deities] will rejoice and gain increased majesty. Again, take some aromatics, mix them together to make a scented paste, and make an effigy of your deity. Offer it *mālatī* flowers, burn resinous aromatics from trees or heartwood aromatics three times daily, and recite with the mantra one hundred and eight times: the mantra [deities] will rejoice and gain increased majesty. Having made this effigy of the deity, place it on a lotus leaf or a plantain leaf or the leaf of a lactescent tree or grass leaves, and make offerings to it not only during the day but also at night. When the ritual is over, dismiss [the deities] as prescribed, dispatching [the effigy] in a large river.

"If you perform the above procedures in accordance with these rules, your deity will rejoice and quickly grant *siddhi*."

Chapter Twenty

Rites for Consecrating the Deity

"Next, once the preliminary service is over, if you wish to increase the majestic virtues of the mantra-lord, you should consecrate him. Take a gold flask or one of silver or copper or a new clay flask, fill it with scented water, and place the five precious objects, flowers, fruits, aromatics, and leaves [inside]; also place the five grains, various unguents, or the powder of heart[wood] aromatics [inside], tie new colored silk around the neck of the flask, and insert branches of the *tāla* tree or branches of lactescent trees. Using the mantra of the lord of the family deities or using the mantra of the family mother, recite it one hundred and eight times and then anoint the crown of the mantra-lord. You should make an effigy of him using gold and so forth and agallochum or sandalwood, place it on a pedestal, and consecrate it. After you have consecrated it, you should then offer things such as flowers and aromatics or offer necklaces and various oblatory articles. Then perform *homa* as an offering and increase the [number of] recitations. If you do this, you will be able to make your deity increase his potency and you will quickly obtain *siddhi*.

"When you perform recitation for the preliminary service, you should [also] anoint your deity—take an *argha* vessel, visualize your deity, and consecrate him. Or when you have finished bathing yourself, you should again meditate on your mantra-lord and consecrate him three times or seven times. At the time of the preliminary service you should not forget [to do this]. Alternatively, also use milk or use ghee or sometimes use honey to fill a flask, then place the seven precious objects and other things [inside] as prescribed, and consecrate your deity—the wishes for which you pray will quickly gain fulfillment."

Chapter Twenty-One

Signs of the Efficacy of One's Prayers

"Next, I shall explain in detail the rules for supplication. On the 620b
eighth day, fourteenth day, or fifteenth day of a dark or bright [half-]month, or on the days of a solar or lunar eclipse and so forth, fast for one day or three days or seven days, bathe and purify yourself, and don new clean robes. If you supplicate [your deity on days] other than these days, you should use the bright [half-]month, recite the *śāntika* mantras, and supplicate him.

"Then at dusk, using hot water and mantras, bathe and purify yourself, remove the grime [from your body], sprinkle [water] on the five places [on the body], and worship your mantra-lord as prescribed. Then offer *argha,* additionally reciting the mantra one hundred and eight times; then, using *jāti* flowers not yet in full bloom, sprinkle them with sandalwood-scent[ed water], and offer these up next. Also make extensive offerings of food, called *udāri* food (= *udāra* food; see Chapter 12), in which the [amount of] curds has been doubled. Make a garland with *mālatī* flowers and offer [this too]. First take some cow's ghee and perform *homa* one hundred and eight times, and then [take] *sarjarasa* [sticks] and again perform *homa* one hundred and eight times.

"Have a young girl twist together a cotton string or a cloth string, take it, and make seven knots, reciting the mantra once for each knot; when the seven knots have all been completed, again recite the mantra seven [times]. [Then] tie [the string] around your upper left arm, lie down on your right side, and meditate on the mantra-lord. After you have obtained instructions [from the mantra-lord] on how to proceed,[88] remain as you please, resting on a couch of cogongrass on top of which flowers have been strewn, and meditate on the figure of your deity.

"If you see in your dreams the lord of your family or the mantra-lord or see the *vidyārāja,* you should realize that these signs are signs of success. Or if you see the Three Jewels or bodhisattvas and the four assemblies (i.e., monks, nuns, laymen, and laywomen) and see them being worshiped, these are signs of *siddhi*. Or if you see yourself reciting mantras and performing [ritual] deeds or see yourself wearing clean white robes and see others coming to worship you, you should realize that a most excellent *siddhi* is close at hand. Or you may see someone climbing a mountain peak or someone riding an elephant or crossing a large river or sea or climbing a fruit tree or riding a lion or a cow, deer, horse, or other animals, or riding any flying bird such as a flying goose or a peacock, or you may see a beautiful woman wearing necklaces and holding a vase of flowers in her hand or walking along [adorned with] perfume, flowers, and a parasol and surrounded [by attendants], or you may receive in your dreams an elephant or horse carriage and precious objects—if you see these signs, they are signs of *siddhi*. Or if you obtain in your dreams things such as flowers, fruits, roots, ghee, milk, curds, and parched rice, or drugs [and other articles] that have been effectuated, these are signs of *siddhi*. At the time of the preliminary service, you may dream of these effectuated drugs [and so forth] or obtain a rosary [in your dreams]—if you obtain these signs, you should realize that you must perform the recitation rite. Or you may see yourself being censed or see [yourself] bathing and purifying [yourself] or see [yourself] wearing necklaces on your person—once you have seen these signs, then perform recitation, and you will quickly [obtain] *siddhi*.

"When performing the recitation rite, take one hundred *jāti*
620c flowers, recite the mantra of the family mother and your own mantra one hundred and eight times together, and offer them. Then take some white sandalwood incense, mantrafy it one hundred times [and offer it too]. If you supplicate [the deity] in this manner, then when you sleep as you please, the mantra-lord will himself manifest signs [in your dreams]

"Again, take the drug *uśīra,* pound it together, and make an effigy of the mantra-lord. [Then] mix some *valmīka,* or ant[hill] earth, and make a vessel, fill it with cow's milk, and place the effigy in it; or, using ghee, milk, and honey, mix them together, put them in the vessel, and [place] the effigy in it. [Then] mantrafy it one hundred and eight times and worship it three times [daily]. If you worship in this manner, your deity will rejoice and you will quickly obtain the manifestation of signs [of success].

"Again, on the eighth day, fourteenth day, and fifteenth day of the dark and bright two [half-]months and on the days of a solar or lunar eclipse and so forth fast, observe abstinence, and make repeated offerings. Using the seven resinous aromatics and the five heart[wood] aromatics, recite the mantra once and perform *homa* once with each aromatic. When you have completed this one thousand two hundred times, you will quickly see signs [of the fulfillment] of the wishes for which you pray.

"If you perform as prescribed the standard rules for supplication explained above in detail, you will quickly gain success, and seeing the signs thereof, you will have no doubts."

Chapter Twenty-Two

Rites for Receiving Mantras

"Next, I shall explain in detail the rites for receiving mantras. Placing both knees on the ground, first make extensive gifts to the venerable *ācārya*. Holding fine flowers in your hands, engender thoughts of respect and receive [the mantra] from the [*ā*]*cārya* three times orally. If the mantra has many [syllables] and you are unable to commit it to memory, you should write it down on a piece of paper with cow bezoar, and having received it, recite it as you please. If you are to receive a mantra at another time after having earlier entered a *maṇḍala*, make extensive gifts to the venerable [*ā*]*cārya* and so forth on a propitious day and then receive it as before. If you receive it correctly in this manner, the mantra will be quickly successful, and even if you do not perform the rites of the preliminary service and immediately recite it, you will still gain success.

"Again, taking a new flask without any imperfections, place flowers, leaves, the seven precious objects, and the five grains [inside], each as prescribed, but without getting it wet, and with thoughts of utmost sincerity perform extensive worship. The *ācārya* first writes the names of mantra-lords on pieces of paper and places them in the flask, which he adorns and worships as in consecration rites. When performing this rite, he fasts and practices abstinence for one day or three days, and he performs this rite at dusk. That is, he copies the names of mantras [on pieces of paper] with cow bezoar, places [the paper] in the flask, offers unguents, flowers, incense, lamps, and food, performs *homa* with his mantra, performing it one hundred and eight times, and makes extensive and earnest requests that the holy hosts protect and listen to him.

"After three full days have elapsed in this manner, [the *ācārya*] makes his disciple take a piece [of paper] out of the flask; beforehand [the disciple] must have washed his body and made it fragrant. He puts an auspicious cogongrass ring on his [right] hand, 621a recites the mantra one hundred and eight times to mantrafy the flask, censes it with incense, makes obeisance with devoted mind, and is made to take a piece [of paper out of the flask], and, after having taken it, he again makes obeisance. If he receives [the mantra] in this manner, he will quickly obtain *siddhi.* If he further recites other mantras, the mantra that he has received will lose its *siddhi.*

"If [the *ācārya*] engenders joy in his mind toward the disciple and confers his own *siddhi*-mantra, [the disciple] should receive it as prescribed in accordance with the rules, and because it has been previously recited [by the *ācārya*], it will not be long before the disciple obtains *siddhi.* First, [the *ācārya*] invokes the mantra-lord and announces [his intention, saying], 'I confer this mantra on this disciple, and I beg you to extend protection to him and quickly grant him *siddhi.*' Holding fragrant flowers in his hands, he recites [the mantra] one hundred times or one thousand times, then summons the disciple and confers it. He also says these words: 'I now transfer this *vidyā*-lord and confer it on my disciple. I beg you to take heed and effect *siddhi* for him.' The disciple should [also] say, 'I have now received the *vidyā*-lord, and I vow never to forget it from this day forth until I reach enlightenment.' [By means of] the rite explained above, whereby the disciple receives the mantra from the teacher, [the disciple] will gain success, but if he receives it [in any other way] apart from this, he will not obtain *siddhi.* If he receives a *siddhi*-mantra in this manner, there is no doubt that he will definitely have success with it.

"If [the mantra] has already been previously endowed with *siddhi,* do not perform the preliminary service. It being thus with mantras, the rites for receiving *siddhi*-drugs and so forth (i.e., drugs and other articles that have already been effectuated) are also the same. Then there may be a person who, after having finished the preliminary service, then, qualified to recite [the mantra], confers it in turn on someone else in accordance with the rules—without doing the preliminary service and by simply performing recitation, the person who has obtained [the mantra] will gain success.

"Someone who would receive a mantra should for the sake of *siddhi* first make extensive gifts to the teacher: flowers, fruits, roots, drugs, fine robes, outer garments, gold, silver, *maṇi*[-gems], assorted precious objects, various grains, flasks full of fine curds, young male and female servants, various articles of bedding, wonderful leather slippers, accoutrements of bodily adornment, drugs [and other articles] that have already been effectuated, elephants, horses, cows and calves, various other vehicles, and even himself he should bring and proffer as gifts. Employed as a servant, he serves [the teacher] for a long time without shirking hard work and, joining his palms devoutly together, he reverently proffers the gifts. If you make gifts in this manner, you will quickly obtain *siddhi*. The various things described in detail above you must first offer up to the *ācārya* and then receive the wondrous words of the mantra."

Chapter Twenty-Three

The Rite for Making Mantras Complete

"Next, if the reciter sees in his dreams the person of the mantra-lord with extra limbs, he should realize that the mantra has extra syllables, while if [the mantra-lord] has missing limbs, he should realize that [the mantra] has missing syllables. Having discerned these signs, he performs the rite for making [the mantra] complete. Or if he sees that the mantra differs from that which he has received and upholds, with the number of syllables, either more or 621b
less, not being the same, and his mind then engenders doubts, he should perform the rite for making [the mantra] complete.

"First write the incorrect mantra on a piece of paper with cow bezoar and, after having worshiped the *vidyārāja*'s mantra as prescribed and protected yourself, place it on the seat of the mantra-lord. Then take some fuel sticks and, following your own ritual but using only plain ghee, you should perform *homa* in order to ask the *vidyārāja* to extend assistance. [Then] spread some cogongrass to make a bed. First make obeisance to the lord of the family deities, then make obeisance to the family mother, then make obeisance to the Buddhas, and make the following pronouncement: 'I beg the Buddhas and holy hosts to extend assistance and protection.' After having made this pronouncement, lie down on the [bed of] cogongrass with your head facing east, and in your dreams your deity will show you signs. On the piece of paper on which [the mantra] has been written with cow bezoar there may be extra [syllables] or there may be missing [syllables]—the deity will rewrite it with cow bezoar, complete with title and notes, and he will also rectify all the extra and missing letters. If the mantra is not incorrect, he will simply say that it is not incorrect. Or he may give instructions in your dreams to complete [the mantra]. When performing this rite, [also] perform the rites for protection in order to ward off demons."

Chapter Twenty-Four

Increasing [a Mantra's] Majesty

"Next, in order to increase the potency [of a mantra], you should perform *homa*. Either using ghee and honey or sometimes using milk, perform [*homa*] with each separately. Alternatively, use sesamum mixed with ghee and do *homa*, or use resinous aromatics mixed with ghee and do *homa*, or use lotus flowers mixed with ghee and do *homa*, or sometimes simply use *sarjarasa*. Or while in the mountains always ingest the five pure [cow products] without eating any other food, [then] take a full hundred thousand flowers of the flower of the family in question, mantrafy each one, and offer it up to your deity; [also offer] fine unguents, incense, flowers, lamps, and food, reciting the mantra eight hundred times for each three times daily for three days—if you worship in this manner, you will increase the [mantra's] potency. Or, using heartwood, burn it as a lamp three times daily for seven days—you will be able to make the mantra increase its potency. Or if you sometimes make offerings of *kāmika* food (see Chapter 12), you will also increase its potency. Rules for recitation, *homa*, and worship such as those explained above are also able to make [the mantra] increase its potency."

Chapter Twenty-Five

Rules for *Homa*

"Next, I shall explain in detail the rules for *homa*, which cause the reciter to quickly obtain *siddhi*.

"In front of an image of the deity make a hearth for [performing] *homa* that is one cubit square, has a rim on [all] four sides, and is a half-cubit deep; [the measurements are] also the same if you make [the hearth] circular. If the place of recitation is indoors, you should go outside and dig the hearth where you can see the figure of the deity [inside]. Make it as prescribed in accordance with the [ritual] deed to be performed (cf. Chapters 13–15). Place things such as fuel sticks, as well as incense and flowers, on the right-hand side and place the *homa* vessels on the left-hand side. 621c

"Using the mantra '[accomplisher of] all deeds,' sprinkle the [above-mentioned] things [with water] and sit on a cogongrass seat. With composed mind and quiet thoughts and holding the *argha* [vessel] in your hands, invoke the *vidyā*-lord. Pour out some *argha* water, pouring a little into the hearth, and then, reciting the mantra once for each flower, offer [flowers] to the mantra-lord. In order to remove pollution, you should recite the mantra of Kīlikīli (= Kīlikīla) and also make his seal, and in order to protect [the ritual site] recite the mantra of Kuṇḍalin and sprinkle some water to purify it. Then use fuel sticks to light the fire, and once you have lit the fire, first invoke Agni (God of Fire), [saying,] 'I now respectfully request Agni, who is foremost, seer among the gods, and esteemed among [those who perform] Brahman practices, to descend to this place and receive *homa*.'[89] Next, recite the [following] mantra; the mantra for invoking Agni is:

> *Oṃ ehy ehi mahābhūta devarṣi dvijasat<tama>tamāgre hitvāhutim āhā<hā>ram asmin saṃnihito bhava agnaye havyakavyavāhanāya svāhā.* (*Oṃ*, come hither! come hither! O great

being, divine sage, and foremost among the truest of the twice-born [i.e., Brahmans]! and accepting oblations and food, be present here! To Agni, conveyor of oblations for the gods and oblations for the ancestral spirits! *svāhā!*) [56][90]

"Having summoned Agni, first sprinkle and purify [the fire] with *argha* water three times, take the five grains, ghee, curds, and other things, mantrafy them with the mantra, and do *homa* three times (i.e., feed the offerings to the fire three times each) in sacrifice to Agni. The mantra for sacrificing to Agni is:

> *Agnaye havyakavyavāhanāya dīpya dīpya dīpaya svāhā.* (To Agni, conveyor of oblations for the gods and oblations for the ancestral spirits! shine, shine! cause to shine! *svāhā!*) [57][91]

"Having made sacrifices of food to Agni, mentally visualize that you lead Agni back to his seat [in the heavens]. Then recite the mantra of Kīlikīli, make his hand-seal, and again purify the fire.[92] All *homa* should be [performed] in this manner. Next, invite your own deity: first recite your deity's mantra once and install him on his seat and, after you have worshiped him as prescribed, [ask him to] deign to accept the *homa*.

"The wood to be used [as fuel] at times of *homa* is as follows: *palāśa* wood, *uḍumbara* (cluster fig) wood, *plakṣa* wood, *nyagrodha* (banyan) wood, *khadira* wood, *arka* wood, *vaikaṅkata* wood, *āmra* (mango) wood, *kāśmīrya* (?) (= *karmarī*?) wood, *śamī* wood, *apāmārga* wood, and *aśvattha* (pipal) wood. [Take] branches of the above twelve kinds of trees one two-finger [hand]span in length: they should all be moist and freshly gathered, and for all *homa* use branches that are straight. Examine the upper and lower [ends], place them fac-
622a ing the same direction, cleanse them with scented water, turn the narrow tip outward, turn the wider lower [end] toward yourself, dip both ends in ghee, and throw them into the hearth.

"When performing the *śāntika* and other rites, follow your own ritual in each case. [Before performing *homa*] first put aside some balls of food, take them, and [then] perform *homa*. These rules apply in all instances. Each day when you prepare food, first put aside one portion of food, place it in front of the deity, wait until the time of *homa,* and take it and use it first. At times of recitation one puts both hands between both knees, and likewise at times of *homa* you should also [sit] like this.

"Take some agallochum four fingers long and as thick as your forefinger, dip it in storax, and do *homa* one hundred and eight [times]: this rite, profound and wondrous, will increase the majesty of your mantras. When you perform this, it is suitable for all [three] families. Alternatively, use bdellium mixed with ghee and do *homa,* again one hundred and eight [times]. Or sometimes simply use *sarjarasa* and perform *homa,* performing it one hundred and eight times. [These rites] are all able to increase the potency of mantras.

"When performing *homa* in order to accomplish mantra rites, first invite the lord of the family deities, then invite your own deity, and then perform *homa* as prescribed. When performing *homa* in order to accomplish mantra rites, first use the mantra of the family mother to protect your deity and then yourself, and then perform *homa* as prescribed. When performing *homa* in order to accomplish mantra rites, you should recite the family heart-mantra when the *homa* is finished in order to increase the power of your mantras. Whenever you perform *homa* in order to accomplish mantra rites, at the start you must always use the large ladle for pouring the oblations [onto the fire], and when you wish to finish also use the large ladle, filling and pouring three times; in between you should use the small ladle. When you are about to finish performing *homa* in order to accomplish mantra rites, use the family heart-mantra to mantrafy the *argha* and offer it.

"Just as the procedures for *homa* are explained in the *maṇḍala* rites, so should you similarly invite [the deities] and perform *homa.* First perform the *ābhicāruka* rite, next perform the *pauṣṭika* rite, and then perform the *śāntika* rite.

"After the *homa* is finished, use your deity's mantra to empower some purified water [cupped in your hand] and sprinkle it over the hearth by circling your hand: do this three times. When the *homa* is completely finished, again invoke Agni so that he may receive the remaining offerings, return and dismiss him as prescribed, and supplicate him as in the rites of invocation. Remove the word 'descend!' (*ehi:* 'come hither!') [in the invocatory mantra] and substitute the word 'return!' (*āgaccha*). Mix all the leftover grain, ghee, honey, curds, and so forth together, use the earlier mantra for sacrificing to Agni (No. 57) to mantrafy [this mixture] three times, and perform *homa.* Then examine the number of syllables in your mantra and recite it [the appropriate number of times (cf. Chapter 18)]. Then do worship, protect your deity, protect yourself, and dismiss [the deities] as prescribed."

Chapter Twenty-Six 622b

Preparing the Appurtenances for Recitation

"Next, I shall explain in detail the appurtenances for success. In order to accomplish mantra [rites], you should first prepare assorted articles and then you should perform the rites of the preliminary service, and if you have already done the preliminary service, you should then recite [mantras].

"[The requisite articles are] namely: assorted unguents and incenses—the five kinds of heart[wood] aromatics are agallochum, [white] sandalwood, red sandalwood, the aromatic *sarala,* and deodar, and the seven resinous aromatics are the aromatic *gandharasa,* the aromatic *sarjarasa,* bdellium, storax, frankincense, the aromatic *śallakī,* and the aromatic *śrīveṣṭaka;* also white mustard seeds, poison, salt, [black] mustard seeds, sesamum oil, cow's ghee, flasks, and copper bowls; the five grains, namely, barley, wheat, rice, pulse, and sesamum; the five precious objects, namely, gold, silver, pearl, conch shell, and red gem (= ruby?); the five drugs, namely, the drug *kaṇṭakārī,* the drug *bṛhatī,* the drug *sahā,* the drug *sahadevā,* and the drug *śvetagirikar[ṇi]kā;* a five-colored cord, namely, [in the colors] blue, yellow, red, white, and black—a cord that has been twisted together by a young girl; a *vajra*-pestle, lampwicks, lampbowls, clay bowls, five kinds of coloring, stakes of *khadira* wood, branches for fuel sticks, margosa-wood bowls, a large ladle and a small ladle, cow bezoar, wootz steel, red sandalwood, a cord for preserving purity, clean bathing robes, the skin of a black deer, *priyaṅgu* flowers, parched rice, wooden shoes, *muñja* (munj) grass, great cogongrass, *śatapuṣpa*—this corresponds to fennel—a basket for gathering flowers, things necessary for food [offerings] such as ghee, honey, granular sugar, and barley sugar, and a rosary.

"The various articles described above are to be all prepared in advance, and then you should perform the preliminary service and recite extensively."

Chapter Twenty-Seven

The Characteristics of Articles for Effectuation

"Next, I shall now explain the articles for effectuation, articles by means of which mantra-*siddhi* [is obtained]. They are, namely, the *cintāmaṇi,* auspicious flask, shower of jewels, hidden treasure, wheel, realgar,[93] and sword. These seven articles are the best among the best: they can bring about the accomplishment of various *siddhi*s, increase merit and virtue, and even [enable one to] consummate the fruit of [becoming] a Dharma-king, not to mention other worldly objectives. The Buddha Family, Lotus Family, and Vajra Family—the mantras of these three families are all endowed with such excellent accomplishments. If you take any one of them, uphold it, and obtain all five [supernatural] faculties, this is deemed a higher *siddhi.* I shall now describe the above-mentioned seven articles in more detail.

"[If you wish to accomplish a rite for the *cintāmaṇi,*] make a gold stand one cubit long (= high?), or else use silver to make it. Carefully decorate it and place a *maṇi*-gem [on top of it]. For the *maṇi* use red glass that shines purely and has no dark marks or [use] a fine crystal, placing it on top of the stand. Those who would effectuate this jewel should recite at night. Next, a drawing of the 622c
stand is given (drawing given in Taishō Edition but omitted here).

"If you wish to accomplish a rite for the auspicious flask, decorate the flask as explained in Chapter [22] 'Rites for Receiving Mantras' without getting it wet and place it on a bannered stand. Next, a drawing of the flask is given—the drawing follows the methods for [drawing] insignia (drawing not given in Taishō Edition).

"If you wish to accomplish a rite for a shower of jewels, once ritual efficacy has been accomplished, simply with a sincere mind you will be able to cause gold, silver, and various assorted jewels to shower down within an area of five *yojanas* (1 *yojana* = approx. 9 miles).

"If you wish to accomplish a rite for hidden treasure, once ritual efficacy has been accomplished, simply with a sincere mind hidden treasure will come forth wherever you direct your thoughts. Pure gold will fill the treasure vault, and even if you give it for the relief of the poor and spend it in various ways, the vault will be inexhaustible.

"If you wish to accomplish a rite for the wheel-sage, make a wheel of wootz steel, round and one two-finger [hand]span in size; the wheel should have six spokes and the outer rim be narrow and sharp. If you follow the rite in this manner, you will quickly obtain *siddhi*.

"If you wish to accomplish a rite for realgar, first take some good bright realgar, like the sun when it first rises, its light a hazy red, or like the hazy glow of molten gold when one refines gold and it turns to liquid. For realgar you should take good [realgar] like this.

"If you wish to accomplish a rite for the sword, first take a sword of wootz [steel], two cubits in length and uniformly four fingers wide [as measured] with the little finger; it should have no blemishes and its color should be dark blue like the feathers of the *cāṣa* (bluejay) bird.

"If you wish to accomplish a Buddha-crown [Family] rite, make [an insignia of] a Buddha-crown with gold just as when drawing an insignia and place it on a bannered stand, using *sphaṭika* (crystal) for the [stand's] support.

"If you wish to accomplish a Lotus [Family] rite, first make a lotus flower with gold, making the flower eight-petaled and one two-finger handspan in size. Alternatively, use silver to make it, or make it with copper, or make it with white sandalwood.

"If you wish to accomplish a Vajra [Family rite], first make a *vajra* with wootz steel, sixteen fingers long, and make it three-pronged at both ends. Alternatively, make it with red sandalwood or make it with the three metals—the three metals are, namely, gold, silver, and copper.

"If you wish to accomplish a rite for orpiment, first take some orpiment like gold leaf in color and reduce a lump of it to pieces; again, [take some that] has a fiery radiance. Orpiment such as this is able to accomplish higher deeds.

"If you wish to accomplish a rite for cow bezoar, take some cow bezoar from a yellow cow.

"If you wish to accomplish a rite for the drug *gairika* (red chalk), first take some of this drug—that like the elecampane in color is 623a
good.

"If you wish to accomplish [a rite for] the drug *srota-añjana* (= *sroto'ñjana:* 'stream' collyrium), that like the droppings of earthworms is good.

"If you wish to accomplish [a rite for] cotton cloth, take some [cotton cloth] that is delicate and soft, remove the hairs, and dye it with saffron.

"If you wish to accomplish [a rite for] the protective cord, take some cotton thread that is very thin, twist three [threads] together, and then twist three [of these strands] together—they should all be twisted toward the right. Alternatively, twist together gold thread.

"If you wish to accomplish a rite for the flower garland, take some *jāti* flowers and make a garland with thread twisted by a young girl.

"If you wish to accomplish a rite for cow-dung ashes, take some dried cow dung from an [*a*]*raṇya,* burn it so that it turns into white ashes, mix it with camphor, and use it.

"If you wish to accomplish a rite for wooden shoes, take some *śrīparṇī* wood, make some wooden shoes, and place a cover on top.

"If you wish to accomplish a rite for the parasol, you should make the covering with the tail [feathers] of peacocks and make the shaft with fresh, straight bamboo.

"If you wish to accomplish [rites for] the bow, arrow, spear, lance, single-pronged stave, and other weapons, you should make each in the same way as that used by people in the world at large.

"If you wish to accomplish [rites for] worldly articles such as saddled horses, carriages, cows, sheep, all birds and animals, and any other articles, you should make them in accordance with what people in general all deem to be best or as is pleasing to the mind or on the basis of your own ritual.

"If you wish to accomplish [a rite for] the *vetāla,* you should take [the corpse of] someone who was born into a family of social rank, was in the prime of life, had no illness, died suddenly, has no scars on his body, and [whose body] has not yet swollen or decomposed and is possessed of all its organs—take a corpse such as this and perform [the rites of] accomplishment: according to your actions, [you will achieve] higher, middling, or lower accomplishments. The article to be taken [for this rite] being thus and your mind without fear, you should perform this rite."

Chapter Twenty-Eight

Taking [Possession of] Articles for Effectuation

"Next, I shall now explain the methods for taking [possession of] articles [for effectuation]. Take the article during the morning on the eighth day, fourteenth day, or fifteenth day of the dark and bright two [half-]months, at the time of a solar or lunar eclipse, or at the time of an earthquake. You should take the articles after having obtained indications [to do so] at times of recitation, or else take the articles after having bathed and purified yourself, fasted and observed abstinence, and sought a favorable indication. [Or] if the required articles mentioned are in a certain locality, take the articles by purchasing them with money without [necessarily] paying the [full] price [but paying according to your means]. Or if at certain times you become aware of increased potency, an endurance of hunger and cold, and various unusual signs, then take the articles at such times. As for the articles of which you take possession, take what is very good, each according to its inherent higher, middling, or lower grade. After you have acquired them as prescribed, you should increase your endeavors and perform the rites of effectuation."

Chapter Twenty-Nine

Cleansing Articles [for Effectuation]

"Next, I shall now explain the methods of cleansing articles [for effectuation] and purifying them by sprinkling. First wash them with the five pure [cow products]; as for those that should not be washed, [just] sprinkle them with the five pure [cow products]. 623b

"Examine the amount of realgar, [make the amount of] the five pure [cow products] the same, and mix them with the powdered [realgar]. Mix orpiment[94] with milk; make powdered cinnabar and mix it with cow's urine; make powdered cow bezoar and mix it with ghee; and mix powdered colors with milk. When preparing the drug *añjana* (collyrium), simply make it into powder. For articles such as the sword and the wheel, use cow-dung water to wash them. As for other [articles] mentioned, wash them with cow's urine.

"With articles that should be washed, first wash them with cow's urine mixed with sesamum water, and after you have finished, wash them with scented water. With other articles for which the proclaimed practice in the world at large is to wash them with water, you should wash them accordingly, or you may wash them with scented water. Then use the mantra '[accomplisher of] all deeds' to mantrafy some water and sprinkle [it over the articles] to purify them. Next, use the family heart-mantra to mantrafy some water and sprinkle [it over the articles] to purify them. Next, use the mantra of the family mother to mantrafy some water and sprinkle [it over the articles] to purify them. As for those articles that should be only washed, first [wash them] with the five pure [cow products], then with sesamum water, and then use scented water. For all things that are to be cleansed it should be [done] in this manner."

Chapter Thirty

The Measurements and Quantities of Articles [for Effectuation]

"Next, I shall explain in detail the measurements of articles for effectuation. Articles for effectuation are, namely, accoutrements of bodily adornment, weapons, and various garments. You should perform [rites of] effectuation with the measurements and quantities [of these articles] normally used in the world at large.

"Moreover, if you wish to accomplish a rite for realgar, take five ounces[95] of [realgar] powder for the highest rite, three ounces for a middling rite, and one ounce for a lower rite. For accomplishing [a rite for] cow bezoar, [take] one ounce for a higher [rite], half an ounce for a middling [rite], and one hundredth of an ounce for a lower rite. For accomplishing [a rite for] orpiment, [take] two ounces for a higher rite, one ounce for a middling rite, and half an ounce for a lower rite. If you wish to accomplish [a rite for] *añjana,* take three hundredths of an ounce for a higher [rite], two hundredths of an ounce for a middling [rite], and one hundredth of an ounce for a lower [rite]. For accomplishing [a rite for] ghee, [take] seven ounces for a higher [rite], five ounces for a middling [rite], and three ounces for a lower [rite]. For accomplishing [a rite for] ashes, [take] five ounces for a higher [rite], three ounces for a middling [rite], and two ounces for a lower [rite]. If you wish to accomplish [a rite for] saffron, the measurements are like those for realgar. In the *antar*[*dhāna*] rites various pilular [drugs] are described, and if you wish to effectuate these, as for their quantity, you should [make] twenty-one pills for a higher [rite], fourteen for a middling [rite], and seven pills for a lower [rite].

"If the measurements of the articles [for effectuation prescribed] in your own ritual are insufficient, you should increase the quantity. Otherwise follow the overall measurements, or comply with your own ritual, or else you may also follow the measurements and quantities prized by the world at large. You should observe the efficacy of your recitation and observe the amounts [used by] your associates, and you should make full preparations [accordingly]. You may [also] be successful by complying with the amount [given] in an indication granted as a special favor by your deity. There are higher, middling, and lower [grades] in rites for *siddhi,* and the quantities and measurements of articles [for effectuation] are also like this [in that they differ according to the grade of the rite being performed]."

Chapter Thirty-One

623c

Rites in the Great Consecration Maṇḍala for Eliminating All Obstructions

"Next, I shall explain in detail the secret and wondrous rites for effectuating articles for effectuation whereby *siddhi* is quickly achieved.

"If you wish to commence a rite of effectuation, you should first prepare the accoutrements for *siddhi,* and then you should increase the majesty of your deity's mantra by means of the *homa* rite and also consecrate yourself. If you wish to consecrate [yourself], construct a *maṇḍala*, worship as prescribed, and after you have performed [self-]consecration, then commence performing the rite of effectuation.

"Next, I shall explain the Great Maṇḍala of Consecration by which one is able to achieve success in all deeds. The rites for purifying the ground and so forth should all be [done] in the manner of the Vidyārāja Maṇḍala described earlier.[96] The *maṇḍala* is square with four corners, and install four entrances. Its size is eight cubits or seven cubits or five cubits [along each side], and open only the west entrance. Clearly demarcate the boundary paths [surrounding each of the three concentric enclosures constituting the *maṇḍala*], using the five colors to draw them: [make the path around the central raised area] like the [central] raised area in width, halve [the width of the path around] the next outer [enclosure], and do the same for [the path around] the next outer [enclosure]. Four cubits outside the west side construct another *maṇḍala* [for performing the actual consecration rites], its size five cubits or four or three [cubits along each side], and open only the east entrance. Or else make the consecration site like the basic Great Maṇḍala but half the size. The lie of the land in any *maṇḍala* should always slope down toward the north entrance: this is said to be auspicious; it is said to be best if the lie of the land in the *maṇḍala* slopes down toward the north. Draw [the lines of the *maṇḍala*] using one color, and outside the [outer] four corners make [a circle of] three-pronged *vajra*s. Within the central raised area draw an eight-petaled lotus flower as prescribed—all *maṇḍala*s should also be like this. Around the outside of the lotus-flower petals draw the wondrous insignia of auspiciousness. In the four entrances draw *vajra*s, and place auspicious flasks in the [four] corners. Do the same also in the outside consecration *maṇḍala*.

"Whenever you wish to consecrate [someone], there are four places in the corners of the encompassing boundary [of the *maṇḍala*] where a flask must be placed. [Additionally] in accordance with your regular mantra or *vidyā* draw the insignia of your own deity in the [central] raised area and place a [fifth] flask [on top]. Draw the insignia of your chief deity in accordance with the family [to which] your mantra [belongs], namely, a Buddha-crown, lotus flower, or *vajra*. You should realize that this rite is most secret. If you do not know the name of your mantra or if it is not connected to any [particular] family, you should place a flask called 'accomplisher of all deeds' or place a flask for 'the accomplishment of objectives' or place a flask called 'mantras' [on white mustard seeds without drawing any insignia].

"Next, outside [the central raised area] on the east side draw the insignia of a Buddha-crown [representing the Buddha Family] with the insignia of the family mother to the right and the insignia of the family heart[-mantra] to the left; then the insignia of a *śakti* (lance [= Tathāgataśakti]) to the right, then the insignia of a tusk (*daṃṣṭra* [= Tathāgatadaṃṣṭra]) to the left, then Ānan[da] to the right, then Subhūti to the left, and install the insignia of sundry mantras and *vidyā*s to the left and right as far
624a as both corners. Next, on the north side draw the insignia of the Bodhisattva Avalokiteśvara [representing the Lotus Family] with the insignia of the family mother to the right and the insignia of the family heart[-mantra] to the left; then the insignia of Lakṣmī

to the right, then the insignia of Tārā to the left, then the insignia of the Bodhisattva Siddhārtha (He Who Has Accomplished His Objective) to the right, then the insignia of the Bodhisattva Mahāsthāmaprāpta to the left, and install the insignia of sundry mantras and *vidyās* to the left and right as far as both corners. Next, on the south side draw the insignia of Vajra[pāṇi representing the Vajra Family] with the insignia of the family mother to the right and the insignia of the family heart[-mantra] to the left; then the insignia of Vajramuṣṭi (Adamantine Fist) to the right, then the insignia of Kuliśāśani (Vajra-Devourer) to the left, then the insignia of a *vajra* to the right, then the insignia of Vajradaṇḍa (Adamantine Staff) to the left, and install the insignia of sundry mantras and *vidyās* to the left and right as far as both corners. Next, to the south of the entrance on the west side draw the insignia of Brahmarāja (King Brahmā) and Brahmaśrīvidyā (Auspicious Spell of Brahmā) along with their retainers as far as the south corner, and to the north of the entrance draw the insignia of the god [Ru]dra and the insignia of his consort along with their retainers as far as the north corner. Next, in the third *maṇḍala* (i.e., the third of the three concentric enclosures constituting the *maṇḍala*),[97] draw the [tutelary] gods of the eight directions, each together with his retainers, and fill their positions [with deities]. Outside the entrance to the second *maṇḍala* (i.e., the second of the three concentric enclosures constituting the *maṇḍala*, where the deities listed above are ranged), draw the *nāga* king Nanda to the right and draw the *nāga* king Upananda to the left. Outside the entrance to the third *maṇḍala* draw the *nāga* king Sunda to the right and the *nāga* king Upasunda [to the left]. Outside the *maṇḍala* draw the insignia of Amṛtakuṇḍalin (Ambrosia Flask).

"After having performed the *maṇḍala* rites as before and having worshiped, you should next perform *homa* for the three kinds of deeds as prescribed. In order to dispel *vināyakas*, you should perform *ābhicāru[ka]* deeds; for your own benefit you should perform *pauṣṭika* deeds; and in order to quell calamities, you should perform *śāntika* deeds. You should perform *ābhicāruka* deeds with the mantra 'accomplisher of all deeds' of the corresponding family, or else use the mantra of Amṛtakuṇḍalin, which is suitable for using with [all] three families; you should perform *pauṣṭika* deeds with the heart-*vidyā* of the corresponding family; and you should perform *śāntika* deeds with the *vidyā* of the mother of the corresponding family. Perform the three kinds of *homa* for the holy ones and gods who have assembled in the *maṇḍala,* using their respective mantras, or perform [*homa*] with the mantra 'accomplisher of all deeds.' Construct the *homa* site to the south of the entrance on the west side of the *maṇḍala.* As in the [standard] *homa* rite, offer ghee and other things one hundred times each, using the mantras for the three deeds, or else increase the number [of times]. In order to increase the majesty of the mantras, you should perform the three kinds of *homa* in this manner. Then worship the mantra [deities] of the three families seven times each; for the lords of the three families you should increase the number [of times]. Alternatively, simply worship the three families one hundred times each, and if you cannot manage this, seven times or three times will also suffice.

"Install your mantra-lord in front of [the lord of] the family
624b deities inside the [central] raised *maṇḍala.* Outside the *maṇḍala* on the east side place in addition the Mother Hārītī, on the south side install Śūlinī, on the west side install Ekajaṭā, on the north side install Kuṭagiri[kā], and make offerings to them in accordance with their likes.

"After having worshiped the mantra [deities] as prescribed and having done *homa,* recite a mantra as appropriate for each of the flasks previously placed [in different parts of the *maṇḍala*], thereby empowering them. For the flask placed in front of your deity again use his mantra to empower it; for the flask inside the [central] raised area you should use the *vidyārāja*'s mantra to effect empowerment; for the flask installed for Kuṇḍalin by the entrance you must also use his mantra to empower it; for the flasks installed in both corners on the east side of the [central] raised *maṇḍala,* use the family heart-mantra for that in the northeast corner and use the mantra of the family mother for that in the southeast corner; for that in the northwest corner use the mantra 'accomplisher of all [deeds]'; and for that in the southwest corner use any mantra.

"After having empowered the above flasks in this manner and having worshiped them, you should then walk around [the *maṇḍala*] in a clockwise direction. As in the rites of consecration explained earlier,[98] here too likewise place [in the flasks signs of] auspiciousness, namely, grain seeds, medicinal herbs, flowers and fruits, twigs and leaves of fragrant trees, garlands of flowers, and jewels—place these in the flasks and use new colored silk to tie around their necks.

"Consecration rites should all be [done] like this. That is, have your associate anoint the crown [of the head] of the practitioner [to be consecrated]—the associate must have recited [mantras] and be pure as prescribed. Alternatively, ask your *ācārya* to give the consecrations. In order to dispel obstructors, first use the flask of Kuṇḍalin, using it for consecration. For the fourth [consecration] you should use [the flask of the deity presiding over] your regular mantra, using it for consecration, and use as you please two other flasks [for the second and third consecrations].[99] When this is finished, you should make use of cow bezoar, unguents, incense, mustard seeds, a cord, bracelets, and garments. When you have finished the consecrations as prescribed, you should again perform *homa* in order to quell obstructions, and when this has been completed, then dismiss [the deities].

"Alternatively, make a small *maṇḍala* of only one color in a flat and clean place, making it perfectly square and two cubits in size. Install the great insignia of the three families [on three sides] and the insignia of a [three-pronged] spear on the west side, and install pure flasks as before. [Then perform] the consecration as prescribed, whereupon you will be free of all obstructions, your deity will rejoice, and it will not be long before you are quickly successful—this is secret and the supreme *siddhi*."

Chapter Thirty-Two

Irradiating Articles [for Effectuation]

"Next, after having finished the consecration as prescribed, you should perform *homa* for twenty-one days or seven days or for one month or as [long as] is appropriate for that [particular] accomplishment or [as long as] is explained in your own ritual. Three times daily, using ghee, honey, and curds mixed with sesamum, you should perform *homa;* alternatively, following your own ritual, 624c you may either offer milk gruel or use boiled rice mixed with curds. Cense the article to be effectuated three times daily with incense, sprinkle it with scented water, and empower it with the mantra while looking at the article with your eyes. [Then] put an auspicious [cogongrass] ring on your finger, lift the article up, and sprinkle cow bezoar and water or white mustard seeds over it. On days of seasonal junctures increase the offerings and offer the article up. If it is to be effectuated during a bright [half-]month, select the fifteenth day, and if it is to be effectuated during a dark [half-]month, select the fourteenth day. In this manner irradiate the article,[100] always using the mantra of the family mother. Then further increase the aromatics, flower garlands, and other things and offer them. Rub your hands with unguent, put a cogongrass ring [around your forearm], hold the article to be effectuated, and recite all night—during [each of] the three watches of the night recite one hundred and eight times. In this manner irradiate the article for effectuation. From start to finish it should all be [done] like this, and if you completely adhere to this rite, you will quickly gain success. The mantra of the Buddha Family for irradiation is:

> *Oṃ teje tejasvini siddhe sādhaya hūṃ phaṭ.* (*Oṃ,* O splendor! splendorous one! accomplished one! cause success! *hūṃ phaṭ!*) [58][101]

The mantra of the Lotus Family for irradiation is:

Oṃ dīpya dīpya dīpaya mahāśriye svāhā. (*Oṃ,* shine, shine! cause to shine! for great auspiciousness! *svāhā!*) [59][102]

The mantra of the Vajra Family for irradiation is:

Oṃ jvala jvālaya bandhu[*ri*] *svāhā.* (*Oṃ,* blaze! cause to blaze! O rounded one [?]! *svāhā!*) [60][103]

"In the rites of the three families always use red *karavīra* flowers, mantrafying them with [one of] the [above] mantras and scattering them over the article [to be effectuated]; alternatively, use *mālatī* flowers or white mustard seeds. At the start, at the end, and in between you should always sprinkle the article in this manner. Or if there is an indication and you see an unusual sign, also scatter [flowers, etc.] in this manner. When you undertake to effectuate [an article], also scatter [flowers, etc.] in this manner, and you will achieve irradiation. If you wish to effectuate articles such as ghee, mantrafy some scented water and use it to sprinkle over the article, whereupon you will achieve irradiation. By such methods irradiate the article, and even if you are not [immediately] successful, you should not discontinue.

"Alternatively, construct a *maṇḍala* and thereby effect irradiation. Purify the ground as before and use the five kinds of colors to construct the *maṇḍala,* four cubits in size and with one entrance open. On the east side of the inner enclosure first place the insignia of a disc, in the northeast corner place the insignia of an almsbowl, and in the southeast corner place the insignia of a *kāṣā*[*ya*] (monk's robes). Next, on the north side place the insignia of a lotus flower, in the northwest corner place the insignia of a *daṇḍa* (staff) stick,
625a and in the northeast corner place the insignia of a *kuṇḍi*[*kā*] (pitcher) flask. Next, on the south side place the insignia of a *vajra,* in the southeast corner place the insignia of a *gadā* (club) stick, and in the southwest corner place the insignia of a *kalaśa* (pitcher) flask. Next, on the west side place the insignia of Vajrāṅkuśa (Adamantine Hook) and Vajramuṣṭi, in the southwest corner place the insignia of Kīlikīla, and in the northwest corner place the insignia of Sumbha.

Then to the right of the disc on the east side place the insignia of the family mother Buddhalocanā; next, to the right of the insignia of the lotus flower on the north side place the insignia of the family mother Pāṇḍaravāsinī; next, to the right of the insignia of the *vajra* on the south side place the insignia of the family mother Māmakī. Next, outside the entrance to the *maṇḍala* place, as described earlier [in Chapter 31], place the insignia of Kuṇḍalin, who is able to crush all hindrances, and worship him as before. Then on the north side place the insignia of Ṣaḍbhuja (Six-Armed One), the insignia of Hayagrīva (Horse-Headed One), the insignia of Tārā, the insignia of Candra, and all the retainers in that family (i.e., the Lotus Family)—install them one after another, and their figures should all be white. Then on the east side place the insignia of Tathāgataśakti, the insignia of Tejorāśi, the insignia of the Vidyārāja Aparājita, and the insignia of his consort Aparājitā. Then on the south side place one after another all the retainers within that family (i.e., the Vajra Family), and on the west side install the insignia of the three families as you please. Next, in the outer enclosure place Kubera and the other great gods of the eight directions, and in the empty places place at will the lords of the mantras 'accomplisher of all deeds' and so forth of the three families. Next, in the central raised area place the insignia of your family lord and, following the explanation in your own ritual, place the article to be effectuated inside [the central raised area], placing it on top of the insignia of the family lord in the central raised area. To the east of the article place the insignia of the mantra [deity], and to the west of the article place the *homa* hearth—the reciter then sits to the west [of the hearth].

"Invoke each [deity] with his own mantra as prescribed and worship them one after another as explained earlier [in Chapter 18]. Once you have finished worshiping them, do *homa* with the *vidyās* of the three family mothers one after another and irradiate the article. Then do *homa* with your own mantra to effect irradiation—among the rites of irradiation *homa* is the best. Whenever you first do *homa*, first mantrafy some scented water with the *vidyā* of the family mother and sprinkle it over the article to purify it, and when the *homa* is finished, again sprinkle it in the same manner. Either use the heart-*vidyā* of Māmakī or use the mantra of the Four-Syllable Vidyārāja—these are suitable for using in [all] three families—and do *homa* to effect irradiation.[104]

"In accordance with the mantra that you use, when you perform *homa* first recite the mantra for a while, next recite phrases of supplication, then recite the mantra for the middle period, then recite phrases of supplication, then again recite the mantra, and once again add phrases of supplication. In this manner insert phrases of supplication in three places in [the recitation of] mantras—[after] the initial, middle, and final parts—and lastly add the words
625b *'hūṃ phaṭ svāhā.'* [Phrases of supplication are,] namely, *'jvala'*
<emit light>, *'jvālaya'* <cause to emit light>, *'siddhi'* <success>, *'sādhaya'* <cause success>, *'dīpya'* <shine>, *'dīpaya'* [<cause to shine>], *'p[r]ataptānām'* <[of/for] those who are shining>, *'teja'* <gloss>, *'tejaya'* <cause to gloss>, *'vardhaya'* <cause to increase>, *'mā vilamba'* <do not delay>, *'āviśa'* <enter>, *'rakṣa'* <protect>, *'saṃnidhim'* <cause auspiciousness to be present>, *'guru'* <best>,[105] and *'hūṃ phaṭ svāhā'*—with phrases of supplication such as these irradiate the article. There is also no harm in repeating various [phrases of supplication] before, after, and during [the recitation of the mantra].

"After the *homa* is finished, you should next mantrafy some white *karavīra* flowers and scatter them over the article to effect irradiation. Alternatively, mantrafy red *karavīra* flowers or use white mustard seeds or use *sumanā* flowers to effect irradiation. First rub your hands with unguent and hold the article [in your hands]; next mantrafy some flowers and scatter them [over the article], then scatter white mustard seeds [over the article], then burn incense and cense it, and then mantrafy some scented water and sprinkle [it over the article]—you should know this procedure. During the three watches of the night—first, middle, and last—mantrafy some scented water with the mantra of your chief deity, mantrafying it and sprinkling [it over the article], and when you have finished sprinkling while reciting your own mantra, do *homa* and recitation as before until sunrise.

"If you completely adhere to this rite, you will quickly gain success. If you irradiate articles [for effectuation] and yourself in this manner, you will definitely quickly gain success. Even if the article is small, you will still obtain great efficacy, and if you completely adhere to this rite, the article will increase and become purified. For this reason you should perform the rite of irradiation. This is called the secret rite of all accomplishments. On days of seasonal junctures you should perform this rite of irradiation, and on other days effect irradiation at any time. When you have completed the [requisite] number of recitations [for the preliminary service] and wish to perform rites of accomplishment, you should first perform in full the rite of irradiation on the first night, and then you will be successful."

The Susiddhikara Sutra, Fascicle Two.

Fascicle Three

Chapter Thirty-Three

Differentiating the Times for *Siddhi*

"Next, I shall now clarify the periods auspicious for success as they have been explained. Knowing these, the practitioner seeks *siddhi*. 625c

"The [auspicious] periods are the eighth month, twelfth month, first month, second month, and fourth month [of the lunisolar calendar]: on the fifteenth day of the bright [half-month] of these five months you should perform [rites for] higher accomplishments. During the fourth month there are invariably difficulties caused by rain, during the second month there are difficulties caused by wind, and during the first month there are various [other] difficulties; it is only during the twelfth month that there are no difficulties, and during the eighth month there are difficulties caused by thunder, hail, and lightning. The difficulties described above are all signs of success. During these five months seek to perform only [rites for higher] accomplishments, and you should also perform *śāntika* deeds. Then on the fifteenth day of the dark [half-month] of these five months you should perform rites for both middling and lower accomplishments, and you should also perform both *pauṣṭika* deeds and *ābhicāruka* deeds.

"At the time of a lunar eclipse effectuate the very best articles, while the time of a solar eclipse is suitable for articles for higher, middling, and lower accomplishments. On the fifteenth[106] day or the seventh or the first or the thirteenth day or the third day of a [half-]month you should perform [rites of] accomplishment and all deeds. If you [wish to] perform [rites for] the highest accomplishments, you should select the times of the best lunar mansions and planets; [the times of] rites for middling and lower [accomplishments] should be known by analogy with this. Moreover, among the lunar mansions Devil's Mansion (Puṣya) is the best, but if you are performing [rites for] fierce accomplishments, then have recourse to times of fierce lunar mansions and planets. Alternatively, complying with [times suitable for] rites for the three kinds of deeds, perform what is to be accomplished also in accordance with the three deeds, or else follow the explanation in your own ritual, or rely on instructions from your own deity. Moreover, during the period from the first day to the fifteenth day of the twelfth month[107] you should perform all [rites of] accomplishment and [all] deeds. Alternatively, selecting a day specified by your deity or the thirteenth day of the dark or bright [half-months] of the various months, you will also gain success.

"The seventh month and eighth month correspond to the latter part of the rainy season, and at this time you should perform *śāntika* rites. The ninth month and tenth month correspond to the first part of winter, and at this time you should perform *pauṣṭika* rites. The third month and fourth month correspond to the latter part of spring, and at this time you should perform *ābhicāruka* rites. The first month and second month correspond to the first part of spring, and this time is suitable for all deeds. The fifth month and sixth month correspond to the first part of the rainy [season], and if you should desire success at all costs [at this time], perform [rites for] lower *siddhi*. Likewise, in the latter parts of spring, winter, and the rainy [season] you should also accomplish the three kinds of *siddhi*. Among these, nine grades are differentiated, and they are allocated [to different times] accordingly.

"The first watch of the night is the time for lower accomplishments, the middle watch of the night is the time for middling accomplishments, and the last watch of the night is the time for higher accomplishments. The first watch of the night is the time for performing *śāntika* deeds, the middle watch of the night is the time for performing *ābhicāruka* deeds, and the last watch of the night is the time for performing *pauṣṭika* deeds. In these three deeds nine grades are differentiated: know their times accordingly and distinguish between higher, middling, and lower [accomplishments] in the signs that appear at the time. 626a

"Moreover, at the time of a solar or lunar eclipse you should perform rites without considering the [proper] times. Times of lunar and solar eclipses are most suited to any fierce accomplishments and *ābhicāruka* deeds. Whenever commencing [rites of] accomplishment, fast for three days, two days, or one day—[the distinctions between] higher, middling, and lower deeds should be known according to the [number of fasting] days (i.e., three days for higher deeds, two days for middling deeds, and one day for lower deeds)."

Chapter Thirty-Four

Completing the Preparations for [Rites of] Accomplishment

"Next, I shall explain the elements of [rites of] accomplishment that may be lacking in your own ritual.

"If you fear that your physical strength is not up to it, you must not fast. If you wish to undertake [a rite of] accomplishment after having completed the [requisite] number of recitations, you must further [perform] recitation and *homa,* [make] various offerings of flowers, aromatics, and eulogies, and visualize your own deity.

"Take some cotton thread, have a young girl twist it into a cord, and, following the earlier procedure [described in Chapter 7], tie seven knots. If you recite [one of] the [following] *vidyās* seven hundred times and tie [the cord] around your waist in the early morning (= in the evening?), then it will prevent seminal loss. The *vidyās* are:

> *Oṃ jaye kumā[ri] śukrabandhani svāhā.* (*Oṃ,* O victorious maiden! you who restrain semen! *svāhā!*) [61]
>
> [Supplication:] *Ehy ehi mama ghane kṣipram āviśa suvrate majjanam abhisaṃśritya vicareta māciram.* (Come hither! come hither! enter my body quickly, O very virtuous one! and having taken refuge in my marrow, may you pervade it before long!)
>
> *Oṃ rakṣāṃ kuru kuruṅgini svāhā.* (*Oṃ,* protect [me], Kuruṅginī! *svāhā!*) [62]
>
> *Oṃ kulaṃdhari bandha [bandha] hūṃ phaṭ.* [63 = No. 19]

"Kumārī's *vidyā* (No. 61) is for using with the Buddha Family, Kuruṅginī's *vidyā* (No. 62) is for using with the Lotus Family, and Māmakī's *vidyā* (No. 63) is for using with the Vajra Family. After the initial, middle, and final parts [of the recitation], recite the formula of supplication, and if there is no formula of supplication in your own ritual, you should take [that given above (i.e., *Ehy ehi...*)] and insert it. Moreover, use these three *vidyās* for their respective families. Tie the mantrafied cord [around your waist] either every day or when performing the rite of irradiation; you should [also] tie it on when constructing a *maṇḍala,* at times of recitation, and at times of seasonal junctures—in all these instances you must promptly tie it on.

"Then, in order to remove torpor, you should mix some eye ointment [using] *srota-añjana, sūkṣmai*[*lā*], camphor, *pippa*[*lī*] (long pepper), Brahman cinnamon, the aromatic *tagara,* and natural sugar: take an equal amount of each, pound and sift them into powder, mix [the powder] with foam from a horse's mouth, grind it finely, and then mantrafy it with [one of] these [following] *vidyās* one hundred times. If, at times of [performing rites of] accomplishment, you wash your face several times and rub your eyes with [this] ointment, you will dispel lethargy and torpor and, should hindrances arise, you will see them all from afar. The *vidyā* for the Buddha Family is:

626b *Oṃ jvala locani svāhā.* (*Oṃ,* blaze! O seeing one! *svāhā!*) [64]

The *vidyā* for the Lotus Family is:

Oṃ vilokini svāhā. (*Oṃ,* O observing one! *svāhā!*) [65]

The *vidyā* for the Vajra Family is:

Oṃ bandhuri dīpte svāhā. (*Oṃ,* O rounded one [?]! shining one! *svāhā!*) [66]

Use these *vidyās* of the three families in all instances.

"If there is a reciter who is now on the point of success but has tired of recitation, he should mix some white sandalwood unguent with water, mantrafy it seven times with the family heart-*vidyā,* and drink three handscoops.

"When wanting [to perform rites of] accomplishment, first sprinkle your body with water, and [then] you should apprehend a favorable sign, whereupon you may perform [rites of] accomplishment. The favorable signs are, namely, a *śaṅkha* (conch), a wheel, a hook, a fish, a dextrorsal mark (*svastika*), a white lotus flower, a banner, a *svastika* mark, a full flask, a *wan*-letter mark (*śrīvatsa*), a *vajra*-pestle, or a flower garland, or seeing a righteous woman with jewelry adorning her body, or seeing a pregnant woman or someone holding up clothing, or seeing a joyful young girl, or seeing a Brahman of pure conduct wearing new white robes, or seeing a carriage, an elephant, a horse, or roots, drugs, and fruits, or seeing an unusual event, or hearing the sound of thunder, or hearing a voice reciting the Vedas, or hearing various musical sounds like blowing a conch or blowing a horn, or hearing the sound of a peacock or the sounds of auspicious birds such as the falcon, partridge, goose, and parrot, or hearing the sounds of fine speech and comforting advice such as 'Begin!', 'Happiness!', and 'Success!', words pleasing to the mind, or seeing propitious clouds, a flash of lightning, a gentle breeze, drizzle, or flowers raining down from the heavens, or there being a pleasant fragrance, or seeing a corona or rainbow.

"Among these signs, those that descend from the heavens represent higher accomplishments, those that appear in the sky correspond to middling accomplishments, and those that appear on the ground represent lower accomplishments, and in these three [types of] signs nine grades are differentiated. Manifestations such as the above are all auspicious, and if you see something contrary to these, then you will not succeed. Once you have seen these signs, engender profound joy, and with such a mind you should perform [rites of] accomplishment."

Chapter Thirty-Five

Inviting Deities to Empower the [Article for] Effectuation

"Next, I shall explain the rite for invoking [deities] to effectuate [the article for effectuation]. The times, constellations, planets, and auspicious signs such as were described earlier have been extensively explained elsewhere in rites for constructing *maṇḍala*s and in rites of accomplishment. When unfavorable signs appear, if you do *homa* with cow's ghee one hundred times using the *vidyā* of the family mother and then perform the rite, you will also be able to accomplish *siddhi*.

"You should also have recourse to the *maṇḍala* sites that were differentiated earlier to perform [rites of] accomplishment. In the case of higher accomplishments perform them on a mountaintop, 626c
in the case of middling accomplishments perform them beside a pond, and in the case of lower accomplishments perform them anywhere; otherwise you should perform them at sites that are compatible with the mantra. If you do not have recourse to these sites, success will be a little slow.

"If you perform all Buddhist mantras inside a *caitya* with *śarī*[*ra*] relics, they will all be successful. The Eight Great Caityas such as [that at] the Buddha's birthplace are the very best among [sites for gaining] success. Moreover, at the site of [the Buddha's] enlightenment (*bodhimaṇḍa*) there are no hindrances whatsoever, and it is well suited to success; even the king of demons is unable to cause any hindrance there, let alone other kinds [of beings]. Therefore, all mantras will certainly be successful [there].

"Whenever it is a case of fierce accomplishments, perform them in a cemetery; otherwise you should perform [rites for fierce] accomplishments in an empty house or in a shrine occupied only by a single deity or at the foot of a solitary tree or beside a river. If you wish to accomplish [the rites of] female *yakṣas*, perform them in a grove; if you wish to accomplish the rites of *nāga* kings, perform them beside a spring; if you wish to accomplish rites for wealth, perform them on top of a building; if you wish to accomplish the rites of [divine] messengers, perform them at places where people congregate; and if you wish to accomplish rites for entering holes, perform them inside a cave. These are the sites for success, secret and differentiated.

"After having selected and decided on the site, you should first fast. [Then] you should purify the site in accordance with the rite for purifying the site of a *maṇḍala* or in accordance with the rites for a recitation chamber, for if the site is clean, you will quickly obtain miraculous efficacy. First, with the mantra 'accomplisher of all deeds' or using Kuṇḍalin's mantra, mantrafy some white mustard seeds and other things and scatter them over the ground to ward off hindrances. Using *khadira* wood, make four stakes, one two-finger [handspan] in size; sharpen one end like a single-pronged [*vajra*-]pestle, rub the stakes over with red sandalwood unguent, and then tie a dark red string around them. Using the *vajra*-stake seal, hold them with clenched fist, mantrafy them with this mantra [for the *vajra*-stake (No. 35/41)] one hundred times, and drive them into the four corners with the tip of the stake slightly visible. Make a white banner and hang it from the top of a long bamboo pole on the east side of the *maṇḍala*.

"Mantrafy iron filings one hundred times with the 'adamantine fence' mantra (No. 39) and make [figures of] three-pronged *vajras*, [their tips] all touching one another, around the *maṇḍala* so as to form an adamantine fence. Then mantrafy iron filings one hundred times with the 'adamantine hook-enclosure' mantra (No. 40) and again make [figures of] three-pronged *vajras*, each placed crosswise on top of the *vajras* [arranged] endways, around the *maṇḍala* so as to form an adamantine hook-enclosure (i.e., canopy).

"As for the entrance to the outer *maṇḍala*, protect the entrance with Kuṇḍalin's mantra and with the insignia of a *vajra;* as for the entrance to the second enclosure, protect the entrance with the

Mother Hārītī; and as for the entrance to the central raised enclosure, protect it with Aparājita. These gatekeepers can be used for [all] three families; alternatively, use one of them to protect [all] 627a
three entrances. These three holy ones are able to crush all hindrances, and there is none who is able to destroy them. They are the secret ones who protect the article for effectuation.

"In the center of the [central] raised area bury the five precious objects and other things. If you are constructing a *maṇḍala* at places where people congregate, you should not bury these five precious objects and other things—simply place them under the article to be effectuated. If you are constructing a *maṇḍala* in a courtyard, indoors, or in a Buddha-hall, it is also the same. In the case of the above five (= four?) sites, if you simply mantrafy scented water and sprinkle it [over the site], then it will be purified; it is not necessary to dig the ground. If you perform these rites in your regular recitation chamber, you will quickly gain success, but it is not at all appropriate to perform rites of accomplishment in a cavity, nor is it appropriate to perform them in a dilapidated house.

"When you wish to construct the *maṇḍala,* seven days beforehand at dusk visualize the deities with thoughts of veneration as if they were before your eyes and invoke them, saying:

> 'All deities within the three families and deities in this [scriptural] treasury together with your retainers! For a long time I have been doing recitation and *homa* and firmly maintaining moral conduct, and with this sincerity I worship you deities: I beg you seven days hence to descend to the ritual site. Taking pity on me, accept these meager offerings and with great compassion bring me success!'

"In this manner invoke [the deities] at the [proper] time for the full seven days and then perform the rites. Every day in the evening also make separate offerings of *argha,* flowers, incense, food, and eulogies to the world-protecting gods of one quarter, and it should be [done] likewise for all the [other] three quarters.

"Furthermore, rub your hands with unguent, mantrafy your

hands, hold the article [to be effectuated] in them, and invite [the deities into] it. Then cense the article with burning incense and invite [the deities into it]. Then also fast, select a favorable time and day, construct an abridged *maṇḍala,* and use it to invite [the deities into] the article.

"[Either use variegated powders] or use only one color to make a circular *maṇḍala.* Open only one entrance [on the west side], and in the center place an eight-petaled lotus flower two cubits in size. Next, make the other outer enclosure as large or small as you like. First, in the inner enclosure place the lords of the three families, and to the north of the entrance on the west side place Maheśvara and his consort. To the right of the Buddha [on the east side] place Tejorāśi and to his left place Buddhalocanā; next, to the right of Avalokiteśvara [on the north side] place Mahāśrī and to his left place Ṣaḍbhujā; next, to the right of Vajra[pāṇi on the south side] place Māmakī and to his left place the *vidyārāja*'s heart[-mantra]. To the south of the entrance on the west side place the *krodha* Kīlikīli and Vajrāṅkuśī. [The deities] given above are all to be installed in the inner enclosure. Next, in the outer enclosure place the gods of the eight directions, and also place the lords of the mantras 'accomplisher of all deeds' and so forth. In the two inner and outer enclosures you should install all the mantra-lords that you revere in your mind and other cherished [deities]. To the north of the outer entrance place Kuṇḍalin and to the south of the
627b entrance place Aparājita. Invite each with his heart-mantra and worship them.

"Place a full *kalaśa*-flask on top of the lotus flower [in the center of the *maṇḍala*] and place the article for effectuation on top of it. Alternatively, place a casket on top of the lotus flower and put the article inside, or place a clay vessel on top of the lotus flower and put the article inside, or put the article in a pile of flowers and place that on top of the lotus flower.

"Then, holding it in your hands, mantrafy the article one thousand times or one hundred times. Next, mantrafy some flowers and throw them over the article. Next, mix bdellium with ghee and burn it to cense [the article]. Next, sprinkle a little scented water over the article. Next, mantrafy the article with the *vidyā* of the family mother and [also] mantrafy the article with the mantras of each of all the deities in the *maṇḍala*. Next, do *homa* with cow's ghee or using cow's milk, or else mix ghee, honey, and sesamum and perform *homa;* lastly, do *homa* with boiled rice mixed with curds. *Homa* should be done with all the things mentioned in your own ritual; take each and perform *homa* repeatedly with all the mantras [of the deities] in the *maṇḍala,* and in each case sprinkle the article with scented water that has been mantrafied with a mantra. As in the rite for irradiating articles [for effectuation] explained earlier [in Chapter 32], here too similarly mantrafy your eyes, look at the article with them, and recite the mantra in your mind. If you perform the rite in this manner, the article will then become [empowered by the deities] invoked. For whatever articles you perform the rite of invocation, you will quickly gain success, and with all the rites of worship and sacrifice in your own ritual you should for each perform this rite of invocation in full.

"[This] *maṇḍala* is both suitable for taking possession of the article [for effectuation] and also suitable for irradiating the article. If you perform [rites of] effectuation in it, obstructors will also not achieve their purpose. It is also suitable for purifying the article and, by means of the consecration rite, it is both suitable for consecrating the article and also suitable for consecrating oneself. This is an excellent *maṇḍala,* secret and able to accomplish all deeds. If you perform these rites, it will not be long before you gain success."

Chapter Thirty-Six

Rites for Redressing Deficiencies

"I shall now explain the rites for redressing deficiencies [in your practice]. After having acquired the article [for effectuation], bathe three times daily, worship, perform *homa,* and hold the article in your hands three times [daily], change your robes three times [daily], and fast on days of seasonal junctures, being sure to augment all the rites of worship and so forth; make obeisance, repent, rejoice [in the good of others], call upon [the Buddhas for instruction], and make vows three times [daily], read the scriptures and construct a *maṇḍala* three times [daily], take refuge and receive the precepts three times [daily], and protect yourself three times [daily]. If you perform the rites in this manner, you will assuredly gain success. Or if through negligence you should cause deficiencies to occur, then you should recite the *vidyā* of the family mother twenty-one times, whereupon [the requirements for redressing the deficiencies] will be satisfied. If you are deficient in this rite, your accomplishments will also be deficient. If there is [still] any defi- 627c
ciency, you must further recite one hundred thousand times; then you should construct [one of] these [following] *maṇḍalas* to redress the earlier deficiencies, and after that you should perform [the rites of] accomplishment.

"The *maṇḍala* [of the Buddha Family] is square with four corners, and install four entrances; demarcate the boundary paths as explained earlier [in Chapter 31]. On the east side place the Buddha, to his right place Buddhorṇā (Buddha-Tuft [= Tathāgatorṇā]), to his left place Buddhaśakti (Buddha-Spear [= Tathāgataśakti]), to the right place Buddhamaitrī, to the left place Buddhalocanā, to the right place Uṣṇīṣacakravartin (Buddha-Crown Wheel-King), to the left place Sitātapatroṣṇīṣa (White-Parasol Buddha-Crown), to the right place [the Buddha-Crown] Tejorāśi (Tejorāśyuṣṇīṣa), to the left place Vijayoṣṇīṣa (Victorious Buddha-Crown), to the right place Abhyudgatoṣṇīṣa (Transcendent Buddha-Crown), to the left place Subhūti, to the right place Ānan[da], in the southwest corner place an almsbowl, in the northwest corner place a monk's staff, outside the entrance place the Mother Hārītī to the right and place Aparājita to the left, and outside the *maṇḍala* place the 'accomplisher of all deeds'; in the center place a disk, on top of which you place the effectuated article, or else you place your own deity; in the outer enclosure place the gods of the eight directions, and on both sides of the [outer] entrance [on the west side] place the *nāga* kings Nanda and Upananda.

"Invite each [deity] with his own mantra or else invite them all together with the family heart-*vidyā*, worship them as prescribed, and then do *homa*. [To represent] the deities, either place their insignia or place their seat [in the corresponding position in the *maṇḍala*]. After having made a purificatory fire with your own mantra, do *homa* with ghee and honey one hundred and eight times; then do *homa* one hundred times with boiled rice mixed with curds and with sesamum, in each case using your own mantra. Once this is finished, again recite [the mantra] one hundred times.

"This is the secret rite for redressing faults. The things offered must all be sweet-smelling, and for the food offered use an *udāra* oblation together with granular sugar mixed with curds. If you perform this rite, the deities will all be satiated and rejoice, and you will [quickly] gain success. You should construct this *maṇḍala* and worship the deities not only to redress deficiencies but also every half-month or on days of seasonal junctures or every day: [the deities] will all be satiated and quickly grant you success. At times when you cannot manage [to do all the above], do it to the best of your ability.

"[Next,] this [following] rite for the Lotus Family is exactly the same as the rite for the *maṇḍala* of the Buddha Family described above, only you modify [the *maṇḍala*] to make it circular, with its size as you please. On the east side place Avalokiteśvara, to his right place the Vidyārāja Hayagrīva, to his left place Viśvarūpa, to

the right place Trinetra (Three-Eyed One),[108] to the left place Caturbhuja (Four-Armed One), to the right place Ṣaḍbhuja, to the left place Dvādaśabhuja (Twelve-Armed One), to the right place Sarvāśāparipūraka (Wish-Fulfilling One), also to the right place Yaśovatī, to the left place Mahāśrī, to the right place Tārā, to the left place Candra, to the right of the nearby entrance (i.e., the entrance to the central enclosure) place Śvetā, and to the left place Pāṇḍaravāsinī, in the center place a lotus flower, and outside the *maṇḍala* place the 'accomplisher of all deeds' of this family. This is the rite for the *maṇḍala* of the Lotus Family for redressing 628a
deficiencies.

"[Next,] this [following *maṇḍala* of the] Vajra Family is also like the *maṇḍala* of the Buddha Family described earlier, and it must be made square, with its size as you please. On the east side place Vajradhara, to his right place the *vidyārāja*, to his left place Māmakī, to his right place the *krodha* Kuṇḍalin, to the left place Vajrāṅkuśī, to the right place [Vajra]daṇḍa, to the left place Mahābala (Great Strength), to the right place [Vajra]muṣṭi, to the left place Sumbha, to the right place Devāṅga, to the left place Padanikṣepa, to the right place the [female] *krodha* Fire, to the right (= left?) of the nearby entrance place Vajrabhairavanetra (Adamantine Fearsome-Eyed One), to the right of the nearby entrance place Vajrāparājita (Adamantine Invincible One), and outside the *maṇḍala* place the 'accomplisher of all deeds' of this family. The other [deities in the] outer enclosure and the rites of worship are all as explained earlier. This is the rite of the Vajra Family for redressing deficiencies.

"Once you have finished worshiping in this manner, seek to obtain a favorable dream and [then] in the early morning bathe, don clean white robes, and make offerings of parched rice, green *kuru* (= *kuśa?*) grass, and sweet-smelling white flowers to the site where the *maṇḍala* has been constructed, after which you completely smear it with cow dung and then perform *saṃpāta-homa*.

"On your right-hand side place *kuru* grass, firewood, ghee, honey, sesamum, and boiled rice—all the things for *homa* are placed on the right; on your left-hand side place the *argha* vessels. Place the ladle for scooping up ghee and the ladle for scooping up [other] things [directly] in front, and then place melted ghee in front of the ladles. Using the mantra 'accomplisher of all deeds,' sprinkle these things [with scented water]. [Then] invite the chief deity of the family, install him, and worship him. [Then,] using your own mantra, invite your own deity with *argha* and also install him. In front of you place the ghee, in front of the ghee position the fire, and between the ghee and the fire place the article for effectuation: first yourself, then the ghee, then the article, then the fire, and then your own deity and the chief deity of the family—you must know the order for placing the above fivesome. To the left of the family lord place the *vidyā* Tejanī and to the right place the 'accomplisher of all deeds': place them in the order [given] in the *homa* rite explained earlier. [Then] first spread green *kuru* grass, set down boiled rice mixed with curds, scatter parched rice, offer a *svasti[ka]* oblation, and worship with sweet-smelling incense, after which you perform the act of *homa* as prescribed.

"Place the article to be effectuated in a vessel of gold or a vessel of silver, copper, stone, *śaṅkha*-conch, wood, or *valmīka* earth. Spread leaves of the *aśvattha* tree and place the vessel on top. Alternatively, spread leaves of lactescent trees or leaves of the *arka* tree or leaves of the plantain tree or lotus leaves or new clean cotton—spread whatever you have acquired. Furthermore, first spread five layers of leaves on the ground, place the article for effectuation [on top], and then cover the article with [another]
628b five layers of leaves, or you may [use] a parasol or various clothes or [other] assorted things [to cover it]—[the covering] should be known according to the vessel in which [the article] has been placed. Then perform the *saṃpāta* rite with an undistracted mind.

"Mentally illuminate the article and sprinkle it. Take a ladle in your hand, slowly scoop up some ghee, and hold it over the article; recite your mantra, and when you reach the syllable '*svā*' [of *svāhā*], pour [the ghee] into the hearth; when you utter the syllable '*hā*' [of *svāhā*], then touch the article [with the ladle] and return [the ladle] to the ghee vessel. In this manner go back and forth between the three points (i.e., ghee vessel, article for effectuation, and hearth), touching the article without interruption. This is called the '*saṃpāta-homa* rite' (*saṃpāta:* 'contact'). Do it one thousand times or one hundred times or, taking into consideration the length of the mantra and the grade and importance of the accomplishment, do [this] *homa* twenty-one times: this is known as the general frequency limit.

"During the *saṃpāta*[*-homa* rite] completely moisten the article with the ladle, making it quite smooth and glossy. When you first set down the article, first sprinkle it with water, then hold it and mantrafy it, then look at it with your eyes, and then present offerings; after the *homa* is finished, you should do the same again. If any of the three kinds of signs of success (i.e., flames, smoke, or heat) expounded in the *maṇḍala* for effectuation should appear when you perform this rite, then you must immobilize it, and you should realize that it will not be long before you gain success.

"If the article is large, place it on your right-hand side, but if it is suitable for taking in your left hand, place it on your left-hand side and do *saṃpāta* for it. If you are effectuating an article that is a sentient being, make an image of it, touch it on the head with the ladle, and perform *homa;* if you are effectuating yourself, touch the crown [of your own head] with the ladle and perform *homa;* and if you are performing *saṃpāta* for someone else, simply call his name and perform *homa*. There is, moreover, a threefold distinction among articles for effectuation: (1) you simply call its name, (2) you set it apart by covering it with something, or (3) it is exposed and visible to the eye.

"For all such [articles] use ghee to perform *homa,* and if you cannot obtain ghee, you should use cow's milk or ghee mixed with milk, or else use the three sweet [substances]. Alternatively, observing the distinctions between [rites of] accomplishment, you should use curds; otherwise do *homa* using whatever is mentioned in your own [ritual], or do *homa* for weapons with sesamum oil. If you are effectuating a *vetāla,* you should use heartwood aromatics and do *homa,* or use storax and other resinous aromatics. Or, observing the distinctions between [different] articles and the distinctions between [rites of] accomplishment, you should take the varieties of aromatic substances that conform with the rite and perform *homa.* If you are effectuating dog's flesh,[109] then use its fat, and [do] likewise with other types of flesh. [In the case of flesh] the article for effectuation may also be drawn and placed in front of you.

"By means of the *saṃpāta* rite explained here or in accordance with the *homa* rite explained earlier, you should extensively perform the *saṃpāta* rite, doing *homa* for the article [to be effectuated]. After having done so, you will quickly gain success.

"Once you have finished doing *saṃpāta,* rinse [the article] to make it clean, after which you consecrate it as prescribed, and once
628c you have finished consecrating it, worship and safeguard it and place it in front of your deity. Further, add various [offerings of] food and worship your deity, and you should also offer sacrifice to the world-protectors of the eight directions. You must also make offerings as prescribed to the *homa* site, after which you bathe yourself using soap powder and *āmla* (tamarind) as prescribed. At midday hold the article in your hands and apply recitation to it. In addition, also prepare separately the cord [for tying around the waist] and as before mantrafy it as prescribed; the armlet, robes, ashes, white mustard seeds, and water you must [also] mantrafy all individually as before. When you wish to perform [a rite of] accomplishment, you must first mantrafy these articles for self-protection so as to provide for later use. If you mantrafy the articles for self-protection in this manner, at the time of [a rite of] accomplishment they will then all have a [miraculous] effect wherever they are used. Therefore, you should first mantrafy them beforehand in preparation. Flowers and other articles of offering you must also mantrafy as prescribed and place them nearby.

"Next, construct a *maṇḍala* as [prescribed], worship as prescribed, and perform [rites of] accomplishment. Using the mantra 'accomplisher of all deeds,' mantrafy a five-colored boundary rope and tie it around the tops of the four stakes [in the four corners]. Mantrafy a flask with Kuṇḍalin's mantra, place it in front of the outer entrance, and tie both ends of the rope tied [around the four stakes] somewhat loosely around the neck of the flask. Whenever you leave or enter [the *maṇḍala*], raise the rope while thinking of Kuṇḍalin and pass through. You may either mantrafy the rope with Kuṇḍalin's mantra or you may take a mantra from your own ritual to mantrafy it.

"In accordance with the rites for warding off hindrances explained earlier, first purify the site and then perform the [following] rites. At this time offer sacrifices to the world-protecting great gods of the eight directions and their retainers outside [the *maṇḍala*]. Place a *vajra* on top of the [above-mentioned] flask or else put twigs with fruit [in it]. Either mantrafy the flask and rope with [the mantra of] the *vidyārāja* of the corresponding family or mantrafy them with the family heart[-mantra] or with [the mantra of] the family mother, and thereby protect the site. Alternatively, install all the pledge-insignia (*mudrās*) of that family, each in its proper position, and thereby ward off hindrances.

"Mantrafy the stakes one hundred times with the 'adamantine stake' mantra (No. 35/41) and make one end of the stakes into the shape of a three-pronged [*vajra*-]pestle or the shape of a single prong. Having done so, drive them into the four corners outside the pure [recitation] chamber or, if constructing a *maṇḍala*, drive them into the [four] corners of the [outer] boundary path. This is called the 'adamantine stake rite' and is able to accomplish all deeds.

"For [drawing] the *maṇḍala* either use dried powdered colors or use various fragrant powders or use paint, and use a brush of cow's hairs to draw it. Draw three-pronged pestles outside the corners, make figures of three-pronged pestles right around the boundary paths [surrounding the *maṇḍala*], and use the 'adamantine fence' mantra (No. 39) to mantrafy them. Then in the middle of these pestle figures along the [outer] boundary further place pestles crosswise—you should do this all around [the boundary]. This is

called the 'adamantine hook-enclosure,' and use the 'adamantine hook-enclosure' mantra (No. 40) to mantrafy it. Once you have done
629a this, there is nothing that can breach it. Therefore, the rites of accomplishment are performed within it. In each entrance and outside each entrance place a *vajra*.

"The rites of accomplishment are either performed inside the pure [recitation] chamber, or else a *maṇḍala* is constructed on open ground. In size it is five cubits or seven or eight [cubits], or, taking into consideration the deed to be accomplished, make it to conform with the scale of the deed. In the entrances place a *vajra,* in the corners place a flask, and in front of the outer entrance place the flask 'accomplisher of all deeds.'

"Inside on the east side place the insignia of the Dharma-wheel; to the right place Buddhalocanā, and to the left place Buddhorṇā; to the right place the insignia of a tusk (= Tathāgatadaṃṣṭra), and to the left place the insignia of a *śakti* (= Tathāgataśakti); to the right place the five Buddha-Crowns, installing them one after another to the left and right; install all the deities in the Buddha Family as you please one after another to the left and right; and lastly place Ānan[da] and Subhūti on both sides. Next, in the nearby entrance at the bottom (i.e., on the west side) place Aparājitā. Next, on the east side of the outer enclosure place the Vidyārāja Siddhārtha, on the north side place the Honored One Mahāsthāmaprāpta, on the south side place the Honored One Mañjuśrī (Wondrous Auspiciousness), and on the west side place the Honored One Kuñjara; on the east side to the right place the god Brahmā and the gods of the realm of form, and to the left place Indra and [the gods] above as far as Paranirmitavaśavartin (He Who Controls the Transformations of Others) and the earth-dwelling gods [of the realm of desire]; in the southeastern quarter place Agni and the seers who form his retinue; in the southern quarter place King Yama and the *piśācas*, *pūtanas* (class of demons), and *mātaraḥ* (Mothers) who form his retinue; in the southwestern quarter place the god Nairṛti and the *rākṣasas* who form his retinue; to the south of the entrance on the west side place the god Varuṇa and the hosts of *nāgas* who form his retinue, and to the north of the entrance place Pṛthivī (Earth God[dess]) and the *asuras* who form her retinue; in the northwestern quarter place Vāyu (God of Wind) and the *garuḍas* who form his retinue; in the northern quarter place the heavenly king Vaiśravaṇa (Much-Hearing One) and the *yakṣas* who form his retinue; and in the northeastern quarter place the god Īśāna and the *kumbhāṇḍas* who form his retinue. Then in one place on the east side place the heavenly son Āditya (Sun) and the planets and so forth, and in one place on the west side place the heavenly son Candra (Moon) surrounded by the lunar mansions. In the crook on both sides of the west entrance place the *nāga* kings Nanda and Upananda, and install the mantras and *vidyās* of all the messengers and their like in the Buddha Family on the four sides of the outer enclosure as you please.

"Then invoke [the above deities] as prescribed, worship them one after another, and do *homa* and recitation. In the very center [of the *maṇḍala*] place your own deity or the article for effectuation. Here too you should perform one after another the acts of self-protection and so forth just as they were explained in the *maṇḍala* rites. This is the *maṇḍala* of the Buddha Family for effectuating articles, and all hindrances are unable to achieve their purpose. If 629b
you perform the rites inside it, you will quickly gain success and all the deities will increase their protection.

"[Next,] construct a *maṇḍala* with the five colors as before, only modify it to make it circular. In the center of the east side of the inner enclosure place the insignia of a lotus flower; to the right place the *vidyās* of the Seven Tārās, and to the left place the Seven Śrīvidyās; next, to the left and right place the Six Great Vidyārājas; to the right place Pāṇḍaravāsinī, and to the left place Yaśovatī; on both sides of the nearby entrance place the Vidyārājñī Ekajaṭā (Single Hair-Lock) and the Vidyārāja Hayagrīva; in front of the outer entrance place the flask 'accomplisher of all deeds'; in the entrances and corners place *vajras*, and in the center [of the *maṇḍala*] place a lotus flower; in the outer enclosure place the god Brahmā, Indra, Maheśvara, and the Gods of Pure Abode, as well as the Bodhisattva Vimalagata (Untainted Conduct), the Bodhisattva Raśmimālin (Radiant Garland), the Bodhisattva Adorned One, the *nāga* king Ananta (Unlimited One) and the *nāga* kings Sunda and Upasunda, the king of *vidyādhara* seers Śaṅkhin together with *vidyādhara* seers, and the world-protectors of the various quarters as before; and install the mantras and *vidyās* of all classes of messengers of this family (i.e., the Lotus Family) as you please—this too is just like the procedure for installing [deities] explained earlier. [This is the *maṇḍala* of the Lotus Family for effectuating articles, and] all obstacles are unable to achieve their purpose; you should perform the rites of effectuation inside it.

"[Next,] construct [a *maṇḍala*] square as before and with boundary paths as before. On the east side of the inner enclosure place Susiddhikara, to his right place the Vidyārājñī Kuliśāśanā (Vajra-Devourer), and to his left place the Vidyārājñī Vajramuṣṭi; to the right place the Vidyārāja Sumbha, and to the left place the Vidyārāja Kīlikīli; to the right place the Honored One Vajra, and to the left place Vajradaṇḍa; to the right place Vajramudgara or [Adamantine] Hammer, and to the left place Vajraśṛṅkhala; to the right place the Vidyārājñī Vajrāṅkuśī, and to the left place the Vidyārājñī Māmakī; on the east side of the outer enclosure place the messenger Superior Wisdom, the messenger Adamantine Wisdom, Maheśvara and his consort, and the heavenly king Vaiśravaṇa and *yakṣas*; in front of the [outer] entrance place the flask 'accomplisher of all deeds'; and in the outer enclosure install one after another the mantras and *vidyās* of all the messengers of the Vajra Family, *bhūtas*, *piśācas*, *gandharvas*, *mahoragas*, *vidyādhara* seers, and the world-protectors of the eight directions.

"Then invoke [the above deities], worship them as prescribed, do *homa* and recitation, and commence [the rites of] effectuation. For [invoking] the deities that you invoke, you should use the *vidyārāja*'s mantra or use the *vidyā* of the family mother, and place a flask for each of all the deities that you invite into the *maṇḍala*. This rite of effectuation [for the *maṇḍala* of the Vajra

Family for effectuating articles] is just like all the rites of the previous *maṇḍalas*.

"Even if someone who performs [rites of] effectuation in these [three foregoing] *maṇḍalas* has not performed all the rites of self-protection, he will still obtain *siddhi*, for the deities have their own vow: 'If he who asks us to betake ourselves to the *maṇḍala* wor- 629c
ships with a devout mind as prescribed, we will grant him what he desires.' Therefore, here you should realize that there will be no hindrances and [the deities] will invariably provide protection. If you use the family heart-mantra and [the mantra of] the family mother or use the *vidyārājñī* [presiding over] the mantra 'accomplisher of all deeds' as well as the mantras within [the family] for self-protection, using them to invoke [the deities] and protect yourself and the [ritual] site, you will quickly gain success. These are the secret rites of the three families.

"Next, I shall further explain the secret *maṇḍala* common to the three families. Place *vajras* along the [outer] boundary path as prescribed, place the insignia of the family lord in the center, place the lord of your own mantra in front of him, or place a *kalaśa*-flask as [explained] earlier, put the article [for effectuation] in a vessel or suchlike, and place it on top of the flask. On the east side of the inner enclosure place the Tathāgata's insignia, on the north side place Avalokiteśvara's insignia, on the south side place Vajra[dhara]'s insignia, and on the west side place Rudra to the right and place the heavenly king Vaiśravaṇa to the left. Here too install [the deities] one after another just as in the Vidyārāja Maṇḍala explained earlier.[110] To the right [of the Tathāgata's insignia on the east side] place the *vidyā* of the family mother, and to the left place the *vidyā* 'accomplisher of [all] deeds'; [the corresponding *vidyā*s of] the two Lotus and Vajra Families are similarly [placed] to the left and right [of the insignia of Avalokiteśvara and Vajradhara on the north and south sides respectively]. On the west side place Gaurī to the right and place Lakṣmī to the left; in both corners on the east side place an almsbowl and a *cīvara* (monk's robe); in both corners on the north side place a *daṇḍa*-stick and a *kuṇḍi[kā]*-flask; in both corners on the south side place a *vajra* and a *mudgara* (hammer); and in both corners on the west side place a [*tri*]*śūla* (trident) and a gemmed flask. In front of the outer entrance [on the west side] set aside a separate spot and place Aparājitā [there]; in front of the entrance on the east side place the Mother Hārītī; in front of the entrance on the south side place Kuṭagirikā; in front of the entrance on the north side place Ekajaṭā; and in the outer enclosure place [various] insignia right around as you please.

"Invoke and worship [the deities] as prescribed. This is the secret *maṇḍala* for all [three families], and the articles for which you perform [rites of] effectuation inside it will all obtain *siddhi*. Even [the demon] Mūrdhaṭaka (Head-Goer) is unable to achieve his purpose here, let alone the other *vināyaka*s. With fine unguents, flowers, lamps, and various food [offerings] recite, irradiate, and worship: here too you should do just as in the worship rites explained for recitation and for *maṇḍala*s, and if you perform them inside a pure [recitation] chamber, it is the same again. You should increase fourfold the various offerings for the *maṇḍala*-lord: this is a secret method. Once you have finished worshiping, you should next offer sacrifice outside as prescribed by burning lamps with ghee, their wicks fresh and clean. Everything offered to your deity must be offered up as *argha*. If you perform the rites in this manner, you will quickly obtain [miraculous] efficacy.

"Mantrafy some white mustard seeds with the *vidyārāja*'s mantra, or else use the mantra 'accomplisher of all deeds' or use an
630a efficacious mantra that you have recited previously to mantrafy [the mustard seeds] and place them in the vicinity of the article for effectuation: if you use them to ward off hindrances, [the hindrances] will immediately disperse. Using the insignia of the family lord, also place it to the left [of the article], or simply mantrafy a large sword and place it to the left.

"In each of the eight directions position a man. First, the person in the eastern quarter adopts the attire of Śakra, holds a *vajra* in his hand, and is identical in appearance to Śakra; the person in the southern quarter adopts the attire of Yama and holds a *daṇḍa*-stick in his hand; the person in the western quarter adopts the attire of the king of *nāgas* (i.e., Varuṇa) and holds a noose in his hand; the person in the northern quarter adopts the attire of Vaiśravaṇa and holds a *gadā*-stick; the person in the northeastern quarter adopts the attire of Īśāna and holds a trident in his hand; the person in the southeastern quarter adopts the attire of Agni, his appearance similar to that of a seer, and holds a *kuṇḍi*[*kā*] and a rosary in his hands; the person in the southwestern quarter adopts the attire of the king of *rākṣasas* (i.e., Nairṛti) and holds a sword horizontally in his hand; and the person in the northwestern quarter adopts the attire of Vāyu and holds a banner in his hand. Śakra is white in color, Yama black in color, the king of *nāgas* red in color, Vaiśravaṇa golden in color, Īśāna white tinged with yellow in color, Agni the color of fire, the king of *rākṣasas* the color of darkish clouds, and Vāyu blue in color; the garments that they wear are also all like this. These persons must have all received the precepts, be extremely pure, have great courage, be proficient in the rites of self-protection, be upright in appearance, be in the prime of life, and be well-built; the weapons that they hold must have all been mantrafied; and they have flower garlands entwined around their necks and both shoulders, are provided with white mustard seeds, and are quite familiar with the signs of hindrances.

"If a hindrance should occur, then they scatter some white mustard seeds and strike it down with them, or else they throw their flower garlands at it, or, if the hindrances are many and show [cause for] great fear, they should point at them from a distance with the weapons that they hold. If they are pressed [by a hindrance], they should strike at it with their weapons, scatter white mustard seeds, and throw their flower garlands. When they point and strike at them with their weapons, they must not move from their positions; if they move from their positions, [the hindrance] will achieve its purpose. Therefore, they must not move from their positions.

"Mantrafy, worship, and place on your person all the insignia for self-protection in this [scriptural] treasury that are difficult to overpower. If enormous and pernicious hindrances approach, you yourself should use those insignia and hurl them at them. Or if you mantrafy some white mustard seeds with an efficacious mantra that you have hitherto been reciting and fling them at the hindrances, and they still do not desist, then you should go outside [the *maṇḍala*] and offer sacrifice as prescribed to that host of hindrances with fine and also plentiful food.

"Among all the protective rites there are altogether nine kinds: dispelling hindrances, binding the terrestrial sphere [below the ritual site], binding the sphere of space [above the ritual site], binding the *maṇḍala* sphere, binding the [four] quarters [around the ritual site], binding the adamantine fence, binding the adamantine hook-enclosure, protecting the article [for effectuation], and protecting your
630b own person. By these means you eliminate hindrances, and when performing [rites of] accomplishment you must keep all such rites in mind.

"Alternatively, if you cannot provide for the above persons to protect the [eight] directions, you should place [in each of the eight directions] the weapon corresponding to that direction, and if you cannot manage this either, place a *nārāca* (iron arrow) weapon in the [eight] directions or place a drawn bow with arrow set in the [eight] directions. Alternatively, in order to assist the adept, station in the entrance someone who clearly comprehends the teachings of the [scriptural] treasury and possesses wisdom and expedient means, whose recitation is efficacious, and whose moral conduct is pure: he will assist in performing [ritual] deeds and will dispel hindrances, and he will also help with everything in the inner enclosure and outer enclosure.

"All preparations must be completed by dusk, and as soon as the sun has set, you commence [the rites of] accomplishment. If you become tired midway through, go outside the *maṇḍala*, rinse your mouth with water, use Kuṇḍalin's mantra to mantrafy some water, and drink three handscoops; alternatively, mantrafy a small quantity of ghee with the heart-mantra of the chief deity [of the *maṇḍala*] and drink this—all your exhaustion will be relieved. Then mix *pippa*[*lī*] with honey, mantrafy it using the *vidyā* of the mother of the Buddha Family, and rub your eyes with it: even if the hindrance of torpor should arise, it will immediately be relieved.

"First, stand facing toward the east with a sincere mind, visualize the deities, take refuge in them, and invoke them. If you obtain a favorable sign from among the three kinds of auspicious omens (i.e., flames, smoke, or heat), perform [the rites of] accomplishment with a joyful mind. The [grade of the] accomplishment will correspond to the omen that you see, and therefore the practitioner must observe the omens.

"First you should visualize for a moment the Vidyārāja Susiddhikara and then circle in a clockwise direction the flask 'accomplisher of all deeds' [placed at the entrance to the *maṇḍala*]. When you enter the *maṇḍala*, pass by each flask that you encounter by circling it in a clockwise direction, and once you have reached [the center of the *maṇḍala*] make obeisance with head bowed to the deities and look all around [at all the deities]. Offer *argha* to each [deity] with his own mantra or offer it up with the family heart-mantra. The mantra-lords that are invoked should be invoked with the *vidyārāja*'s mantra, and the *vidyārāja* that is invoked should be invoked with the *vidyārājñī*['s mantra]. Once they have been invoked, display the seal of each and recite their mantras or *vidyā*s, or else simply display one seal for all and recite the [corresponding] mantra or *vidyā*. If you act in this manner, you will quickly obtain *siddhi*.

"The article for effectuation may be placed in an *argha* vessel or placed on top of a flask or held in your hands cupped together or simply retained in your mind or placed in a vessel of *valmīka* [earth] or placed on a leaf: place it right in front of the chief deity [of the *maṇḍala*] in the inner [enclosure]. Smear all vessels for the [article to be] effectuated with cow bezoar. Next, use white mustard seeds to effect protection, and then mantrafy some *mālatī* flowers and offer them to the article. On account of your having smeared [the article with] cow bezoar, it becomes immobilized; by using mustard seeds it becomes protected; and with the offering of flowers it becomes irradiated—these three kinds of rites should be performed one after another, and they must not be omitted.

"Place the article for effectuation in front of the chief deity—no
630c other object must be [placed] in between to separate them. Use two kinds of methods to protect the article for effectuation: the first is, namely, hand-seals, and the second is white mustard seeds. In order to quickly render the article for effectuation efficacious, repeatedly offer items such as *argha,* flowers, and incense as well as curds—you should make offerings repeatedly. The person for assisting with the effectuation always remains in his position in order to protect the article.

"Once you have installed the article and made offerings to it in this manner, then hold it in your hands or look at it with your eyes and recite slowly with an undistracted mind, repeatedly irradiating the article as you do so. Continuing in this manner, recite right through the night, and you must not allow any interruptions. During the three watches of the night make successive offerings with *argha* and so forth. If you have to go outside [the *maṇḍala*] to rinse your mouth, make the assistant sit in your stead in front of the article and continue reciting. If the [officiating] reciter should forget anything, his assistant must redress all the omissions.

"If a great hindrance should occur while reciting, the assistant should repel the hindrance, and if he is unable to resist it, the practitioner should himself scatter white mustard seeds so as to ward off the hindrance while the assistant mantrafies the article. If this hindrance should at the time appear in the eastern quarter as heavy rain and lightning, you should realize that it is a hindrance from Śakra; if this hindrance should appear in the southeastern quarter as a large flame-colored person or a [bright] sun like [the sun during] daytime, you should realize that it is a hindrance from Agni; if this hindrance should appear in the southern quarter as the figure of a most terrifying corpse that howls in a loud voice, holds a large sword in one hand, has its nose completely cut off, holds a skull in its [other] hand containing human blood which it drinks, and has a fire burning on top of its head, you should realize that it is a hindrance from Yama; if this hindrance should appear in the southwestern quarter as urine raining down, with the urine defiling the *maṇḍala,* and as various most terrifying figures, you should realize that it is a hindrance from Nairṛti; if this hindrance should appear in the western quarter as rain, thunder, lightning, hail, and so forth, you should realize that it is a hindrance from the king of *nāgas* (i.e., Varuṇa); if this hindrance should appear in the northwestern quarter as a great black wind rising, you should realize that it is a hindrance from Vāyu; if this hindrance should appear in the northern quarter as great *yakṣas* and female *yakṣas* who torment the practitioner, you should realize that it is a hindrance from the heavenly king Vaiśravaṇa; if this hindrance should appear in the northeastern quarter as strange figures with elephant's heads, pig's heads, and dog's heads and each holding a large mountain, you should realize that it is a hindrance from Īśāna; if gods should appear up above endowed with great majesty, you should realize that it is a hindrance from the gods above; and in the case of a hindrance [appearing] down below, with the earth moving and cracking, you should realize that it is hindrance from the *asuras*. When performing [rites for] higher accomplishments, these hindrances will appear, and such hindrances will appear in the middle [watch] of the night. The appearance of any hindrance to higher accomplishments is all the larger, and middling and lower accomplishments should be known accordingly [with medium-sized hindrances occurring for middling accomplishments and smaller hindrances occurring for lower accomplishments].

"The higher, middling, and lower signs [of success] correspond to the three watches of the night: if [their occurrence] tallies with 631a
the [proper] time, you will be successful, and if it does not tally with the [proper] time, you will not be successful. The three kinds of signs are, namely, heat, smoke, and light (i.e., flames). These three signs should appear one after another. In the case of a higher accomplishment it will have all three signs, in the case of a middling

accomplishment it will have the first two signs, and in the case of a lower accomplishment only the first sign will appear.

"Alternatively, if your recitation is sincere and the three signs appear one after another during the first watch of the night, then immobilize the light [representing the highest sign] with the *vidyā* of the family mother or immobilize the sign with the heart[-mantra] of the *vidyārāja* and smear or sprinkle [the article for effectuation] with some mantrafied cow bezoar or hold it in your hand; alternatively, sprinkle it with ghee, or scatter flowers or white mustard seeds over it, or simply sprinkle water over it to immobilize the sign, whereupon you will fulfill your wishes if you then make use of it. Or if [the sign] appears during the first [watch of the] night, then effect immobilization [of the sign] and recite, and when the proper time comes, you may make use [of the article]. Middling accomplishments should [also] be known accordingly.

"In the first [watch of the] night lower *siddhis* are accomplished, in the middle [watch] of the night you obtain middling accomplishments, and when dawn breaks you obtain higher accomplishments. If a middling accomplishment is accomplished during the middle [watch] of the night, once you have immobilized it as prescribed, you may make use of it even when daybreak comes; lower accomplishments should be known accordingly.

"It is not propitious if you do not make use of anything that has been effectuated at the proper time. If you immediately neither use nor immobilize an article even though it has been effectuated, and if you still do not make use of it when dawn comes, then the article will be like a withered flower or like bad food and will not be fit for use. An article into which you have invoked a mantra [deity] by means of recitation will also lose its efficacy once the [proper] time has passed. In addition, in the case of an article for effectuation that has not been effectuated even though the first sign has appeared, if you immobilize the sign at the time and later also perform the rites of irradiation and so forth, as well as worshiping and consecrating it on days of seasonal junctures, then it will become effectuated. [But] if it is [still] uneffectuated after three years, you should realize that the article cannot be effectuated. The [time] limit for rites for higher accomplishments is three years, in the case of middling accomplishments it is the sixth month, and in the case of lower accomplishments the time is not limited. Auspicious rites of effectuation [for divine images] are also the same as this."

Chapter Thirty-Seven

Rites for Retrieving an Article for Effectuation That Has Been Stolen

"I shall now explain the rites for retrieving an article that has been stolen. Once the article has been effectuated or while you are performing [the rite of] effectuation, the article may be stolen, and at the time of the theft you may either see the figure [of the thief] or you may simply lose the article without seeing the thief. You then neither select a [propitious] day or lunar mansion nor fast and, generating wrath, you should quickly perform this *maṇḍala* rite at once.

"Using the ashes of a burned corpse, make [the *maṇḍala*] triangular with only the west entrance open. Place your own deity in front of the outer entrance. In the eastern corner of the inner enclosure place the Vidyārāja Susiddhikara; to the right place
Vajrakrodha (Adamantine Wrath), to the left place Mahāroṣaṇa 631b
(?) (Great Wrath), to the right place Vajramuṣṭi, to the left place Vajrāṅkuśī, to the right place Vajrakīlikīla, to the left place Bhīma, to the right place Jaṭa, to the left place Piṅgala, to the right place Aśani, to the left place Śṛṅkhala, to the right place Vijaya, to the right of the entrance place Kāli[ka], to the left of the entrance place Nandimukha, to the left place Vajrasena (Adamantine Army), to the right place Subāhu, and also install the other *mahākrodhas* and so forth. For the sake of success install them one after another, invoke them as prescribed, and worship them one after another with red-colored flowers, red food, and so forth. You should here perform the *ābhicāruka* rite that was explained earlier. With exquisite flowers and so forth you should worship as prescribed your own deity placed outside the entrance. In the outer enclosure place the gods of the eight directions and place sundry messengers and other deities of the corresponding family—these you must also worship in this manner.

"In the center [of the *maṇḍala*] perform the *homa* rite: the hearth is triangular and everything [else] is as [explained] earlier. Smear seven thin sticks of *khadira* [wood] with your own blood and do *homa* with them, or else use margosa wood or use firewood left after burning a corpse and do *homa* with it. After the fire is alight, mix your own blood with the ashes of a burned corpse and do *homa* with it; also mix together the four kinds [of substances, namely,] poison, your own blood, mustard-seed oil, and red (i.e., black) mustard seeds, and do *homa* with them. Then take these four kinds of substances, make an effigy of the person who stole the article, and sit on top of it or tear it to pieces with your left hand and perform *homa*. Those who are able to suppress their anger and who understand the rites should perform this rite.

"If the person who stole the article, stricken with terror, brings [the article] and personally delivers it to the practitioner, then [the practitioner] should bestow fearlessness on him and then perform the *śāntika* rite for him—if he does not perform it, [the thief] will die. Alternatively, [although the thief himself may not appear] the article that was taken will be secretly placed in front of the deity [by the outer entrance] with more added to it.

"Then again, if you wish to recover the article for effectuation a long time after it was stolen, then you should construct this *maṇḍala* for accomplishing all deeds common to the three families. Make it square, and install the insignia of the Vidyārāja Susiddhikara in the center. On the south side of the inner enclosure place Vajrakrodha, Mahāroṣaṇa (?), Māmakī, Vajrāṅkuśī, [Kuliśa]śani, Vajramuṣṭi, Vajrānala (Adamantine Fire), Vajramudgara, Vajrabhīma (Adamantine Fearsome One), Vajraśṛṅkhala or [Adamantine] Chain, Kīlikīla, Vajramati (Wisdom-Vajra), and Aparājitā, and also place the *mahākrodhas*, messengers, and mantra-lords of great majesty—install them one after another on the south side. On the north side of the inner enclosure place Sarvāśāparipūraka, Avalokiteśvara, the Vidyārāja Hayagrīva, Bahubhujamukha (?) (Many-Faced and Many-Handed One), Citrarūpin (Able to Manifest Many Forms), Yaśovatī, Mahāśrī

(Great Auspiciousness), Lakṣmī, Śvetā, Pāṇḍaravāsinī, Tārā, 631c
Candra, Bala, and all the mantras, *vidyās*, messengers, and so forth—install each as prescribed one after another. On the east side of the inner enclosure place Uṣṇīṣacakravartin (Golden-Wheel Buddha-Crown) and the other Buddha-Crowns, Buddhorṇā, Buddhalocanā (= Tathāgatalocanā), Buddhaśakti (= Tathāgataśakti), Buddhadaṃṣṭra (= Tathāgatadaṃṣṭra), and Buddhamaitrī, as well as Aparājita and other *vidyārājas*, the mantra 'accomplisher of all deeds' and other mantras, and messengers—install each as prescribed one after another on the east side. [The deities] on both sides of the nearby entrance and outside the entrance are again installed as before as prescribed. In the outer enclosure [place] the gods of the eight directions; to the south of the west entrance place the heavenly king Brahmā and his retainers, and to the north of the west entrance place Maheśvara and his consort together with Gaṇapati and other retainers; also [place] the Seven Mātaraḥ or Mothers, the Eight Nāga Kings and their retainers, the *asura* king and his retainers, those who take refuge in the Buddha, and gods of great majesty—install each as prescribed one after another in the outer enclosure, invoke them with utmost sincerity, and worship them one after another.

"On the outer west side place a *homa* hearth, make an effigy with wax of the person who stole the article, place it in a winnowing basket, and, following the *ābhicāru[ka]* rite, invoke [the deities], offer sacrifice to them, worship them, and do *homa;* then cut the effigy [to pieces] with a sword and perform *homa*. Alternatively, follow the *ābhicāru[ka]* rite explained for this family (i.e., the Vajra Family) and act accordingly, or if your deity has himself stolen [the article] and does not grant you success, also do the same.

"Performing [this] rite during the period from the fifth day to the fourteenth day of a dark [half-]month is said to be best. Also flog the effigy with a stick and broil it with fire; beat it in various violent ways, stab its limbs with *madana* thorns in accordance with the rite for adamantine stakes, rub salt mixed with black mustard-seed oil all over its body, and torment it and inflict injury on it as you please. Then wrap the effigy in clothes used for covering a corpse and tie it with a red cord, offer red-colored flowers, mantrafy your own eyes, and gaze at it with enraged eyes—insert phrases of censure in the mantra and beat it every day. If [the thief] should bring the article back, then you should stop.

"You should perform this violent rite during the middle [watch] of the night. Using *kovidā[ra]* wood, smear it with black mustard oil and perform *homa*. Also mix poison, your own blood, [white] mustard oil, salt, and black mustard seeds all together, intone the name of the person who stole the article, and perform *homa* eight hundred times, or else simply mix salt with your own blood and perform *homa*. Torment [the thief] in this manner, and if he does not return the article, then you should further perform a violent rite for causing death—perform all the rites for killing explained in the *ābhicāru[ka]* rites, inserting phrases
632a of killing in the mantras.

"If [the thief] brings the article back, then halt the rite on account of his begging your indulgence. If he has already used the article and brings something else instead, again halt the [ritual] deeds. Or if he has already used the article and has nothing in its stead, but only comes to repent and apologize, again halt the [ritual] deeds and grant him forgiveness. If he has either lost it or shared it with others and brings back whatever is left, again halt the [ritual] deeds and grant him forgiveness.

"You should perform *homa* with the mantra of Vajravidāra[ṇa], or else perform *homa* with [the mantra of] Mahāroṣaṇa (?) or with [the mantra of] the *krodha* Ucchuṣma (?) (Impure One), or perform *homa* with the mantra for recovering lost articles given for the corresponding family. These three mantras (i.e., the mantras of Vajravidāraṇa, Mahāroṣaṇa, and Ucchuṣma) are, moreover, suitable for using with all three families.[111] [There is also this] mantra:

> *Namo ratnatrayāya, namaś caṇḍavajrapāṇaye mahāyakṣase<na>nāpataye, oṃ hara hara vajra matha matha vajra*

> *dhuna dhuna vajra hana hana vajra paca paca vajra dala dala vajra dāraya dāraya vajra [vi]dāraya vidāraya vajra chinda chinda vajra bhinda bhinda vajra hūṃ phaṭ.* (Homage to the Three Jewels! Homage to Violent Vajrapāṇi, great general of the *yakṣas*! *Oṃ,* seize, seize, O *vajra!* destroy, destroy, O *vajra!* shake, shake, O *vajra!* slay, slay, O *vajra!* roast, roast, O *vajra!* split, split, O *vajra!* tear, tear, O *vajra!* tear [asunder], tear asunder, O *vajra!* cut, cut, O *vajra!* split, split, O *vajra! hūṃ phaṭ!*) [67][112]

"Once you have obtained the article or once you have obtained a substitute, then protect the article and also protect yourself, and on days of seasonal junctures you should perform the rites of irradiation and so forth one after another. With the article of a middling accomplishment and [the article of] a lower accomplishment [as well as the article of a higher accomplishment], you should offer one part to the World-honored One; you should offer one part to your *ācārya;* you should go outside the *maṇḍala* and, taking one part, offer it to previously accomplished [adepts]; you should give one part to your associates; and take the fifth part and make use of it yourself. Alternatively, divide it into two parts and use one part yourself and offer one part to the [other] four.[113] The rites for un[divided] articles are all like this.

"First offer up *argha* to the [World-]honored One and so forth and then take that portion [for your own use]. In the case of the portion for the previously accomplished [adepts], make offerings of *argha* double its value and take it for your own use: its price is offerings. If your *ācārya* is not present, reimburse the value of his portion and make use of it yourself: its price is engendering shame [of one's sins] in one's mind—this is its price. When you go outside the *maṇḍala* to offer the previously accomplished [adepts their portion], you should say these words: 'Previously accomplished ones, accept your portion!' Holding *argha* in your hand, you should intone this a second and a third [time]. If there is no one to take it, then you should take it and give it to your associates, and you must

632b not harbor any doubts [when doing so]: because they are of sincere mind, because they worship, because they firmly observe the precepts, and because they attend on the practitioner, they are previously accomplished persons, and therefore they are worthy of receiving that portion. When you intone this three times, the associates should respond in this manner: 'We are indeed previously accomplished ones.' The practitioner [then] divides the article himself and gives it to his associates.

"If the article is small [in quantity] and cannot be divided—[for example,] *añjana* and cow bezoar cannot be divided—you should perform the division mentally and make use of it yourself. There are [also] articles such as those that are used only by a single person and cannot be divided—wheels and swords are so—and you should act in accordance with the [rite of] effectuation explained in your own ritual. Paintings and statues can also not be divided. Even if the quantity of the article for effectuation in your ritual is small, add to the quantity at will, perform [the rite of] effectuation, and give it to your associates. Alternatively, follow the quantity of the article [used by] previously accomplished persons and perform [the rite of] effectuation: even if you halve it, you will still gain success. Otherwise you must adhere to the amount explained in your ritual.

"When the practitioner divides the article and gives it to his associates, he should do so saying, 'You will be driven hard by me in various ways,' and after they have agreed, then he should give it to them. Or if you have effectuated [the article] for yourself alone, anything is permissible with regard to the benefiting of other people if it accords with the teachings of this [scriptural] treasury or other rites. When sharing [the article] among your associates, divide the article with moderation according to their services, and you should be impartial.

"Once the article has been effectuated, you should first worship your own deity, engender profound shame [of your sins], and earnestly invoke him again, whereafter you may divide it. The rites for all [three] families are like this. Middling and lower accomplishments should [also] be known accordingly. Engender profound shame [of your sins], worship [your deity] with reverence, and give away your possessions. The instructions that are received depend on the circumstances, and by such deeds you reimburse the value of the article.

"Once the article has been effectuated, first offer *argha* and [then] share [the article] as prescribed. Recite your own mantra, make the [corresponding] hand-seal, and mentally visualize your deity, as well as reciting the mantras of the *vidyārāja* and his consort and visualizing them too, and then make use of the article.

"You will [be able to] ascend into the sky at will; if you arrive at a place of many seers, there will be none able to injure or belittle you; even though you may have enemies, again there will be none able to harm you. The adept will constantly think of his deity—this he should not forget; he must constantly keep the effectuated article in mind or look at it with his eyes; because he recites the *vidyārāja*'s mantra, the seers will revere him, and because he recites the consort's *vidyā,* he will have no fears; making the *samaya* seals, making the family seals, and looking at the article with his eyes—he should not neglect any of these. When he meets a seer, he should first pay his respects and inquire about him, saying, 'Welcome!', 'Peace!', or 'From where have you come?', and if he [in turn] is questioned, he replies with fine words.

"When roaming through the sky, you should not pass over a
divine shrine, nor should you pass over a solitary tree, a crossroads, 632c
an abode of seers, a city, a sacrificial altar, an assembly place for Brahmans, or even the abode of a host of seers engaged in evil practices. If you pass over these out of self-conceit, you will be certain to fall [to the ground]. If you fall because of negligence, then you should recite the *vidyārāja*'s mantra and think of him—if you have already fallen or are about to fall, you will then regain your original position. Although the sky has no shape or color, with divine vision you will see the way, and you will, for example, be like an adept who arrives as soon as he has aroused his mind or who arrives while remaining motionless in meditation. Therefore, you travel along the paths of previously accomplished [adepts].

"Through the strength of your merit garments [will appear] of their own accord and [you will have] palaces as you please; you will have use of wooded gardens with flowers and see various birds, heavenly maidens will disport, sing, dance, and make music, [you will enjoy] various sensual pleasures, and lights will blaze [just like] the wishing *kalpa* tree (*kalpataru*), which is able to fulfill all wishes. For a resting place precious stones will form a seat, a canal will flow below, and soft grass will cover the ground; [you will have] various necklaces, accoutrements of bodily adornment, and [means of] enjoyment; auspicious trees will bear fruit of ambrosia, and whatever the mind desires or thinks of, everything will appear before you. But even once this has happened, you must constantly protect yourself—this you should not forget.

"You should reside in pure groves, on mountaintops, on islands in the sea, or on river islets. By means of the play [of your supernatural faculties] you should reside in these places, and then you will experience excellent states as [described] above. Or else you may reside together with a host of previously accomplished seers.

"Now, if you perform the rites for *siddhi* in full as explained earlier but the article is not effectuated, immobilize it as prescribed or safeguard it and put it away; [then] further perform the rites of preliminary recitation as before and once again perform the rites of effectuation. If it is [still] not effectuated after having done this, redouble your efforts, recite still more, and perform the rites of effectuation. If you do this a full seven times and it is still not effectuated, you should perform these [following] rites—it will definitely be effectuated.

"That is to say, beg for food, apply yourself diligently to recitation, generate great respect [for the Buddhas], and visit the eight holy sites [associated with the Buddha Śākyamuni], making obeisance as you proceed, or else read the *Mahāprajñā[pāramitā]-sūtra* either seven times or one hundred times, or take special things and donate them to the Sangha. Alternatively, beside a river entering the sea or on an island in the sea you should make stupas one cubit [high] and a full one hundred in number: in front of each stupa

recite as prescribed a full one thousand times, and if the final one-hundredth stupa should emit light, you will know that if you perform the rite [of effectuation, the article] will definitely be effectuated. Then again, make one thousand stupas and recite one thousand times in front of each: once the number [of recitations] has been completed, then even though [you have may committed the five] sins that bring immediate [retribution],[114] [the article] will be effectuated of its own accord without your having to perform any rites. Furthermore, if you recite any mantra one *koṭi* (ten million) times, [the article] will definitely be effectuated. If you per- 633a
form recitation for a [fixed] period for twelve years, you will again be successful in everything even though you may be guilty of grave sins; even if the rite is incomplete, you will gain success in everything.

"Furthermore, once the number of recitations and the [requisite] period have been completed, then you should perform *homa* for increasing [the majesty of the deities], or else construct this *maṇḍala* for accomplishing all deeds and perform the four kinds of *homa* (*śāntika, pauṣṭika, ābhicāruka,* and *vaśīkaraṇa* [subjecting others to one's will]) inside it. Either on a mountaintop or in a place where a herd of cows has previously lived or on an islet in the Ganges River, make the ground level and construct a *maṇḍala* one hundred and eight cubits in size. Place one hundred and eight flasks; erect pillars to form entranceways in the four entrances, and in front of each entrance construct a gemmed stand variously adorned; make garlands with fine flowers and twigs and attach them to the entrance pillars and to the tops of the banners in the corners; burn lamps using ghee, a full one hundred and eight [in number], right around the site; lay out the *maṇḍala,* burn fine aromatics in one hundred and eight censers, and place them around the site. One side of the inner enclosure is seven cubits [wide] in size, while one side of the outer enclosure is three cubits [wide], and the remainder corresponds to [the raised area in] the center. The invocation, worship, and so forth are all as before; as for the *homa* rite, it will next be explained separately: in the center place a *kalaśa*-flask [mantrafied] with your own mantra and perform the *homa* rite on the four sides of the flask.

"Place the deities of the Buddha Family right along the east side of the inner enclosure, place the deities of the Lotus Family right along the north side, place the deities of the Vajra Family right along the south side, and place the god Rudra and the heavenly king Vaiśravaṇa, each with his retainers, on the west side. If the inner enclosure cannot hold the messengers and other deities described earlier, they should be placed in the outer enclosure. Place the gods for protecting the [eight] directions and their retainers each in their proper positions. First place the lords of the three families, Rudra, and the heavenly king Vaiśravaṇa in their respective positions and then place the *vidyārāja, vidyārājñī,* mantra-lord 'accomplisher of [all] deeds,' and messengers of each—install them one after another. In front of the outer entrance place the Honored One Kuṇḍalin and place the Honored One Aparājitā.

"Construct the *maṇḍala* in this manner as prescribed, and when you have finished, perform invocation [of the deities] using the heart[-mantra] of the family in question and worship them one after another. Then perform recitation in the four quarters, and then perform the *homa* rite in the hearths situated on the four sides of the flask [in the center], each in accordance with the corresponding family. This is called '*homa* for increasing [the majesty of] the deities.' For the food offerings use *udāra* oblations. When you have finished performing this, all the deities will achieve increased [majesty].

"Once you have finished reciting and performing *homa* in this manner, do further *homa* with ghee using the mantra of the family mother; then, using the mantra of your own deity, mix milk gruel with ghee and perform *homa;* in addition, using the mantra of the family mother, mix sesamum with the three sweet [substances] and perform *homa;* and, using the mantra of the family mother, also use
633b ghee to do *homa*. Once you have finished performing these rites, all the deities will be satiated, achieve increased [majesty], and be completely satisfied, and they will all rejoice and quickly grant success.

"If you construct this *maṇḍala* up to seven times, you will definitely be successful. [However,] if you recite and visit the [Eight Great] Stupas as before up to seven times and construct this *maṇḍala,* but are [still] not successful, then torment your deity with the *ābhicāruka* rite. Make an effigy of him with wax, take his mantra, and recite it. First recite the mantras of the family mother and *vidyārāja* and insert the mantra of your deity in between. [Then] do *homa* by means of the *ābhicāruka* rite. Rub the effigy with mustard-seed oil, whereupon [the deity] will catch a virulent fever, and if you turn [the effigy] upside down, his whole body will be in pain. Flog [the effigy] angrily and beat it with flowers. Using the above two mantras, perform worship with an angry mind. [This] rite for punishing your deity is, for example, just like that for punishing demons. Perform such rites in accordance with the teachings; they must not be done arbitrarily. If the deity comes and appears in front of you and grants you success, stop doing the above deeds once your wish has been fulfilled and perform the *śāntika* rite.

"Alternatively, mix poison, your own blood, sesamum oil, salt, and red (i.e., black) mustard seeds all together and do *homa* right through the night. Your deity will then be terrified and cry out, saying, 'Stop, stop! Don't, don't! I'll grant you success!'

"If, after having performed the rites in this manner for three days, [the deity] has still not come and granted success, then boost your courage and with a fearless mind cut off some of your own flesh and do *homa* three times. Your deity will then come and beg your forgiveness, and your mind's desires will be granted fulfillment. If there have been any faults of omission [in your performance of the rites], he will explain them all. Even though you may have committed the five [sins that] bring immediate [retribution], if you cut off [your own] flesh and do *homa* for nine nights, [the deity] will definitely come and grant you success. This is a rite in which you do battle with mantras, and you should perform it with a fearless mind and having protected yourself as prescribed—it will certainly not be in vain. Once you have gained success, then you should promptly perform the *śāntika* rite. If [the deity] has mentioned some transgressions [on your part], then you must make up for the omissions.

"Among all the deeds of accomplishment, this *maṇḍala* is the best: inside it you perform the three kinds of deeds (i.e., *śāntika, pauṣṭika,* and *ābhicāruka*) and obtain the three kinds of results (i.e., higher, middling, and lower); inside it you should perform all deeds as well as *homa* and punish your deity as you would chastise demons. Every time you worship use new things for everything, and likewise with the things for *homa* too. You should not be negligent in this rite; bathe and purify yourself, protect yourself as prescribed, and do not be contemptuous [of others]. Clearly understanding the teachings of the [scriptural] treasury, you should punish your deity by means of this rite: if you act contrary to it, then you will bring about your own demise."

The Susiddhikara Sutra, Fascicle Three.

Notes

1 Literally, "knowledge/spell-king." The primary meaning of *vidyā* is "knowledge" or "science," but it also came to mean "magical power" and "spell," and in this latter sense of spell or mystic formula it is similar in meaning to *mantra* and *dhāraṇī*. A *vidyārāja* thus represents a personification of what was believed to be an especially potent spell, and he normally assumes a fearsome appearance in order to subjugate and convert obdurate nonbelievers; his female counterpart is called a *vidyārājñī*, or "spell-queen," generally translated as "spell-consort" in Chinese, but frequently rendered as "spell-king's consort" in the *Susiddhikara-sūtra*. Similar terms appearing in the *Susiddhikara-sūtra* are "mantra-lord"/"mantra-consort" and "*vidyā*-lord," although in many cases these terms appear to be broader in meaning than *vidyārāja*/*vidyārājñī*.

2 The chapters that would seem to provide the answers to the questions are indicated in parentheses.

3 Literally, "knowledge/spell-holder"; beings either human or supernatural who are possessed of magical power (*vidyā*).

4 It is not made clear what the "basic mantra of this scripture" is, and its identity was to become a subject of considerable discussion among Japanese exegetists.

5 Strictly speaking, the Chinese equivalent of "family" (*pu;* Sanskrit *kula*) means "part," "class," "section," "division," etc., but following general usage it is here translated as "family." In the *Susiddhikara-sūtra* and other early Buddhist Tantric texts the deities are organized into three such groups or families (Buddha, Lotus, and Vajra), but later four, five, and even six families evolved, with each family including a "lord," "mother," *vidyārāja, mahākrodha, uṣṇīṣa*, messengers, etc. It should also be noted that in a number of passages the Tibetan equivalent of the Chinese *pen-pu* ("family in question") is *rgyud* (Sanskrit *tantra*) or *cho ga* (Sanskrit *vidhi*), suggesting that *pu* could perhaps also mean something like "ritual manual," but since this remains conjectural, *pu* has tentatively been translated as "family" throughout.

6 The Japanese manuscript gives two mantras and reads as follows:

The heart-mantra with three *hūṃ* syllables is:

Oṃ krodhana hūṃ jaḥ.

The mantra of Sarasvatī is:

Oṃ śruti smṛti dhāraṇi hūṃ haḥ.

Mantrafy water three times with this mantra and sprinkle it over your body to purify yourself.

The Tibetan refers to the "heart-mantra with three *hūṃs*" but does not give the mantra itself.

7 The Tibetan does not give mantras [2]–[10].

8 This mantra lacks a salutation; see mantra [45] in Chapter 18. The Japanese manuscript gives an abridged version of this mantra: *Namo ratnatrayāya, oṃ kaṭe vikaṭe kaṭa kaṭaṃkaṭe bhagavati vijaye svāhā* (cf. mantra cited in n. 68).

9 Japanese manuscript: *Namo ratnatrayāya, namaś caṇḍavajrapāṇaye mahāyakṣasenāpataye, namo lokadhātriye, namaḥ śaṃkare śāntikare ghuṭṭa ghuṭṭa ghuṭṭini ghātaya ghuṭṭini svāhā* (cf. mantras cited in n. 69, n. 104).

10 Japanese manuscript: *Namo 'pratihatoṣṇīṣāya sarvatrāparājitāya, śamaya śamaya śānti tati* (?) *dharmarājabhāṣite mahāvidye sarvārthasādhani svāhā.*

11 Japanese manuscript: *Oṃ amṛtodbhavodbhava namaḥ.*

12 The Japanese manuscript gives the standard form of this mantra: *Namo ratnatrayāya, namaś caṇḍavajrapāṇaye mahāyakṣasenāpataye, oṃ sumbha nisumbha hūṃ gṛhṇa gṛhṇa hūṃ gṛhṇāpaya hūṃ ānaya ho bhagavan vidyārāja hūṃ phaṭ.*

13 Japanese manuscript: *Oṃ huru huru caṇḍāli mātaṅgi svāhā.*

14 Japanese manuscript: *Namo ratnatrayāya, namo mahāśriyāye, oṃ śākye samaye sauviye* (or *saumiye*?) *siddhe siddhe sādhaya śive śive śivaṃkare śivaṃ me āvaha sarvārthasādhani svāhā.* A similar mantra appears in Chapter 16 of the Tibetan, where it represents the mantra "accomplisher of all deeds" of the Lotus Family (see n. 59).

15 A variant of this mantra appears in Chapter 18 (No. 43); "Great Lord of [Śiva's] Hosts" normally refers to Gaṇeśa. Japanese manuscript: *Namo ratnatrayāya, namaś caṇḍamahāvajrakrodhāya, oṃ huru huru tiṣṭha tiṣṭha bandha bandha hana hana amṛte hūṃ phaṭ.* A similar mantra appears in Chapter 16 of the Tibetan, where it represents the mantra "accomplisher of all deeds" of the Vajra Family (see n. 59).

16 In the Japanese manuscript the remainder of this paragraph is rendered simply as follows: "If, when examining the mantra, it has the word *'śānti-kuru,'* the word *'svasti-kuru,'* the word *'śama,'* the word *'praśama,'* the word *'upaśama,'* or the word *'svāhā,'* you should realize that it is a mantra for the *śāntika* [rite]. If it has the word *'pauṣṭika,'* you should realize that it is a mantra for the *pauṣṭika* [rite]. If it has the word *'kuru,'* you should realize that it is a mantra for the *ābhicāruka* [rite]." The Tibetan

does not give specific examples of words indicative of the three kinds of rites.

17 These final two terms probably represent a misreading of the compound *bhasmī-kuru,* "reduce to ashes!"

18 *Āveśa* refers to the act of causing a deity, spirit, etc., to enter a person, but in Chinese texts it sometimes also signifies by extension the deity, etc., made to enter a person or the person thus possessed, and this would seem to be the case here.

19 A "great *maṇḍala*" (*mahā-maṇḍala*) normally refers to a *maṇḍala* in which the deities are represented by their physical forms, in contrast to a *samaya-maṇḍala,* in which they are represented by symbolic insignia, and a *dharma-maṇḍala,* in which they are represented by symbolic syllables and words; the Tibetan has the plural "great *maṇḍalas*."

20 It is not entirely clear where the teacher's words end, and perhaps the following clause (as far as "...to confer mantras on a disciple") should also be read as part of them.

21 The meaning of "third associate" is not entirely clear. According to Ennin, there are three kinds of associates—those possessed of all the qualities described in the first half of the chapter, those lacking in some of these qualities but still versed in ritual, and the additional associate permitted in certain circumstances—and he equates the "third associate" with this final associate. The Tibetan makes no mention of a "third associate."

22 The "four sites" normally refer to Kapilavastu (or Lumbinī, where Śākyamuni was born), Buddhagayā (present-day Bodhgayā, where he attained enlightenment), the Deer Park (Mṛgadāva [present-day Sārnāth], where he gave his first sermon), and Kuśinagarī (where he died); "the place where the Buddha attained enlightenment" and "the banks of the Nairañjanā River" should thus presumably be counted as one site.

23 Since the later chapters describing *maṇḍalas* (Chapters 31, 32, 35–7) do not give details about how to prepare the site before constructing a *maṇḍala,* this reference to a "chapter on the *maṇḍala*" could perhaps be seen as further evidence supporting the conjecture that the *Susiddhikara-sūtra* originally formed part of a larger text, unless it is meant to refer to the chapters on *maṇḍalas* in other scriptures (which is how it is interpreted by Ennin). However, in view of the fact that the Tibetan simply states that the sites of *maṇḍalas* differentiated according to the (three) families are also suitable for *siddhi,* one should probably not read too much into this reference to a "chapter on the *maṇḍala*" in the Chinese.

24 The Japanese manuscript gives what is probably a defective form of this mantra: *Oṃ hūṃ hana vajra [vajre]ṇa haḥ;* the Tibetan omits *hūṃ*. The following ablutionary rites as described in the Japanese manuscript differ markedly from those prescribed in the Koryŏ and Sung editions and the Tibetan, and the corresponding section of the Japanese manuscript is accordingly translated here:

If you mantrafy the water with this mantra seven times and [then] bathe, no kinds of demons nor any *vināyaka*s will be able to torment you. If you do not mantrafy the water, do not use it. The 'earth' mantra is:

Oṃ nikhana vasudhe svāhā.

Mantrafying some earth seven times with this mantra, you should mix the earth with a little water and stir it. If you then rub it over your body and bathe as prescribed, no *vināyaka*s will be able to torment you. The mantra for warding off *vināyaka*s is:

Oṃ amṛte hana hana hūṃ phaṭ.

Recite this mantra seven times to ward off *vināyaka*s and then bathe. The 'bathing' mantra is:

Oṃ amṛte hūṃ phaṭ. (= [15])

Recite this mantra seven times and bathe at will. When bathing, do not converse in whispers, and you must mentally recite the 'bathing' heart-mantra. The 'bathing' heart-mantra is:

Oṃ haḥ kha li li hūṃ phaṭ.

Recite this mantra until you finish bathing and then scoop up some water and pour it over your head. The 'self-consecration' mantra is:

Oṃ ha kha li li hūṃ phaṭ.

[Reciting] this mantra, scoop up some water with both hands, mantrafy it three times, and pour it over your head. Do this three times. Next, the mantra for tying the hair on the crown [of your head] is:

Oṃ susiddhikari svāhā. (= [16])

Mantrafying your hair three times with this mantra, you should make a topknot on the crown [of your head]. If you are a *bhikṣu,* make a fist with your right hand, stretch out the thumb, and bend the forefinger in an arc so that it presses down on top of the thumb; [recite] the mantra three times and place the seal on top of your head. The 'hair-tying' mantra of the Buddha Family is:

Oṃ śikhi śikhe svāhā.

The 'hair-tying' mantra of the Lotus Family is:

Oṃ śikhe svāhā.

The 'hair-tying' mantra of the Vajra Family is:

Oṃ śikhābhyaḥ (?) *svāhā.*

Next, you should wash your hands, rinse your mouth three times, and bathe your chief deity. The mantra of the Buddha Family for rinsing the mouth, imbibing water, and purifying by sprinkling is:

Oṃ mahājvala hūṃ.

The mantra of the Lotus Family for rinsing the mouth, imbibing water, and purifying by sprinkling is:

Oṃ ṭuṭura (?) *kuru kuru svāhā.*

The mantra of the Vajra Family for rinsing the mouth, imbibing water, and purifying by sprinkling is:

Oṃ jvalita vajriṇi hūṃ.

Once you have finished rinsing your mouth, imbibing water, and purifying by sprinkling, face toward the direction in which your deity resides and visualize your deity, recite his mantra, and make his hand-seal; take three scoops of water and imagine that you bathe your deity and offer up *argha* (oblations), or else recite at will while in the water, and then betake yourself to the ritual site. The 'water-offering' mantra of the Buddha Family is:

Oṃ terare (?) *buddha svāhā.*

The 'water-offering' mantra of the Lotus Family is:

Oṃ bhiri bhiri (?) *hūṃ phaṭ.*

The 'water-offering' mantra of the Vajra Family is:

Oṃ viśvavajre svāhā.

The appearance of the hand-seal [is as follows]: turn the palms of both hands upward with the sides touching each other, press the tips of both thumbs with both forefingers, and slightly bend the remaining six fingers so that they touch each other. Scoop up some water with [this] seal, mantrafy it three times, and reverently bathe your deity. This seal is suitable for using with [all] three families. Then in that [same] place recite your regular mantra as many times as you like: only then may you proceed to your usual site of recitation.

25 The transliteration of this mantra is obviously defective; a fuller version is provided by the Sung edition: *Namo ratnatrayāya, namaś caṇḍavajrapāṇaye mahāyakṣasenāpataye, namo vajrakrodhāya prajvalitadīptadaṃṣṭrotkaṭabhayabhairavāya asimusalavajraparaśupāśahastāya, tad yathā, oṃ amṛtakuṇḍali kha kha kha kha khana khana khana khana khāda khāda khāda khāda khāhi khāhi khāhi khāhi tiṣṭha tiṣṭha hana hana daha daha paca paca gṛhṇa gṛhṇa bandha bandha garja garja tarja tarja visphoṭaya visphoṭaya bhagavann amṛtakuṇḍali mūrdhnaṃ tāḍaya vajraṇa* (= *vajreṇa?*) *sarvavighnavināyakān nivāraya mahāgaṇapatijīvitāntakarāya hūṃ hūṃ phaṭ krodhāhvānaye* (?) *svāhā.* The Tibetan gives a shorter version: *Namo ratnatrayāya, namaś caṇḍavajrapāṇaye mahāyakṣasenāpataye, namo vajrakrodhāya mahādaṃṣṭrotkaṭabhairavāya,*

tad yathā, oṃ amṛtakuṇḍali kha kha khāhi khāhi tiṣṭha tiṣṭha bandha bandha hana hana daha daha garja garja visphoṭaya visphoṭaya sarvavighnavināyakān mahāgaṇapatijīvitāntakarāya svāhā. Cf. mantras [10] and [43].

[26] I have translated this passage in light of the Japanese manuscript, which reads: "On the eighth day, fourteenth day, and fifteenth day of bright [half-]months, on the last day of the month, and on the [first] fifteen days of the eleventh month"; the Koryŏ and Sung editions have "eleventh day" for "eleventh month." According to the Tibetan, "the [first] fifteen days of the eleventh month" in the Japanese manuscript corresponds to "the half-month of miracles" (Sanskrit *prātihārakapakṣa*), which in Chapter 33 of our text is translated as "from the first day to the fifteenth day of the twelfth month" (cf. n. 107), while in Chapter 18 the equivalent of "the half-month of the great miracle" is rendered as "the [first] fifteen days of the first month [of the year]"; in Tibetan traditions, "the half-month of miracles" corresponds to the first fifteen days of the first month of the lunar year.

[27] Japanese manuscript: *Namo ratnatrayāya, namaś caṇḍavajrapāṇaye mahāyakṣasenāpataye, oṃ kīli kīli vajra bhīma<ra>raudra balakīrti* (?) *mahākrodha vijaya nikṛnta hūṃ hūṃ phaṭ phaṭ bandha bandha haḥ* (cf. mantra cited in n. 92).

[28] Japanese manuscript: <salutation same as before> *Oṃ kiri kiri raudriṇi svāhā*. This mantra appears together with the salutation in Chapter 18 of our text as the mantra of the Vajra Family for purifying the rosary ([47]), and in the present context the mantra of Māmakī given in the other texts would seem to be more appropriate.

[29] Instead of this interpolative comment, the Japanese manuscript here inserts the mantras of the Buddha-Mother (Buddhalocanā; [2]) and Pāṇḍaravāsinī (in the version given in n. 8). The Tibetan similarly gives the mantras of Buddhalocanā and Pāṇḍaravāsinī, albeit different versions: the former lacks the salutation, while the latter is more or less identical to mantra [45] but is transliterated only from *tad yathā* onward.

[30] In the Japanese manuscript mantras [20]–[22] are each preceded by *oṃ*.

[31] The Tibetan adds *oṃ* to the start of this mantra (but not to mantras [25]–[28]).

[32] Our text has *che* (*Cudrania triloba*), but I have followed the Japanese manuscript and the Sung edition, which read *po,* variously identified with the thuja, cypress, abies, or juniper; the Tibetan has *shug pa,* denoting a cypress-like juniper (*Juniperus excelsa*), while the Sanskrit *padmaka* refers to a tree of the genus *Prunus*.

[33] Our text would appear to be corrupt here, and I have tentatively followed the Japanese manuscript.

[34] Chapter 26 provides a slightly different list of the seven resinous aromatics, with storax being substituted for camphor; the Tibetan does not here list the seven resinous aromatics individually.

[35] See n. 109.

[36] The Tibetan *mngag gzhug* ("servant," "messenger") suggests *preṣya* or *praiṣya* ("servant"), but *praiṣika* (or possibly *preṣika*) is perhaps a variant form of *preṣaka* (a kind of malevolent supernatural being).

[37] The identity of many of these cakes (or pastries and sweetmeats) is uncertain, but those that can to some degree be identified include the following (given in the order in which they appear in the text): *svastika:* a cake prepared with barley flour; *pūpa:* similar to *apūpa,* a cake made of rice or barley meal cooked in ghee on a slow fire; *vaṭaka:* a round cake made of pulse and fried in oil or butter; *laḍḍu(ka)* (= *modaka*): a sweetmeat made of coarsely ground gram or other pulse mixed with sugar and spices and fried in ghee or oil; *madhuśīrṣaka* (= *madhumastaka*): a cake prepared from wheat flour stuffed with honey and spices and cooked in ghee; *phenaka:* a cake of fine wheat flour coated with sugar; *piṇḍakośaka:* perhaps balls of rice, etc. (*piṇḍa*) shaped like an egg (*kośaka*); *gulapiṣṭaka:* perhaps the same as *guḍapiṣṭa,* a sweetmeat made with flour and sugar; *śaṣkulī:* a large round cake prepared with rice flour, sugar, and sesamum and cooked in ghee or oil; *parpaṭa:* a thin cake made of rice or pulse flour and baked in grease; *pūpa[pūrṇa]* (*pūrṇa* supplied by the Japanese manuscript, the Sung edition, and the Tibetan): presumably a type of "filled" (*pūrṇa*) cake; *māṣapūpa:* presumably a cake made with beans (*māṣa*); *vidagdhaka:* cf. *vidagdha,* "burned up, scorched"; *lāvaṇikā:* presumably a cake prepared with salt (*lavaṇa*); *garbhotkarikā:* presumably a type of *utkarikā,* a sweetmeat made with rice flour, milk, treacle, and ghee; *kukkuṭī:* literally, "hen"; *haṃsa:* literally, "swan, goose"; *sikthikā:* boiled rice kneaded into a ball; *śrīpūraka:* presumably a type of *pūraka* (ball of meal) or perhaps a type of *pūrikā* (a kind of cake); *veṣṭikā:* a cake of wheat flour stuffed with gram pulse mixed with spices; *guḍapūraka:* presumably a type of *pūraka* (ball of meal) containing sugar (*guḍa*); *citrapūpa* (or *citrāpūpa*): a "speckled" (*citra*) cake; *kharjūra:* cf. *kharjūrikā,* a kind of sweetmeat presumably containing dates (*kharjūra*); *guḍaparpaṭaśṛṅgāṭa:* presumably a triangular (*śṛṅgāṭa*) thin cake (*parpaṭa*) containing sugar (*guḍa*); *garbhitapiṇḍapūpa:* presumably a type of *pūpa* cake in the form of stuffed (*garbhita*) balls of rice, etc. (*piṇḍa*); *rājahaṃsa:* literally, "king-goose/swan"; *sarjaka:* first change in warm milk when mixed with buttermilk; *ghṛtapūraka:* presumably the same as *ghṛtapūra,* a sweetmeat made with flour, milk, and coconut and fried in ghee (*ghṛta*); *kosalikā:* cf. *kosalī,*

balls of pasted meat covered with grains of rice and fire-roasted; *saṃpuṭa:* literally, "hemisphere"; *ṣāḍava:* a sweet preparation of sour fruits reduced to thick consistency; *hariṇī:* literally, "doe"; *śakuna:* literally, "bird"; *mīna:* literally, "fish"; *parṇibhṛṣṭaka:* reappears below in the same chapter in the presumably correct form *parṇabhṛṣṭaka* and is glossed as "baked (*bhṛṣṭa*) leaves (*parṇa*)"; *dvīpikā:* although the name of a plant (*Asparagus racemosus*), the Tibetan *gzig,* "leopard," suggests an association with *dvīpin,* "tiger, leopard"; *jalahāstinīya:* cf. *jalahastin,* "water elephant"; *karkapiṇḍaka:* presumably a type of ball of rice, etc. (*piṇḍaka*); *vaṭṭikā:* perhaps *vaṭikā,* a round cake made of pulse fried in oil or butter; *gajakarṇikā:* literally, "tip of elephant's ear."

38 Tibetan *śrīveṣṭa*. Since *śrīveṣṭa* or *śrīveṣṭaka* refers to the resin of *Pinus longifolia,* this is perhaps an error for *śrīveṣṭikā,* presumably a type of *veṣṭikā* (see n. 37).

39 A sweet cake fried with ghee or oil.

40 A thin crisp cake (probably = *parpaṭa;* see n. 37).

41 The meaning of *hsien* ("manifest") as used here is unclear; the Tibetan reads "those which are incompatible and not named" (*gang dag 'gal dang ma smos dang…*).

42 A type of *piṣṭaka* (cake made of flour) prepared with sesamum (*tila*).

43 See n. 38; the transliteration *śrīveṣṭakā* rather than *śrīveṣṭaka* further supports the conjecture that it is an error for *śrīveṣṭikā*.

44 Presumably dishes served with *pūpa* cakes.

45 The meaning of this clause is uncertain; the Japanese manuscript has simply "dried out by wind."

46 Sanskrit *vitasti:* a unit of measurement equal to the distance between the tips of the extended thumb and little finger; it represents a long span in contrast to the shorter *pradeśa* (see n. 51) and is equivalent to twelve *aṅgula*s (see n. 49).

47 I.e., make oblations by casting offerings into the fire. The term *homa* can refer either to the entire ritual procedure for making burnt offerings or, more specifically, to the actual act of casting fuel sticks and other offerings into the fire, as is here the case.

48 Sanskrit *hasta:* a unit of measurement equal to the distance from the elbow to the tip of the middle finger and equivalent to two *vitasti*s.

49 Sanskrit *aṅgula:* a unit of measurement equal to a finger's breadth.

50 "Buddha-crown" is the standard Chinese translation of the Sanskrit *uṣṇīṣa,* a class of deities generally believed to be personifications of the protuberance (*uṣṇīṣa*) on the crown of the Buddha's head, although strictly speaking they are personifications rather of *dhāraṇī*s believed to embody the power of the light rays emitted from the Buddha's head.

51 Literally, "two fingers broken." Here and elsewhere it corresponds to the Sanskrit *pradeśa,* a unit of measurement equal to the distance between the tips of the extended thumb and forefinger; it represents a short span in contrast to the longer *vitasti* (see n. 46).

52 See n. 109.

53 The Chinese has "Six-Hundred-Eyed One," but I take "six" (*liu*) to be an error for *yün* ("called"). It might also be noted that whereas the Tibetan interprets the *aśani* of Kuliśāśani in the sense of "thunderbolt," the Chinese takes it as a derivative of the root *aś,* "to eat," both here and below, and the Tibetan interprets the compound Mahāmari (= Mahāmara?) as *mahā-amara,* "great immortal one," while the Chinese has read it as *mahā-mara,* "great death."

54 *Śālabhañjikā* means "woman plucking [the twigs of] a sal tree," and such figures are found carved on archways in India, but it also came to signify a tree spirit.

55 *Argha* signifies the act of respectfully receiving a guest (or deity) with various offerings, but it can also refer to the offerings themselves, some of which are given below; often, however, the offering consists only of water (*arghya*).

56 Possibly an abbreviation of *śuktikā,* "mother-of-pearl."

57 Tibetan *drag cing gtum la pha rol gnon* = Sanskrit Ugracaṇḍaparākrama? A deity named Sole Victor is also mentioned in Chapter 18, but there the corresponding Tibetan is *dpa' bo gcig pu* (= Sanskrit Ekavīra). The meaning of the Chinese *ch'i-chia,* which I have tentatively equated with Tibetan *drag* and translated as "violence," is uncertain.

58 These mantras are not given as such in the Chinese, but they do appear immediately below in the Tibetan; see n. 59.

59 Instead of mantras [29]–[34], the Japanese manuscript and the Sung edition give three mantras used when performing *homa.* The corresponding passage is accordingly translated here (cf. Chapter 25 of our text):

> The mantra of the Buddha Family for inviting Agni is:
>
> *Oṃ agnaye havyakavyavāhanāya svāhā.*
>
> Recite this mantra three times to invoke Agni, burn food [offerings], and worship him. The mantra for *homa* is:
>
> *Oṃ agnaye havyakavyavāhanāya dīpya dīpya dīpaya svāhā.*
>
> Next, hold some cow's ghee, and each time you mantrafy it with this mantra, burn some (i.e., feed it to the fire): complete this three times to worship Agni. The mantra of Krodhavajra (= Vajrakrodha?) of the Vajra Family is:
>
> *Oṃ kīli kīli vajrakrodha hūṃ phaṭ.*
>
> Each time you mantrafy some food with this mantra, burn the food for Agni.

By performing [this] rite you will dispel the obstructors in the ground.

The Tibetan, on the other hand, gives the mantra "accomplisher of all deeds" for each of the three families:

Namo ratnatrayāya, namaś caṇḍavajrapāṇaye mahāyakṣasenāpataye, namaś caṇḍavajrakrodhāya, oṃ hulu hulu tiṣṭha tiṣṭha bandha bandha hana hana amṛte hūṃ phaṭ svāhā.

Oṃ traṃ bandha svāhā.

Namo mahāśriye, oṃ śame samaye saume siddhi siddhi sādhaya śive śivaṃkari āvaha sarvārthasādhani svāhā.

These presumably represent the corresponding mantras of the Vajra, Buddha, and Lotus Families respectively, but according to the *Susiddhikarasādhanasaṃgraha* the first of these three mantras is the mantra of Amṛtakuṇḍalin and the mantra "accomplisher of all deeds" for the Vajra Family is: *Oṃ kīlikīla vajra hūṃ phaṭ.*

60 The Tibetan omits this mantra.

61 The Tibetan here gives the mantras of the *vidyārāja*s of the three families, which correspond (with minor differences) to mantras [5]–[7]

62 The Japanese manuscript and the Sung edition have *vajraprākāra* ("O adamantine fence!") for *vajraprākāraṃ,* and it is this form that is usually found in transliterations of this mantra in other Chinese texts; the Tibetan omits mantras [39]–[43].

63 The Japanese manuscript and the Sung edition have *visphurād* ("by glittering"?) for *visphura,* and it is this form that is usually found in transliterations of this mantra in other Chinese texts.

64 Japanese manuscript and Sung edition: *Oṃ vajrakīla hūṃ phaṭ.*

65 Japanese manuscript and Sung edition: *Oṃ kīli kīli vajra hūṃ phaṭ.*

66 Cf. mantra [10] and n. 15. Japanese manuscript and Sung edition: *Namo ratnatrayāya, namo vajrakrodhāya mahābalaparākramāya sarvavighnavināśanāya, oṃ huru huru tiṣṭha tiṣṭha bandha bandha hana hana amṛte hūṃ phaṭ.*

67 The Japanese manuscript and the Sung edition omit the salutation (*namo bhagavate uṣṇīṣāya*); the Tibetan omits mantras [44]–[46].

68 Cf. mantra [3]. Japanese manuscript and Sung edition: *Oṃ kaṭe vikaṭe kaṭaṃkaṭe kaṭa vikaṭa kaṭaṃkaṭe bhagavati vijaye svāhā* (cf. mantra cited in n. 8).

69 Japanese manuscript and Sung edition: *Namo lokadhātriye, namaḥ śaṃkare śāntikare ghuṭṭa ghuṭṭa ghuṭṭini ghātaya ghuṭṭini svāhā* (cf. mantra cited in n. 9).

70 Cf. n. 57.

71 What is termed here and below "initial recitation," "preliminary recitation," or "preliminary service" corresponds to the Sanskrit *pūrvasevā* ("prior/preliminary service/worship") and refers to the initial session of devotions that a practitioner must perform when he is first given a mantra.

72 The Tibetan gives the mantra of Ucchuṣma: *Namo vajrāya, oṃ vajrakrodhamahābala hana daha paca vidhvaṃsaya ucchuṣmakrodha hūṃ phaṭ.*

73 The Tibetan Chapter 16 ends here, and Chapter 17 starts with the following mantra: *Oṃ ekajvalavajrapāṇi hūṃ samayam anusmara hūṃ phaṭ svāhā.*

74 Although our text has "Dharma-Buddha" (*fa-fo*), I follow the Japanese manuscript and the Sung edition, which read "(all) Buddhas" (*chu-fo*). There are further instances below where *fa* in our text is clearly an error for *chu*.

75 The Japanese manuscript and the Sung edition (which give the mantra of the Vajra Family after that of the Lotus Family) omit the salutation (*namo...mahāyakṣasenāpataye*). *Kiri kiri* could equally well be read *kīli kīli,* but I have tentatively followed the Tibetan.

76 Japanese manuscript and Sung edition: *Oṃ adbhute vijaye siddhe siddhārthe svāhā;* Tibetan: *Namo ratnatrayāya, oṃ adbhute vijaya siddhi siddhārthe svāhā.*

77 The Tibetan adds a salutation: *Namo ratnatrayāya, nama āryāvalokiteśvarāya bodhisattvāya.*

78 The Tibetan has "thumb" for "forefinger," as do also the Japanese manuscript and the Sung edition, which in addition provide a more detailed description of the positions of the fingers when working the rosary:

> With the thumb of the right hand press the tip of the ring finger, stretch the middle finger and little finger straight out, bending them slightly, and with the forefinger press against the side of the upper phalange of the middle finger; the left hand is also the same.

79 The Japanese manuscript and the Sung edition have [*sid*]*dhe siddhe* for *siddhe,* while the Tibetan has *sādhaya sādhaya* for *sādhaya. Siddhe* could also be taken to mean "O success!"

80 Japanese manuscript and Sung edition: *Oṃ* [*va*]*sumati śriye padmamālini svāhā.*

81 The Japanese manuscript, the Sung edition, and the Tibetan all have "thirty-two syllables." There are frequent discrepancies between the texts with regard to numerical references, but these differences have generally not been noted.

[82] Here and below *vidyā* (or mantra) is often used metonymically to refer to the deity personifying or presiding over the *vidyā* (or mantra).

[83] It is not entirely clear whether or not the "undergarment" mentioned here represents one of the "three robes" as is normally the case (Ennin counts it separately), but, following the Tibetan, I have assumed that it is.

[84] Cf. n. 26.

[85] The Tibetan inserts *oṃ* before *viśuddhe*.

[86] The Japanese manuscript and the Sung edition add a salutation: *Namo ratnatrayāya, nama āryāvalokiteśvarāya bodhisattvāya mahāsattvāya mahākāruṇikāya.*

[87] The Tibetan omits *prabhāvati.*

[88] The Tibetan has "...after you have *prayed for* commands...," which would seem to fit the context better, assuming that the instructions or commands take the form of dreams as described below.

[89] These words of invocation are a loose translation of the first part of the following mantra.

[90] Our text has *havyakavyavāhutiya* for *havyakavyavāhanāya*. The Tibetan translates *ehy...bhava* and gives the mantra as follows: *Oṃ agnaye havyakavyavāhanāya svāhā.* The Japanese manuscript and the Sung edition omit the mantra with the comment "as above," presumably referring to the similar mantra cited in n. 59.

[91] Tibetan: *Oṃ agnaye havyakavyavāhanāya dīpya dīpaya svāhā.* The Japanese manuscript and the Sung edition again omit the mantra with the comment "as above," presumably referring to the similar mantra cited in n. 59.

[92] The Tibetan here inserts the following mantra of Kīlikīli: *Oṃ kīli kīli vajrabhīmaraudripatrita* (?) *mahākrodha vijaya nikṛnta hūṃ phaṭ bandha bandha svāhā* (cf. mantra cited in n. 27).

[93] Here and below all three Chinese recensions regularly confuse realgar and orpiment, and in the translation this error has been corrected on the basis of the Tibetan. That this is an error is confirmed by the analogies given below when describing the colors of realgar and orpiment.

[94] The Chinese correctly has "orpiment" here.

[95] Chinese *liang:* a unit of weight equivalent to approximately sixteen grams, but popularly equated with an ounce; Tibetan *srang* (Sanskrit *pala*), to which the unit of capacity *ho* occurring toward the end of Chapter 18 also corresponds.

[96] The "Great Maṇḍala of Consecration" is the first *maṇḍala* to be described in the *Susiddhikara-sūtra,* and therefore this reference to the "Vidyārāja

Maṇḍala described earlier" could be regarded as evidence that the *Susiddhikara-sūtra* originally formed part of a larger text; see also n. 23.

97 In ordinary Sanskrit usage, *maṇḍala* simply means "circle," and in a Tantric context it refers not only to a sacred enclosure in its entirety but also to the series of concentric enclosures, set within a square and often circular, that make up the overall *maṇḍala*. Judging from the fact that the deities are here arranged along the east, north, south, and west sides of the second of these enclosures, it would appear that in the present instance these concentric enclosures are square rather than circular.

98 This possibly refers to Chapter 20, although the Tibetan has a more general import: "the rites for consecration that are explained in *maṇḍalas*."

99 It is not entirely clear how many consecrations are performed, but since the Tibetan has "lastly" for "fourth," I have assumed that four consecrations are performed, although Ennin describes it as a "seven-flask consecration."

100 "Irradiate" is here used in the sense of causing an object to generate radiant energy or magical power (*tejas*), thereby sanctifying it and increasing its magical efficacy.

101 The Japanese manuscript and the Sung edition omit *teje.*

102 The Tibetan inserts *āviśa* after *dīpaya.*

103 Tibetan: *Oṃ jvala jvala jvālaya bandhuri hūṃ phaṭ.*

104 The Tibetan gives Māmakī's *vidyā* and heart-mantra and what presumably corresponds to "the mantra of the Four-Syllable Vidyārāja": *Namo lokadhātriye, namaḥ śaṃkare śāntikare ghuṭṭa ghuṭṭa ghuṭṭini ghuṭṭaye ghuṭṭini svāhā* (cf. mantra cited in n. 9); *Oṃ kulaṃdhari bandha bandha hūṃ phaṭ* (= [19]); *Oṃ vajra hūṃ phaṭ.*

105 What I have tentatively read as *guru* could also be read *kuru* ("do!"), in which case it should probably be understood in conjunction with the preceding *saṃnidhim* as *saṃnidhiṃ kuru* ("be present!").

106 The Japanese manuscript, the Sung edition, and the Tibetan all have "fifth" for "fifteenth."

107 Following the Japanese manuscript and the Sung edition, I take *shih cheng erh yüeh* ("tenth, first, and second months") in our text to be an error for *shih-erh yüeh* ("twelfth month"), which according to the Tibetan corresponds to the Sanskrit *prātihārakapakṣa* (see n. 26).

108 Following the Japanese manuscript, the Sung edition, and the Tibetan, I take *erh-mu* ("two-eyed") in our text to be an error for *san-mu* ("three-eyed").

[109] Tibetan *sha chen* = Sanskrit *mahāmāṃsa:* human flesh (literally, "great flesh"). Because of the similarities between the characters for "dog" (*ch'üan*) and "great" (*ta*), it is possible that the Chinese *ch'üan-jou,* "dog's flesh," is a scribal or typographical error for *ta-jou,* "great flesh," but it is more likely to have been a deliberate mistranslation in deference to Chinese sensibilities. Likewise in Chapter 15 "dog's flesh or pig's flesh" corresponds to the Tibetan *sha chen la sogs pa,* "great flesh and so forth," and in Chapter 11 "the fat of dog's flesh" corresponds to the Tibetan *tshil chen gyi snum,* "oil of great fat" (i.e., human fat).

[110] Cf. n. 96.

[111] The Japanese manuscript and the Sung edition here insert brief instructions with three mantras for performing a *homa* rite similar in content to the passage quoted in n. 59.

[112] The Japanese manuscript, the Sung edition, and the Tibetan all add *daha daha vajra* after *hana hana vajra;* the Tibetan also has *dhāraya dhāraya* (or *dāraya dāraya*) *vajra dāruṇa dāruṇa vajra* for *dāraya dāraya vajra*.

[113] Literally, "four places." According to the Japanese manuscript and the Sung edition, the second part is offered to the four assemblies of monks, nuns, laymen, and laywomen. This interpretation of "four places" is not supported by the Tibetan, and therefore I have tentatively taken it to refer to the aforementioned four recipients of the divided article other than oneself.

[114] The five cardinal sins of killing one's father, killing one's mother, killing an arhat, causing the Buddha's body to bleed, and causing disunity in the Sangha.

Bibliography

Giebel, Rolf W. "*Soshitsujikara-kyō* genten kenkyū shotan—kanji on'yaku bugon gange tō no suitei kanbon o chūshin ni—." *Tōhōgaku,* No. 99, 2000. Gives Sanskrit reconstructions of fourteen verses of the *Susiddhikara-sūtra* preserved in Chinese transliteration.

Hopkins, Jeffrey, translator and editor. *The Yoga of Tibet—The Great Exposition of Secret Mantra: 2 and 3.* London: George Allen & Unwin, 1981. Contains many quotations and summarizations of passages from the Tibetan translation of the *Susiddhikara-sūtra.*

Ōyama, Ninkai. "Soshitsuji-kyō ni kansuru ichi kōsatsu." *Mikkyō Bunka,* Vol. 140, 1982. Dates earliest copy of the Japanese manuscript version to the mid-eighth century.

Takada, Ninkaku. "Shōbodai-zō *Soshitsujikara jōjuhō shū* no kenkyū—shosa tantora no shishi nenju shidai—." *Kōyasan Daigaku Ronsō,* Vol. 12, 1977. Japanese translation of Varabodhi's *Susiddhikara-sādhanasaṃgraha.*

Takada, Yorihito. "*Soshitsujikara-kyō* 'Shōmon-bon' no kōsatsu." *Mikkyōgaku,* No. 32, 1996. Discusses the relationship between the three Chinese recensions.

Glossary

Akaniṣṭha Heaven: The highest of the eighteen heavens of the realm of form (*rūpa-dhātu*). *See also* three realms.

Akṣobhya ("Immovable One"): One of the five Buddhas of the Vajradhātu Maṇḍala. *See also* Amoghasiddhi; Lokeśvararāja; *maṇḍala;* Ratnasaṃbhava; Vairocana.

Amoghasiddhi ("Infallible Success"): One of the five Buddhas of the Vajradhātu Maṇḍala. *See also* Akṣobhya; Lokeśvararāja; *maṇḍala;* Ratnasaṃbhava; Vairocana.

arhat: One who has freed himself from the bonds of birth and death by eliminating all passions. The highest spiritual ideal of early Buddhism.

Avalokiteśvara: The bodhisattva who represents great compassion. *See also* bodhisattva.

bodhisattva: One who has engendered the profound aspiration to achieve perfect enlightenment (*bodhicitta*) on behalf of all sentient beings. The spiritual ideal of the Mahayana. *See also* Mahayana.

Buddha Family: One of the three groups or "families" (*kula*) into which the deities of early Tantric Buddhism are organized. *See also* Lotus Family; Tantric Buddhism; Vajra Family.

dhāraṇī: Originally, the ability to comprehend and retain the Buddhist teachings. It also came to refer to special verbal formulae believed to encapsulate the essence of the teachings and have great power. *See also* mantra.

dharma-kāya. See tri-kāya.

dharma-mudrā. See mudrā.

Dharma-realm (*dharma-dhātu*): Literally, the objects (dharmas) of the mind in general. It also means the entire universe, or the fundamental spiritual reality underlying all the illusions and things of the phenomenal world. *See also* three realms.

Esoteric Buddhism: *See* Tantric Buddhism.

evil destinies: Three of the six modes of cyclic existence (samsara) in which sentient beings transmigrate in retribution for evil deeds: (1) hell, (2) the realm of hungry ghosts (*preta*s), and (3) the realm of animals. The other three modes are the realms of humans, of demigods (*asura*s), and of gods.

Great Hell of Immediate Retribution (Avīci): The lowest and most painful of the various levels of hells.

Great Vehicle. *See* Mahayana.

Jambūdvīpa: Also Jambudvīpa. In Indian cosmology, the continent to the south of Mount Sumeru (or Meru) and the home of human beings.

karma-mudrā. See mudrā.

Lokeśvararāja ("Lord and King of the World"): One of the five Buddhas of the Vajradhātu Maṇḍala. *See also* Akṣobhya; Amoghasiddhi; *maṇḍala;* Ratnasaṃbhava; Vairocana.

Lotus Family: One of the three groups or "families" (*kula*) into which the deities of early Tantric Buddhism are organized. *See also* Buddha Family; Tantric Buddhism; Vajra Family.

māha-mudrā. See mudrā.

Mahāvairocana. A designation of the chief deity in Tantric Buddhism, corresponding to the *dharma-kāya* and to be distinguished from Vairocana (although the two are sometimes used interchangeably). *See also* Tantric Buddhism; *tri-kāya;* Vairocana.

Mahayana ("Great Vehicle"): A form of Buddhism that developed in India around 100 B.C.E and which exalts as its religious ideal the bodhisattva, the great being who is willing to delay his own enlightenment until he can save all sentient beings. Such selfless compassion becomes possible only when the practitioner grasps the central Mahayana doctrine of emptiness and so realizes that "self" and "others" are not separate. *See also* bodhisattva.

Maitreya: The future Buddha, currently still a bodhisattva. *See also* bodhisattva.

maṇḍala ("circle"): In Tantric Buddhism, a square or circular site in which deity-images, etc., are installed for the performance of rituals. It also came to refer to pictorial representations of these arrangements of deities. *See also* Tantric Buddhism.

Mañjuśrī: The bodhisattva who represents wisdom. *See also* bodhisattva.

mantra: A mystic or incantatory formula used in the rituals of Tantric Buddhism. *See also dhāraṇī;* Tantric Buddhism.

māra: The original meaning of *māra* is "death," and it also came to signify the personification of death or the Evil One (Māra). In Buddhism four types of *māra*s, or demons, are distinguished: (1) the five aggregates, (2) mental afflictions, (3) death, and (4) the king of demons in the

Paranirmitavaśavartin Heaven. *See also* Paranirmitavaśavartin Heaven.

mudrā ("seal"): Generally, a ritualistic hand gesture used in the rituals of Tantric Buddhism. Sometimes four types are distinguished: (1) *mahā-mudrā* ("great seal")—images of deities as they are visualized in their physical form; (2) *samaya-mudrā* ("pledge-seal")—seals in the sense of hand gestures; (3) *dharma-mudrā* ("dharma-seal")—incantatory formulae or seed-syllables representing the verbal counterparts of the deities; and (4) *karma-mudrā* ("action-seal")—activities characteristic of each deity.

nirmāṇa-kāya. *See tri-kāya.*

nirvana: The final goal of Buddhist aspiration and practice, a state in which passions are extinguished and the highest wisdom attained.

own-nature: The quality of having a permanent, unchanging existence independent of causes and conditions.

Paranirmitavaśavartin Heaven: The sixth heaven in the realm of desire (*kāma-dhātu*). *See also* three realms.

prajñā: Nondiscriminating or transcendental wisdom, the understanding of things as they actually are. One of the *pāramitās* (perfections) of a bodhisattva. *See also* bodhisattva; six *pāramitās*.

Prajñāpāramitā ("perfection of wisdom"): The name of a body of Mahayana literature that emphasizes the doctrine of emptiness. Also the name of a goddess personifying this body of literature. *See also* Mahayana.

pratyekabuddha: A sage who attains enlightenment by observing the principles of causation and dependent arising by himself. He attains enlightenment without the guidance of a teacher, and he intends neither to guide others nor to expound the teaching to others.

Ratnasaṃbhava ("Jewel-born One"): One of the five Buddhas of the Vajradhātu Maṇḍala. *See also* Akṣobhya; Amoghasiddhi; Lokeśvararāja; *maṇḍala;* Vairocana.

Śākyamuni: The historical Buddha who lived in India in the fifth century B.C.E., and whose life and teachings form the basis of Buddhism.

samādhi: A state of meditative concentration and focusing of thought on one object.

Samantabhadra ("Universally Good"): A bodhisattva who represents the ultimate principle, meditation, and the practice of all Buddhas. The embodiment of adherence to vows of great compassion. *See also* bodhisattva.

samaya: In Tantric Buddhism, the "pledge" of the "coming together" of a divinity with the practitioner, or a symbolic representation of the pledge. *See also* Tantric Buddhism.

samaya-mudrā. See mudrā.

saṃbhoga-kāya. See tri-kāya.

siddhi: "Accomplishment" or "success," many different varieties of which are enumerated in Tantric scriptures. *See also* Tantric Buddhism.

six *pāramitās* ("perfections"): virtues cultivated by a bodhisattva on the way to complete enlightenment. They are: (1) giving (*dāna*); (2) morality (*śīla*); (3) forbearance (*kṣānti*); (4) effort or energy (*vīrya*); (5) meditation (*dhyāna*); and (6) wisdom (*prajñā*). *See also* bodhisattva.

śrāvaka: Originally, a disciple of the historical Buddha, one who directly heard his teachings. Later used as a general term for followers of early Buddhism, to distinguish them from adherents of Mahayana and Tantric Buddhism. *See also* Mahayana; Tantric Buddhism.

Tantric Buddhism: A form of Buddhism that evolved through the blending of the teachings of Mahayana Buddhism with the techniques for realization described in texts called *tantras*, involving the extensive use of mantras, *mudrās*, *maṇḍalas*, and ritual. In its form as it has developed in East Asia in particular, it is often referred to as Esoteric Buddhism. *See also* Mahayana; *maṇḍala;* mantra; *mudrā.*

Tathāgata: An epithet for a Buddha. It came to be interpreted as "one who has gone to (*gata*) or come from (*āgata*) the truth of thusness (*tathatā*)," i.e., "one who embodies the truth of thusness."

three bodies. *See tri-kāya.*

three families. *See* Buddha Family; Lotus Family; Vajra Family.

Three Jewels: The Buddha, the Dharma (the Buddha's teachings), and the Sangha (the community of his followers).

three realms (*tri-dhātu*): The three spheres of transmigratory existence: (1) the realm of desire (*kāma-dhātu*), i.e., the world of everyday consciousness accompanied by desires; (2) the realm of form (*rūpa-dhātu*), in which desires have been eliminated but the physical body remains; and (3) the realm of nonform (*ārūpya-dhātu*), in which the physical body no longer exists.

tri-kāya: The three bodies, or manifestations, of a Buddha, consisting of the *dharma-kāya* ("Dharma-body"), which is ultimate truth; the *saṃbhoga-kāya* ("enjoyment body"), a symbolic personification of the Dharma-body that a Buddha assumes both as a reward for eons of ascetic practice and in order to expound the Dharma to bodhisattvas and others; and the *nirmāṇa-kāya* ("transformation body"), an "incarnate" or "historically manifested" body of a Buddha such as Śākyamuni that appears in the world to guide sentient beings in a manner adapted to their situations and abilities.

udāna: A joyous or inspired utterance, generally in verse.

Vairocana ("He Who Is Like the Sun" or "Resplendent One"): One of the five Buddhas of the Vajradhātu Maṇḍala. *See also* Akṣobhya; Amoghasiddhi; Lokeśvararāja; *maṇḍala;* Ratnasaṃbhava.

vajra: Originally it referred to a thunderbolt or to a very hard metal identified with the diamond, and hence it is often used as an analogy for something hard and indestructible. It also refers to a ritual instrument similar in shape to a short scepter and having one, three, or five prongs at each end.

Vajra Family: One of the three groups or "families" (*kula*) into which the deities of early Tantric Buddhism are organized. *See also* Buddha Family; Lotus Family; Tantric Buddhism.

Vajrapāṇi ("Vajra-in-Hand"): A bodhisattva who is in Tantric Buddhism generally equated with Vajrasattva. *See also* bodhisattva; Tantric Buddhism; Vajrasattva.

Vajrasattva ("Adamantine Being"): A bodhisattva associated with the awakening of the aspiration for enlightenment (*bodhicitta*) and considered to epitomize the ideals of Tantric Buddhism. *See also* bodhisattva; Tantric Buddhism.

Index

E

F

G

N

O

P

Y

A List of the Volumes of the BDK English Tripiṭaka (First Series)

Abbreviations

Ch.: Chinese
Skt.: Sanskrit
Jp.: Japanese
Eng.: Published title
T.: Taishō Tripiṭaka

Vol. No.		Title	*T.* No.
11-III	*Ch.*	Jên-wang-pan-jo-po-lo-mi-ching (仁王般若波羅蜜經)	245
	Skt.	Kāruṇikārājā-prajñāpāramitā-sūtra (?)	
11-IV	*Ch.*	Pan-jo-po-lo-mi-to-hsing-ching (般若波羅蜜多心經)	251
	Skt.	Prajñāpāramitāhṛdaya-sūtra	
12-I	*Ch.*	Ta-lo-chin-kang-pu-k'ung-chên-shih-san-mo- yeh-ching (大樂金剛不空眞實三麼耶經)	243
	Skt.	Adhyardhaśatikā-prajñāpāramitā-sūtra	
12-II	*Ch.*	Wu-liang-shou-ching (無量壽經)	360
	Skt.	Sukhāvatīvyūha	
	Eng.	The Larger Sutra on Amitāyus (In The Three Pure Land Sutras)	
12-III	*Ch.*	Kuan-wu-liang-shou-fo-ching (觀無量壽佛經)	365
	Skt.	Amitāyurdhyāna-sūtra	
	Eng.	The Sutra on Contemplation of Amitāyus (In The Three Pure Land Sutras)	
12-IV	*Ch.*	A-mi-t'o-ching (阿彌陀經)	366
	Skt.	Sukhāvatīvyūha	
	Eng.	The Smaller Sutra on Amitāyus (In The Three Pure Land Sutras)	
12-V	*Ch.*	Ti-ts'ang-p'u-sa-pên-yüan-ching (地藏菩薩本願經)	412
	Skt.	Kṣitigarbhapraṇidhāna-sūtra (?)	
12-VI	*Ch.*	Yao-shih-liu-li-kuang-ju-lai-pên-yüan-kung- tê-ching (藥師琉璃光如來本願功德經)	450
	Skt.	Bhaiṣajyaguruvaiḍūryaprabhāsapūrva- praṇidhānaviśeṣavistara	
12-VII	*Ch.*	Mi-lê-hsia-shêng-ch'êng-fo-ching (彌勒下生成佛經)	454
	Skt.	Maitreyavyākaraṇa (?)	
12-VIII	*Ch.*	Wên-shu-shih-li-wên-ching (文殊師利問經)	468
	Skt.	Mañjuśrīparipṛcchā (?)	
13-I	*Ch.*	Miao-fa-lien-hua-ching (妙法蓮華經)	262
	Skt.	Saddharmapuṇḍarīka-sūtra	
	Eng.	The Lotus Sutra	
13-II	*Ch.*	Wu-liang-i-ching (無量義經)	276

Vol. No.		Title	*T.* No.
13-III	*Ch.*	Kuan-p'u-hsien-p'u-sa-hsing-fa-ching (觀普賢菩薩行法經)	277
14–19	*Ch.*	Ta-fang-kuang-fo-hua-yen-ching (大方廣佛華嚴經)	278
	Skt.	Avataṃsaka-sūtra	
20-I	*Ch.*	Shêng-man-shih-tzŭ-hou-i-ch'eng-ta-fang-pien-fang-kuang-ching (勝鬘師子吼一乘大方便方廣經)	353
	Skt.	Śrīmālādevīsiṃhanāda-sūtra	
20-II	*Ch.*	Chin-kuang-ming-tsui-shêng-wang-ching (金光明最勝王經)	665
	Skt.	Suvarṇaprabhāsa-sūtra	
21–24	*Ch.*	Ta-pan-nieh-p'an-ching (大般涅槃經)	374
	Skt.	Mahāparinirvāṇa-sūtra	
25-I	*Ch.*	Fo-ch'ui-pan-nieh-p'an-liao-shuo-chiao-chieh-ching (佛垂般涅槃略説教誡經)	389
25-II	*Ch.*	Pan-chou-san-mei-ching (般舟三昧經)	418
	Skt.	Pratyutpannabuddhasammukhāvasthitasamādhi-sūtra	
	Eng.	The Pratyutpanna Samādhi Sutra	
25-III	*Ch.*	Shou-lêng-yen-san-mei-ching (首楞嚴三昧經)	642
	Skt.	Śūraṅgamasamādhi-sūtra	
	Eng.	The Śūraṅgama Samādhi Sutra	
25-IV	*Ch.*	Chieh-shên-mi-ching (解深密經)	676
	Skt.	Saṃdhinirmocana-sūtra	
	Eng.	The Scripture on the Explication of Underlying Meaning	
25-V	*Ch.*	Yü-lan-p'ên-ching (盂蘭盆經)	685
	Skt.	Ullambana-sūtra (?)	
25-VI	*Ch.*	Ssŭ-shih-êrh-chang-ching (四十二章經)	784
26-I	*Ch.*	Wei-mo-chieh-so-shuo-ching (維摩詰所説經)	475
	Skt.	Vimalakīrtinirdeśa-sūtra	
26-II	*Ch.*	Yüeh-shang-nü-ching (月上女經)	480
	Skt.	Candrottarādārikāparipṛcchā	

Vol. No.		Title	*T.* No.
26-III	*Ch.*	Tso-ch'an-san-mei-ching (坐禪三昧經)	614
26-IV	*Ch.*	Ta-mo-to-lo-ch'an-ching (達磨多羅禪經)	618
	Skt.	Yogācārabhūmi-sūtra (?)	
27	*Ch.*	Yüeh-têng-san-mei-ching (月燈三昧經)	639
	Skt.	Samādhirājacandrapradīpa-sūtra	
28	*Ch.*	Ju-lêng-ch'ieh-ching (入楞伽經)	671
	Skt.	Laṅkāvatāra-sūtra	
29-I	*Ch.*	Ta-fang-kuang-yüan-chio-hsiu-to-lo-liao-i-ching (大方廣圓覺修多羅了義經)	842
29-II	*Ch.*	Su-hsi-ti-chieh-lo-ching (蘇悉地羯囉經)	893
	Skt.	Susiddhikaramahātantrasādhanopāyika-paṭala	
	Eng.	The Susiddhikara Sutra (In Two Esoteric Sutras)	
29-III	*Ch.*	Mo-têng-ch'ieh-ching (摩登伽經)	1300
	Skt.	Mātaṅgī-sūtra (?)	
30-I	*Ch.*	Ta-p'i-lu-chê-na-chêng-fo-shên-pien-chia-ch'ih-ching (大毘盧遮那成佛神變加持經)	848
	Skt.	Mahāvairocanābhisambodhivikurvitādhiṣṭhāna-vaipulyasūtrendrarāja-nāma-dharmaparyāya	
30-II	*Ch.*	Ching-kang-ting-i-ch'ieh-ju-lai-chên-shih-shê-ta-ch'eng-hsien-chêng-ta-chiao-wang-ching (金剛頂一切如來眞實攝大乘現證大教王經)	865
	Skt.	Sarvatathāgatatattvasaṃgrahamahāyānābhi-samayamahākalparāja	
	Eng.	The Adamantine Pinnacle Sutra (In Two Esoteric Sutras)	
31–35	*Ch.*	Mo-ho-sêng-ch'i-lü (摩訶僧祇律)	1425
	Skt.	Mahāsāṃghika-vinaya (?)	
36–42	*Ch.*	Ssŭ-fên-lü (四分律)	1428
	Skt.	Dharmaguptaka-vinaya (?)	
43, 44	*Ch.*	Shan-chien-lü-p'i-p'o-sha (善見律毘婆沙)	1462
	Pāli	Samantapāsādikā	
45-I	*Ch.*	Fan-wang-ching (梵網經)	1484
	Skt.	Brahmajāla-sūtra (?)	

Vol. No.		Title	T. No.
45-II	*Ch.*	Yu-p'o-sai-chieh-ching (優婆塞戒經)	1488
	Skt.	Upāsakaśīla-sūtra (?)	
	Eng.	The Sutra on Upāsaka Precepts	
46-I	*Ch.*	Miao-fa-lien-hua-ching-yu-po-t'i-shê (妙法蓮華經憂波提舍)	1519
	Skt.	Saddharmapuṇḍarīka-upadeśa	
46-II	*Ch.*	Fo-ti-ching-lun (佛地經論)	1530
	Skt.	Buddhabhūmisūtra-śāstra (?)	
46-III	*Ch.*	Shê-ta-ch'eng-lun (攝大乘論)	1593
	Skt.	Mahāyānasaṃgraha	
	Eng.	The Summary of the Great Vehicle	
47	*Ch.*	Shih-chu-p'i-p'o-sha-lun (十住毘婆沙論)	1521
	Skt.	Daśabhūmika-vibhāṣā (?)	
48, 49	*Ch.*	A-p'i-ta-mo-chü-shê-lun (阿毘達磨俱舍論)	1558
	Skt.	Abhidharmakośa-bhāṣya	
50–59	*Ch.*	Yü-ch'ieh-shih-ti-lun (瑜伽師地論)	1579
	Skt.	Yogācārabhūmi	
60-I	*Ch.*	Ch'êng-wei-shih-lun (成唯識論)	1585
	Eng.	Demonstration of Consciousness Only (In Three Texts on Consciousness Only)	
60-II	*Ch.*	Wei-shih-san-shih-lun-sung (唯識三十論頌)	1586
	Skt.	Triṃśikā	
	Eng.	The Thirty Verses on Consciousness Only (In Three Texts on Consciousness Only)	
60-III	*Ch.*	Wei-shih-êrh-shih-lun (唯識二十論)	1590
	Skt.	Viṃśatikā	
	Eng.	The Treatise in Twenty Verses on Consciousness Only (In Three Texts on Consciousness Only)	
61-I	*Ch.*	Chung-lun (中論)	1564
	Skt.	Madhyamaka-śāstra	
61-II	*Ch.*	Pien-chung-pien-lun (辯中邊論)	1600
	Skt.	Madhyāntavibhāga	
61-III	*Ch.*	Ta-ch'eng-ch'êng-yeh-lun (大乘成業論)	1609
	Skt.	Karmasiddhiprakaraṇa	

Vol. No.		Title	*T.* No.
67, 68	*Ch.*	Miao-fa-lien-hua-ching-hsüan-i (妙法蓮華經玄義)	1716
69	*Ch.*	Ta-ch‘eng-hsüan-lun (大乘玄論)	1853
70-I	*Ch.*	Hua-yen-i-ch‘eng-chiao-i-fên-ch‘i-chang (華嚴一乘教義分齊章)	1866
70-II	*Ch.*	Yüan-jên-lun (原人論)	1886
70-III	*Ch.*	Hsiu-hsi-chih-kuan-tso-ch‘an-fa-yao (修習止觀坐禪法要)	1915
70-IV	*Ch.*	T‘ien-t‘ai-ssŭ-chiao-i (天台四教儀)	1931
71, 72	*Ch.*	Mo-ho-chih-kuan (摩訶止觀)	1911
73-I	*Ch.*	Kuo-ch‘ing-pai-lu (國清百録)	1934
73-II	*Ch.*	Liu-tsu-ta-shih-fa-pao-t‘an-ching (六祖大師法寶壇經)	2008
	Eng.	The Platform Sutra of the Sixth Patriarch	
73-III	*Ch.*	Huang-po-shan-tuan-chi-ch‘an-shih-ch‘uan-hsin-fa-yao (黃檗山斷際禪師傳心法要)	2012A
73-IV	*Ch.*	Yung-chia-chêng-tao-ko (永嘉證道歌)	2014
74-I	*Ch.*	Chên-chou-lin-chi-hui-chao-ch‘an-shih-wu-lu (鎭州臨濟慧照禪師語録)	1985
	Eng.	The Recorded Sayings of Linji (In Three Chan Classics)	
74-II	*Ch.*	Wu-mên-kuan (無門關)	2005
	Eng.	Wumen’s Gate (In Three Chan Classics)	
74-III	*Ch.*	Hsin-hsin-ming (信心銘)	2010
	Eng.	The Faith-Mind Maxim (In Three Chan Classics)	
74-IV	*Ch.*	Ch‘ih-hsiu-pai-chang-ch‘ing-kuei (勅修百丈清規)	2025
75	*Ch.*	Fo-kuo-yüan-wu-ch‘an-shih-pi-yen-lu (佛果圜悟禪師碧巖録)	2003
	Eng.	The Blue Cliff Record	

Vol. No.		Title	T. No.
76-I	*Ch.*	I-pu-tsung-lun-lun （異部宗輪論）	2031
	Skt.	Samayabhedoparacanacakra	
76-II	*Ch.*	A-yü-wang-ching （阿育王經）	2043
	Skt.	Aśokarāja-sūtra (?)	
	Eng.	The Biographical Scripture of King Aśoka	
76-III	*Ch.*	Ma-ming-p'u-sa-ch'uan （馬鳴菩薩傳）	2046
76-IV	*Ch.*	Lung-shu-p'u-sa-ch'uan （龍樹菩薩傳）	2047
76-V	*Ch.*	P'o-sou-p'an-tou-fa-shih-ch'uan （婆藪槃豆法師傳）	2049 (7)
76-VI	*Ch.*	Pi-ch'iu-ni-ch'uan （比丘尼傳）	2063
76-VII	*Ch.*	Kao-sêng-fa-hsien-ch'uan （高僧法顯傳）	2085
76-VIII	*Ch.*	Yu-fang-chi-ch'ao: T'ang-ta-ho-shang-tung-chêng-ch'uan （遊方記抄: 唐大和上東征傳）	2089-
77	*Ch.*	Ta-t'ang-ta-tz'ŭ-ên-ssŭ-san-ts'ang-fa-shih-ch'uan （大唐大慈恩寺三藏法師傳）	2053
	Eng.	A Biography of the Tripiṭaka Master of the Great Ci'en Monastery of the Great Tang Dynasty	
78	*Ch.*	Kao-sêng-ch'uan （高僧傳）	2059
79	*Ch.*	Ta-t'ang-hsi-yü-chi （大唐西域記）	2087
	Eng.	The Great Tang Dynasty Record of the Western Regions	
80	*Ch.*	Hung-ming-chi （弘明集）	2102
81–92	*Ch.*	Fa-yüan-chu-lin （法苑珠林）	2122
93-I	*Ch.*	Nan-hai-chi-kuei-nei-fa-ch'uan （南海寄歸内法傳）	2125
	Eng.	Buddhist Monastic Traditions of Southern Asia	
93-II	*Ch.*	Fan-yü-tsa-ming （梵語雑名）	2135
94-I	*Jp.*	Shō-man-gyō-gi-sho （勝鬘經義疏）	2185
94-II	*Jp.*	Yui-ma-kyō-gi-sho （維摩經義疏）	2186
95	*Jp.*	Hok-ke-gi-sho （法華義疏）	2187

Vol. No.		Title	*T.* No.
96-I	*Jp.*	Han-nya-shin-gyō-hi-ken （般若心經秘鍵）	2203
96-II	*Jp.*	Dai-jō-hos-sō-ken-jin-shō （大乘法相研神章）	2309
96-III	*Jp.*	Kan-jin-kaku-mu-shō （觀心覺夢鈔）	2312
97-I	*Jp.* *Eng.*	Ris-shū-kō-yō （律宗綱要） The Essentials of the Vinaya Tradition	2348
97-II	*Jp.* *Eng.*	Ten-dai-hok-ke-shū-gi-shū （天台法華宗義集） The Collected Teachings of the Tendai Lotus School	2366
97-III	*Jp.*	Ken-kai-ron （顯戒論）	2376
97-IV	*Jp.*	San-ge-gaku-shō-shiki （山家學生式）	2377
98-I	*Jp.*	Hi-zō-hō-yaku （秘藏寶鑰）	2426
98-II	*Jp.*	Ben-ken-mitsu-ni-kyō-ron （辨顯密二教論）	2427
98-III	*Jp.*	Soku-shin-jō-butsu-gi （即身成佛義）	2428
98-IV	*Jp.*	Shō-ji-jis-sō-gi （聲字實相義）	2429
98-V	*Jp.*	Un-ji-gi （吽字義）	2430
98-VI	*Jp.*	Go-rin-ku-ji-myō-hi-mitsu-shaku （五輪九字明秘密釋）	2514
98-VII	*Jp.*	Mitsu-gon-in-hotsu-ro-san-ge-mon （密嚴院發露懺悔文）	2527
98-VIII	*Jp.*	Kō-zen-go-koku-ron （興禪護國論）	2543
98-IX	*Jp.*	Fu-kan-za-zen-gi （普勧坐禪儀）	2580
99–103	*Jp.*	Shō-bō-gen-zō （正法眼藏）	2582
104-I	*Jp.*	Za-zen-yō-jin-ki （坐禪用心記）	2586
104-II	*Jp.* *Eng.*	Sen-chaku-hon-gan-nen-butsu-shū （選擇本願念佛集） Senchaku Hongan Nembutsu Shū	2608
104-III	*Jp.*	Ris-shō-an-koku-ron （立正安國論）	2688

Vol. No.		Title	*T*. No.
104-IV	*Jp.*	Kai-moku-shō (開目抄)	2689
	Eng.	Kaimokushō or Liberation from Blindness	
104-V	*Jp.*	Kan-jin-hon-zon-shō (觀心本尊抄)	2692
104-VI	*Ch.*	Fu-mu-ên-chung-ching (父母恩重經)	2887
105-I	*Jp.*	Ken-jō-do-shin-jitsu-kyō-gyō-shō-mon-rui (顯淨土眞實教行証文類)	2646
105-II	*Jp.*	Tan-ni-shō (歎異抄)	2661
	Eng.	Tannishō: Passages Deploring Deviations of Faith	
106-I	*Jp.*	Ren-nyo-shō-nin-o-fumi (蓮如上人御文)	2668
	Eng.	Rennyo Shōnin Ofumi: The Letters of Rennyo	
106-II	*Jp.*	Ō-jō-yō-shū (往生要集)	2682
107-I	*Jp.*	Has-shū-kō-yō (八宗綱要)	蔵外
	Eng.	The Essentials of the Eight Traditions	
107-II	*Jp.*	San-gō-shī-ki (三教指帰)	蔵外
107-III	*Jp.*	Map-pō-tō-myō-ki (末法燈明記)	蔵外
	Eng.	The Candle of the Latter Dharma	
107-IV	*Jp.*	Jū-shichi-jō-ken-pō (十七條憲法)	蔵外